Rights Reign Supreme

Rights Reign Supreme

An Intellectual History of Judicial Review and the Supreme Court

JAMES M. MASNOV

McFarland & Company, Inc., Publishers
Jefferson, North Carolina

ISBN (print) 978-1-4766-9052-0
ISBN (ebook) 978-1-4766-4825-5

LIBRARY OF CONGRESS AND BRITISH LIBRARY
CATALOGUING DATA ARE AVAILABLE

Library of Congress Control Number 2022055340

Front cover: Exterior of United States Supreme Court
(Shutterstock/Javier Cruz Acosta)

Printed in the United States of America

*McFarland & Company, Inc., Publishers
Box 611, Jefferson, North Carolina 28640
www.mcfarlandpub.com*

To Christina Marie and Katelynn Rose,
for making life worth living, for pulling me out of myself,
and for being my two favorite people in the world.

Acknowledgments

Expressing gratitude to each and every person who contributed to my success in the production of this work would be an impossible endeavor. Many people both inside and outside of the academy, including friends, family, and colleagues, have provided help and guidance along the way. There are, however, certain individuals I wish to mention and thank for particular assistance and support. This work is the culmination of a long process that stresses my deep interest in the history of political philosophy, legal theory, and constitutionalism, particularly as an early Americanist. There are thus a number of people I wish to thank for the help I have received in the development of my work.

I want to thank the following historians, political scientists, and legal scholars for their guidance, constructive criticism, and support: Bob Reinhardt, Kimberly Jensen, John Rector, Chris Cocoltchos, Mark Henkels, David Doellinger, Thomas Luckett, David Horowitz, Chris Shortell, and Tim Garrison. Each one of them helped me significantly along the way, through peer review, opening doors of opportunity to me that would have been otherwise closed, and providing venues for me to share my work with fellow scholars. I am forever in their debt.

I also sincerely thank each and every person who reads this book. Whether a scholar or curious reader of history, political science, or political and legal theory, I am grateful that there continues to be people in this country and in this world who seek to understand the past, both for the sake of knowledge itself and to better comprehend current and future circumstances. Only through an understanding of where we have been is it possible to know who we are now and where we are going. The importance of historical literacy cannot be overstated. Thank you.

Table of Contents

Preface

This book is a work of intellectual history that chronicles the principle of judicial review: the power of the American judiciary, the United States Supreme Court in particular, to declare laws it finds unconstitutional to be null and void. This awesome power has been as controversial as it has been transformational to the American system of law and governance. This work examines early instances of judicial review around the time of the American Revolution, discourses during the drafting and ratification of the U.S. Constitution, federal instances in the first decade of the new republic, scholarship surrounding the principle, and the trajectory of the Court over the nineteenth, twentieth, and early twenty-first centuries.

The book is not a comprehensive legal history. Instead, it highlights notable instances of judicial review over the centuries and offers something unique by scrutinizing the philosophical antecedents in Europe that proved influential in Colonial America, revolutionary America, and the United States during the early constitutional period. Classical republicanism—rebirthed in Renaissance-era Florence and practiced virtually by accident in England in the seventeenth century—and liberalism, which flowered during the early republic and into the nineteenth century, created a paradoxical synthesis of legal and political thought. These effects cast the American constitutional system as something far different from anything that had preceded it. Judicial review, one of the most unique aspects of the constitutional system of the United States, has rarely been examined through the intellectual history that informed it, until now.

Notable recent works that address judicial review include Keith Whittington's *Repugnant Laws: Judicial Review of Acts of Congress from the Founding to the Present* (2019) and Akhil Reed Amar's *The Words that Made Us: America's Constitutional Conversation, 1760–1840* (2021). While Whittington's *Repugnant Laws* proved useful to this work in its assessment of acts of judicial review throughout American history, it does not do much in considering the intellectual history that informed the principle. Amar's *The Words that Made Us* explores the philosophical discourses

1

during the early decades of the founding but his observations of judicial review in particular are less stressed than his earlier works, such as *America's Constitution: A Biography* (2005). Though the scholarship of these writers is significant and helped to inform this work, their aims were considerably different. The book you are now reading sets itself apart from the recent works of Whittington, Amar, and others by tracing the intellectual and philosophical underpinnings of classical republicanism and liberal individualism, and connects these precepts to the power of judicial review and its evolution into an instrument of rights theory.

Rights Reign Supreme: An Intellectual History of Judicial Review and the Supreme Court is the culmination of years of research, informed by work conducted in graduate school and developed further afterward. Much of this involved investigations into primary sources, including Montesquieu's essays on the separation of powers, early American court cases (both state and federal), the debates at the Philadelphia Convention in 1787, the state ratification debates, the writings of Publius (James Madison, Alexander Hamilton, and John Jay), arguments among the so-called Antifederalists, the natural rights arguments of John Locke in the late seventeenth century and James Wilson in the late eighteenth century, and the writings of Renaissance-era champions of republicanism. This work was further developed through an appraisal of the relevant secondary source literature by historians, political scientists, and legal scholars. To provide similar scope to the scholarship as was done with the history, works from the nineteenth century to the present proved valuable for tracing the discourses regarding judicial review, its merits, and its challenges.

The organization of this book is largely chronological, though not entirely. The introduction analyzes instances of rights assertions during the colonial period and the book then generally follows the timeline of American history, with two notable exceptions. Following Chapter One's primary source analysis of relevant data in the 1780s and 1790s, Chapter Two focuses on the history of judicial review scholarship. This acts as a historiography, essential to any book of academic history, and places the work of this author within the larger context of the discipline. Chapter Three returns to the chronology and the book proceeds thusly until Chapter Seven, where a second digression from the timeline transpires. This is done for the purpose of scrutinizing the philosophical antecedents of American constitutionalism and their relevance to judicial review. Following this, the timeline is restored with a survey of judicial review practice in the twentieth and twenty-first centuries in Chapter Eight, and commentary on judicial review today in the book's conclusion.

The book you are about to read is thus of tremendous scope, with significant ambitions. It is an intellectual history of judicial review, which is itself a unique project. It presents a separate value as well, however. It also acts as a survey of the history of the United States from a perspective never before offered in quite this way. It is a survey of the history from the vantage point of rights values and rights recognition via the judiciary, providing a way to look at the previous centuries in a new light, and with fresh eyes.

Introduction

Ramos *v.* Louisiana *(2020)*

When the United States Supreme Court handed down its decision in the *Ramos* v. *Louisiana* case on April 20, 2020, they affirmed that the right to a jury trial, enumerated in the Sixth Amendment of the U.S. Constitution (and referenced in Article III, Section 2), included the protection against conviction by non-unanimous juries. As a consequence, two states which had allowed for non-unanimous jury convictions for about a century, Louisiana and Oregon, were compelled to comply with the decision.

Evangelisto Ramos had challenged his non-unanimous conviction for second degree murder by a Louisiana jury, maintaining that non-unanimous jury convictions were unconstitutional because they violated essential guarantees outlined in the U.S. Constitution, enumerated in the Sixth Amendment, and incorporated against the individual states via the Fourteenth Amendment. The Supreme Court's majority ultimately agreed with Ramos. Authoring the majority's decision, Justice Neil Gorsuch observed the relevant history:

> The Constitution's text and structure clearly indicate that the Sixth Amendment term "trial by an impartial jury" carries with it *some* meaning about the content and requirements of a jury trial. One such requirement is that a jury must reach a unanimous verdict in order to convict. Juror unanimity emerged as a vital common law right in 14th century England, appeared in the early American state constitutions, and provided the backdrop against which the Sixth Amendment was drafted and ratified. Postadoption treatises and 19th-century American legal treatises confirm this understanding.[1]

The Justice further noted that "the Sixth Amendment right to a jury trial is incorporated against the States under the Fourteenth Amendment.... Thus, if the jury trial right requires a unanimous verdict in federal court, it requires no less in state court."[2]

The majority's decision traces the overtly racist motivations for both

Louisiana and Oregon's non-unanimous jury systems when they were designed in the late nineteenth and early twentieth centuries, respectively:

> Why do Louisiana and Oregon allow nonunanimous convictions? Though it's hard to say why these laws persist, their origins are clear. Louisiana first endorsed nonunanimous verdicts for serious crimes at a constitutional convention in 1898. According to one committee chairman, the avowed purpose of that convention was to "establish the supremacy of the white race," and the resulting document included many of the trappings of the Jim Crow era: a poll tax, a combined literacy and property ownership test, and a grandfather clause that in practice exempted white residents from the most onerous of these requirements…. Adopted in the 1930s, Oregon's rule permitting nonunanimous verdicts can be similarly traced to the rise of the Ku Klux Klan and efforts to dilute "the influence of racial, ethnic, and religious minorities on Oregon juries." In fact, no one before us contests any of this; courts in both Louisiana and Oregon have frankly acknowledged that race was a motivating factor in the adoption of their States' respective nonunanimity rules.[3]

Justice Gorsuch adds further historical context by illustrating the original public meaning of the Sixth Amendment and the other relevant texts during their adoption when he observes that wherever "we might look to determine what the term 'trial by an impartial jury trial' meant at the time of the Sixth Amendment's adoption—whether it's the common law, state practices in the founding era, or opinions and treatises written soon afterward—the answer is unmistakable. A jury must reach a unanimous verdict in order to convict."[4] He further notes that "state courts appeared to regard unanimity as an essential feature of the jury trial. It was against this backdrop that James Madison drafted and the States ratified the Sixth Amendment in 1791. By that time, unanimous verdicts had been required for about 400 years."[5] Crucially, and—for the purpose of this work—most relevant, is Gorsuch's comment regarding how this case connects to notions of justice, rights, and the rule of law. He asks rhetorically, "On what ground would anyone have us leave Mr. Ramos in prison for the rest of his life?" concluding that not a single member "of this Court is prepared to say Louisiana secured his conviction constitutionally under the Sixth Amendment."[6]

The *Ramos* v. *Louisiana* decision is merely one recent example of the judicial branch of the United States exercising its role as arbiter in matters related to separation of powers and governmental overreach through its power of judicial review: the power to nullify state or federal laws repugnant to, and which violate, the U.S. Constitution. Perhaps more importantly, and certainly less discussed generally by historians, is the reason *why* the Court's role is to exercise such power. This brings into focus the objective of this book. The American judiciary has come to occupy a unique and essential aspect of the American project: defender of the

Constitution against the inappropriate and illegal aims of the Executive and Legislative branches among both state and federal powers. Most important of all, however, is an altogether different feature of the Court and of its judicial review power, which is the judiciary's role to act as an instrument of rights theory against the unconstitutional and even democratic elements of the American regime.

Judicial review is itself unique to the American project. There are antecedents to its practice among European powers in earlier centuries, but nowhere has the power of the judiciary to nullify laws become central to a government's design as it has in the United States. The power of judicial review has been attacked as both ahistorical and legally improper by scholars among both the political left and right, depending on the era and circumstances. This book will address such matters by asserting that judicial review is constitutionally appropriate. It will trace its historical significance and enduring legacy in American law, and ultimately contend that its antidemocratic function is not a bug but a feature. Judicial review is an instrument of a uniquely American form of rights theory, informed by centuries of culture and influenced by particular European natural rights theorists during the founding era.

European Antecedents of Judicial Independence and Judicial Review

Among the most noteworthy examples of judicial independence in the centuries preceding the American founding are the jurisprudence of Chief Justice Sir Edward Coke of England in the early seventeenth century and the French parlements under the *Ancien Regime*. Though neither example reaches the level of judicial autonomy and legal authority that the American judiciary achieved in the late eighteenth century and beyond, they are nevertheless valuable for an understanding of both their influence and their discrepancies. By examining relevant instances, their connection to the forms of government and law practiced in England and France, respectively, becomes clearer, as do the reasons as to why judicial review never took hold in these realms in earlier centuries, or even today. In approaching the relevant legal histories of England and France, a deeper understanding will be attained regarding the reasons why the power of judicial review never took root in European states. This will underscore the uniqueness of the feature in the United States and lay the groundwork for apprehending the intellectual history which made judicial review in the United States possible.

In 1610, England's Chief Justice Sir Edward Coke declared in what came to be known as the *Bonham Case* that "when an act of Parliament is against common right and reason, or repugnant, or impossible to be performed, the common law will control it, and adjudge the act to be void."[7] This moment has been referenced by historians and legal scholars alike as an important if fleeting moment when the notion of judicial review entered the scene; fleeting because England did not adopt judicial review in response to Coke's assertion. Some scholars have maintained that Coke did not mean what his words clearly declare. English legal theorists and American historians have attempted over a period of centuries to construe Coke's argument into something almost unrecognizable. In the eighteenth century, William Blackstone rejected the most overt and obvious interpretation of Coke's decision in the *Bonham Case* by claiming that "if the parliament will positively enact a thing to be done which is unreasonable, I know of no power that can control it."[8] Legal scholar John V. Orth has observed that American historian Bernard Bailyn's groundbreaking 1967 work, *The Ideological Origins of the American Revolution*, makes a similar claim. Bailyn offers that "'by saying that the courts might 'void' a legislative provision that violated the constitution, he [Coke] had meant only that the courts were to construe statutes so as to bring them into conformity with recognized legal principles,' that is to say, to give them a reasonable construction."[9]

At that time, Coke was speaking particularly to royal power, as during this era the English Parliament had not risen to its eventual supremacy, and occasionally arguments against a literal interpretation of Coke's words is sometimes framed for this reason. The rise of parliamentary power had not yet asserted itself in England, thus—so the argument goes—Coke's assertion of the court nullifying law is an inappropriate example of judicial review precisely because it was not in opposition to an authoritative representative body. Coke, however, spoke of the court acting as a check against the sovereign, and it is not altogether clear that such a check would be roundly rejected just because the sovereign is made up of a parliament. If Coke did not mean what he said in the *Bonham Case*, the onus is upon critics to offer evidence for a contrary interpretation. The proper course, then, is to otherwise assume Coke meant what he said and not attempt to speak for him. Let us briefly observe the history of the rise of the English Parliament, however, because it will nevertheless help to explain why judicial review never became an English legal principle.

John V. Orth observes that in the early seventeenth century, the Stuart monarchs formulated an attempt for absolute power. Their challengers, in response, combed for a neutralizing force. "Not unnaturally, Coke, the great lawyer and judge, had sought to locate the limits on royal power in the common law.... Despite the fact the king was the font of justice and that English judges were royal appointees…. Coke had sought to use certain powerful medieval concepts, drawn from natural law and customary right, to cabin the sovereign."[10] Such attempts, including Coke's arguments in the *Bonham Case*, would not take hold due to later seventeenth-century events, particularly the English Civil Wars in the middle of the century and the Glorious Revolution in 1688. By the end of the seventeenth century, the foil to royal power in England was not the courts but Parliament. As a result, the courts retained their role as an arm of the executive and never achieved independence. As Orth explains, "The establishment of parliamentary supremacy meant that English courts could never again seriously claim the right to declare statutes void."[11] This is significant because it underscores that the trajectory of English governance going forward was to be an investment in representative government in the form of the English Parliament. This is substantially different to how legitimate political representation, constitution-making, and legal protection would express itself in the American system a century after the Glorious Revolution.

France, under the *Ancien Regime*, had experienced a limited form of judicial independence which was quite novel. The French parlements—which were legal courts and not to be confused with legislative bodies such as England's Parliament—operated for centuries as a limited but nonetheless important check against the power of the French king. Pre-revolutionary France's representative body, the Estates-General (made up of the First Estate: the clergy; the Second Estate: the nobility; and the Third Estate: the commoners), did not convene between the years 1614 and 1789. The years between was an era of absolute rule by the monarch and his only check were the French parlements. Though their challenges were not the final word regarding the law, their judicial independence and ability to (at least) challenge the wisdom and legitimacy of a law decreed by the king was an important precursor to the judicial independence later found in the United States.

Indeed, one of the most important influencers upon American political and legal thought was the eighteenth-century French philosopher Montesquieu. Montesquieu advocated for judicial independence and for the judiciary to act as an entirely separate branch of government in his 1748 work, *The Spirit of the Laws*. Montesquieu had in fact inherited a parlementship in the region of Bordeaux (parlementships were positions bought and sold as property and contributed to the large number of nobles in France; magistrates of the parlements were known as the *nobility of the robe*). He did not care for the position and sold it to a family member. His work in *The Spirit of the Laws* nevertheless reveal his high regard for judicial independence. Montesquieu's arguments for a separation of powers into three different branches were to be of significant importance upon the political philosophy of the American framers, most notably James Madison. In a section of *The Spirit of the Laws* titled "Laws that Compromise Political Liberty: Their Relation to the Constitution," Montesquieu asserted that all "would be lost if the same person, or the same body, whether composed of notables, nobles, or the people, were to exercise these three powers: that of making laws, that of executing political decisions, and that of judging crimes or disputes arising among individuals."[12] We can see, then, in Montesquieu how French notions of judicial independence under the Ancien Regime were influential to American legal theory later in the eighteenth century.

The power of the French parliaments to resist the registration of laws they deemed to be inappropriate exercises of the king's authority, though limited and not the final word, acted to some degree as a moderating influence upon the monarchy. Their privately owned positions as magistrates, known as venal offices, contributed to their sense of independence. Alexis de Tocqueville recognized this point in his work of French history, *The Ancien Regime and the French Revolution*, when he noted that in "no other country of Europe were the regular courts less subservient to the government than France.... The king had virtually no influence on the fate of judges. He could not remove them, transfer them, or even, as a general rule, promote them. In short, he had no hold over them."[13] Tocqueville also described that the "irregular intervention of the courts in government, which often disrupted the orderly dispatch of the public's affairs ... served at times to safeguard liberty" and that judicial "habits had become national habits. The idea that every issue is subject to debate and every decision to appeal was taken from the courts ... only in this one respect did the Ancien Regime contribute to the education of a free people."[14] This crucial aspect of French law and culture suddenly came under threat in the middle of the eighteenth century during the reign of Louis XV, and the parlements were ultimately suspended in 1770. Tocqueville observed that the suspension of the parlements precipitated revolutionary thought. "When the people witnessed the downfall and disappearance of the parlement, which, was nearly as old as the monarchy itself and previously thought unshakeable, they vaguely understood that a time of violence and hazard was approaching, one of those times in which everything becomes possible, when few things are so old as to be respectable or so new that they cannot be tried."[15]

Upon his succession in 1774, Louis XVI sought to ingratiate himself with the people by re-establishing the parlements. The suspension and restoration of the parlements appeared to have, in some way, emphasized the instability of the French system of government. The combination of its lack of legislators, its monarchical fiat, and a relatively independent judiciary that could nevertheless be erased if the king so chose highlighted the precariousness of the entire regime. Perhaps most significant of all, France had never established a constitution for itself the way England had. Keith Michael Baker notes this in his collection of essays, *Inventing the French Revolution* (1990). Baker observes that the "significance of this failure to establish any settled constitutional order in France was the essential lesson" in the work of eighteenth-century historian and royal archivist Gabriel Bonnot de Mably's *Observations of the History of France.*[16] "With the passing exception of Charlemagne, the French had never attempted to discover 'by what laws nature ordered men to achieve their happiness.'... For Mably, the French monarchy—far from being characterized by the existence of fundamental laws—was no more than the historical outcome of their absence."[17]

There is some irony in Louis XVI re-establishing the French parlements, and in the dismissal of them once the French Revolution came. The parlements had represented a significant aspect of the rule of law during the Ancien Regime that was otherwise lacking in France. Louis XVI had re-established them to curry favor with the people when he succeeded to the throne. Because this associated the parlements with the monarchy, however, and because the parlements had a long history associated with the Ancien Regime, they were rejected once the French Revolution commenced and all remnants of the old guard were ultimately abandoned. Revolutionary France saw its future protected and established, not entirely dissimilar to England a century before, through representative bodies enacting legislation, and not through a legal system which secured separation of powers and fundamental individual rights. Judicial independence and judicial review would instead be embraced by a different revolutionary nation across the Atlantic, one which took the lessons of England's progress with representative government and pre-revolutionary France's dalliance with judicial power, and synthesized them into a new configuration, informed by principles of constitutional fidelity, separation of powers, and devotion to the recognition of rights values.

Tensions in American Intellectual History

European natural rights theorists of the seventeenth and eighteenth centuries, including John Locke, Algernon Sidney, and the aforementioned Charles de Secondat Montesquieu, were profoundly influential upon the political philosophy of the American founders during the revolutionary and constitutional periods of the 1770s and 1780s. Other noteworthy influences include the writings of Cato earlier in the eighteenth century. These examples simultaneously gave birth to a new form of liberalism in the nineteenth century while also contributing to a long tradition of classical republicanism which called back to, at least, rights theorists of the Italian Renaissance. A deeper examination of the history of rights theory and its influence upon the American founding will be discussed in Chapter Seven. It will do, for the purposes of this introduction, to simply note that rights theory—in both its classical republican form and its enlightenment liberal form—was intensely persuasive upon American thought in the decades prior to the American Revolution. It appears also to have informed much of the thinking in the post–Revolution period and beyond, even as it drew from, at times, contrasting ideologies.

There are many tensions in the early history of American thought. These tensions are seen often as contradictory forces in conflict with each other. While true, it might be argued that these tensions have actually informed and facilitated the history of rights values throughout the history of the American republic. Rights values are the principles routinely returned to in the history of the American colonies and the United States. These principles are related to notions of justice, equality under the law, dignity, and individual rights. The tensions which define the American experience have informed a recurring conversation about rights values from the seventeenth century to today. These tensions can be understood as occupying five broad categories of American thought: spiritual, philosophical, social, economic, and political.

Spiritual tensions are among the earliest of the North American experience. This includes the religious conflicts which motivated Calvinist Separatists to migrate to North America in the early seventeenth century, their complicated and troubled relationship with Native Americans whom they initially viewed as pagan savages, and their impulse to mission to and convert indigenous Americans to Christianity. Spiritual tensions can also be seen in the internal tensions of Calvinist and Congregationalist thought in conflict with other forms of Protestantism. Protestantism's conception of individual revelation and attaining a personal relationship with God was in some ways divergent from Calvinism's (and Congregationalism's) collectivist form of social conservatism and conception of predestination.

Similar to the spiritual tension between Protestantism's personal relationship with the divine and the Calvinist strain which championed predestination, a *philosophical tension* in American thought expressed itself between beliefs of free will and providence. This philosophical paradox was not limited to the seventeenth century. Members of the revolutionary generation also spoke to notions of free will and God's will almost interchangeably, as though they were not to some degree opposite claims. Nineteenth-century America offered something similar to this in the simultaneous characterization of the boot-strapping, self-made American who nevertheless had a manifest destiny to settle the west and conquer the continent in the name of modernity and progress. Somehow, for centuries, Americans have been examples of self-actualized success stories whose successes were simultaneously pre-ordained and inevitable.

A *social tension* in American thought has also been to no small degree philosophical, and connects to the aforementioned ideologies of classical republicanism and liberal individualism. These two separate and to some extent opposing creeds have informed and complicated the intellectual history of North America and the United States. Classical republicanism's collectivist ideology of civic virtue and sacrifice of personal wants for public benefit runs counter to liberalism's emphasis on the rights and liberties of the individual.

Opposing views regarding commerce between republican pre-revolutionaries in the eighteenth century and the celebration of self-interest and aggregation of capital by nineteenth-century liberals underscore the difference of values between these ideologies. The classical republican/liberal individualist conflict can indeed be viewed as a more direct *economic tension* as well, especially in the late eighteenth and the nineteenth centuries, between agrarian self-sufficiency and the growth of industrial, urban commerce. The well-known economic and political war between Thomas Jefferson and Alexander Hamilton in the 1790s reveals the disparate visions of the two framers. Jefferson's vision of the American nation as one of economically independent yeoman farmers with little need for government who would be the culmination of an American promise of independence from tyranny was utterly at odds with Hamilton's dream of the United States as a British-style commercial power which necessitated a credit system and financial markets. Economic tensions in American thought since the founding have thus been more than merely matters of differences of fiscal opinion. They have themselves been an ideological battle.

Friction within the *political* category of American thought is most relevant to this work, as it most directly highlights constitutional matters and the role the American judiciary has come to occupy. This friction is the precarious balance between the rule of government based on majorities and the rule of law based on individual rights. It is a matter which runs deep within American political thought, yet the topic generally receives little attention among historians. The way a society organizes itself is no small matter. The fact that the United States has affirmed individual rights, sometimes at the expense of popular will, and has done

Tensions in the History of American Thought

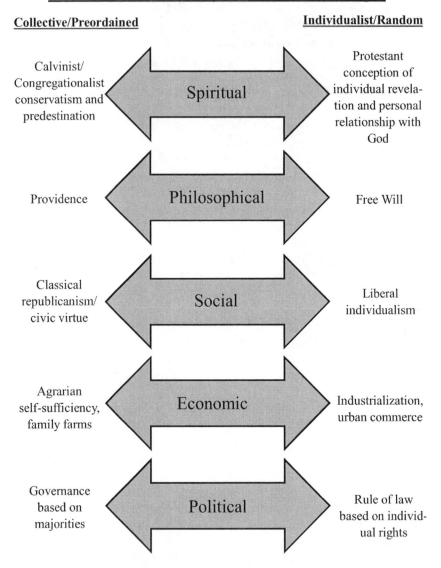

Tensions in the history of American thought.

so by designing its judiciary to be, at least at times, a guardian and protector against majoritarian impulses is certainly historic. Discovering the intellectual history which facilitated such a project is a worthwhile endeavor.

A Brief History of American Rights Values

As stated previously, American rights values are principles returned to time and again throughout the history of the North American colonies and the United States which called for the recognition of equality under the law, dignity for every human being, and individual rights. As early as 1688, individuals and groups in North America challenged institutions and practices which violated such rights values.

On April 18, 1688, the first known written protest against slavery in the New World was drafted. According to the Germantown Mennonite Trust, which oversees the history of Germantown, Pennsylvania, the signers of the Germantown antislavery petition "were disturbed that many of Philadelphia's Quakers chose to own slaves.... Although they had come to the new world to escape persecution, they saw no contradiction in owning slaves." Settlers of Germantown, however, "came from a country unaccustomed to slavery and the German Quakers in the area refused to participate in the slave trade."[18] The petition powerfully states that the practice of slavery was a violation of fundamental rights:

> Now, tho they [slaves] are black, we can not conceive there is more liberty to have them slaves, as it is to have other white ones. There is a saying that we shall doe to all men like as we will be done ourselves; making no difference of what generation, descent or colour they are. And those who steal or robb men, and those who buy or purchase them, are they not all alike? Here is liberty of conscience wch is right and reasonable; here ought to be liberty of ye body, except of evil-doers ,which is another case. But to bring men hither, or to rob and sell them against their will, we stand against.[19]

Rights values informed the language of the American Revolution less than a century later. George Mason's Declaration of Rights for Virginia, adopted as part of its constitutional convention on June 12, 1776, declared that "all men are by nature equally free and independent and have certain inherent rights, of which, when they enter into a state of society, they cannot, by any compact, deprive or divest their posterity; namely, the enjoyment of life and liberty, with the means of acquiring and possessing property, and pursuing and obtaining happiness and safety."[20] Mason's declaration had a direct and almost immediate influence on Thomas Jefferson's Declaration of Independence only a few short weeks later. Jefferson's declaration, on behalf of all thirteen colonies-turned-independent states, asserted that natural rights were inalienable, endowed by one's Creator, and that "among these are Life, Liberty, and the pursuit of Happiness."[21] Jefferson's original draft also condemned the British for the introduction of slavery into the American colonies and for the institution's violation of natural rights:

[The king] has waged cruel war against human nature itself, violating its most sacred rights of life and liberty in the persons of a distant people who never offended him, captivating and carrying them into slavery in another hemisphere or to incur miserable death in their transportation thither. This piratical warfare, the opprobrium of *infidel* powers, is the warfare of the *Christian* king of Britain, determined to keep open a market where *Men* should be bought & sold, he has prostituted negative for suppressing every legislative attempt to prohibit or to restrain this execrable commerce, and that this assemblage of horrors might want no fact of distinguished die, he is now exciting those very people to rise in arms among us, and to purchase that liberty of which he has deprived them: thus paying off former crimes committed against the *Liberties* of the people, with crimes which he urges them to commit against the lives of another.[22]

Natural rights-based arguments against the institution of slavery persisted into the nineteenth century. The New England Antislavery Society's Constitution of 1832, principally drafted by the organization's founder, William Lloyd Garrison, stated, "We hold that man ... cannot be the property of man ... whoever retains his fellow man in bondage, is guilty of a grievous wrong ... [and] a mere difference of complexion is no reason why any man should be deprived of any of his natural rights, or subjected to any political disability."[23] Garrison had earlier been a member of the colonization movement, which sought to free slaves and resettle them in Liberia. However, by the early 1830s he had abandoned colonization in favor of absolute abolition and legal equality. A fellow member of the abolition movement, runaway slave Frederick Douglass, punctuated the absurdity of slavery's basic violation of the natural right of self-ownership by beginning his speeches in the 1840s with "I appear before you this evening as a thief and a robber. I stole this head, these limbs, this body from my master and ran off with them."[24]

The tensions, previously discussed, in the history of American thought at times complemented and emboldened their counterparts. For example, economic and industrial innovation and a burgeoning liberal capitalism in the early nineteenth century, some feared, threatened the virtuousness needed for the republic to survive and thrive. As liberal individualism and modern commerce grew, the classical republicanism many feared was fading from American thought expressed itself in new ways. This included the reform movements of the nineteenth century, often facilitated and led by women. Thus, as individualistic liberalism subsumed notions of civic virtue in some areas, republican virtuousness found new expression in social reform movements. Reformers addressed social ills and political matters as diverse as drunkenness, mental health, the treatment of the incarcerated, poverty, women's rights, and the abolition of slavery. Thus the liberal act of reform in nineteenth-century America was often motivated by a conservative impulse for promoting civic virtue and decency. The process of expanding rights in the history of the United States has similarly been fueled by seemingly oppositional forces: a liberal motivation to expand rights and legal equality, and a conservative rationale to preserve republican virtue to foster a healthy society.

When the convention at Seneca Falls assembled in 1848, nearly all of the women present had participated in the abolitionist movement. The Seneca Falls convention and its Declaration of Sentiments illustrated the connection between the fight to end slavery, arguments for women's equality, and assertions of a tradition already more than a century old in America of declaring the existence of natural rights. The Declaration of Sentiments was deliberately framed so that its arguments for female equality would ring familiar to those of the Declaration of Independence:

> We hold these truths to be self-evident; that all men and women are created equal; that they are endowed by their Creator with certain inalienable rights; that among these are life, liberty, and the pursuit of happiness; that to secure these rights governments are instituted, deriving their just powers from the consent of the governed. Whenever any form of Government becomes destructive of these ends, it is the right of those who suffer from it to refuse allegiance to it, and to insist upon the institution of a new government, laying its foundation on such principles, and organizing its powers in such form as to them shall seem most likely to effect their safety and happiness.[25]

Just as Jefferson had listed the Americans' grievances against the British king, the Declaration of Sentiments included a similar list of grievances on behalf of women against men. "The history of mankind is a history of repeated injuries and usurpations on the part of man toward woman, having in direct object the establishment of an absolute tyranny over her. To prove this, let facts be submitted to a candid world." Included in the list was the deprivation of women's natural right to self-governance. "He has never permitted her to exercise her inalienable right to the elective franchise. He has compelled her to submit to laws, in the formation of which she had no voice."[26]

Seneca Falls is merely one example of a recurring reference to rights values in the American tradition, and it certainly wasn't the last. Martin Luther King's letter from Birmingham Jail asserted the principle that an unjust law is not one that binds in conscience, proclaiming that an "unjust law is a code that is out of harmony with the moral law."[27] King's "I Have a Dream" speech, like the Seneca Falls Declaration of Sentiments, argued in favor of an American rights values tradition laid down by the Declaration of Independence. He referred to the Declaration of Independence as a promissory note and the lack of equal rights under the law for African Americans as a case of "insufficient funds."[28] Civil Rights legislation championed by Dr. King in the 1960s was achieved through such recognition of American rights values. Just a few years later, the Black Panther Party quoted verbatim the first two paragraphs of the Declaration of Independence in its 1966 manifesto. Further, it did not argue that the American system of law was corrupt, but that it had not properly abided by its own mission on behalf of African Americans. "We believe that the courts should follow the United States Constitution so that black people will receive fair trials. The 14th Amendment of the U.S. Constitution gives a man a right to be tried by his peer group. A peer is a person from a similar economic, social, religious, geographical, environmental, historical and racial background."[29]

American Judicial Review: Informed by Intellectual History and Democracy's Limits

Over the course of its history, American thought has, time and again, centered itself upon an awareness of rights values. This emphasis upon the recognition of natural and civil rights is fundamental to the intellectual history of the United States. It has informed the architecture of its legal system and constitutional design. The supreme authority of the United States Constitution, and the power of the courts to compel the executive and legislative branches to a fidelity to the enumerated powers therein, is evidence of more than a scheme of balanced government, important as that is. It acts also as an instrument of rights theory, given to an unelected body to protect the individual rights of citizens against the fleeting passions of majorities. The American legal system's emphasis on rights values, informed by the intellectual history, sets it apart from its European precursors. Sir Edward Coke's assertion of the proper role of the Court to be a bulwark against arbitrary power, and the French parlements' independence under the Ancien Regime, were cases where the power of judicial review could have emerged but did not. The role of the judiciary to act as a viable check against undue executive and legislative action manifested itself in the United States because of its emphasis upon rights values over that of majoritarian will. Unlike England during the Glorious Revolution or France during its revolution a century later, the United States did not assert representative government as the final word on the law, however important representation unquestionably is. This was due both to rights values and to experiences during its own revolution, when the American people learned the limits of representative democracy.

A discussion follows which lays out the early history of debates regarding the legitimacy of judicial review during the American founding, and instances of judicial review in the 1780s and 1790s, predating *Marbury v. Madison* (Chapter One). Subsequent chapters include a historiography of judicial review scholarship (Chapter Two), a noteworthy alternative to judicial review which could have gained ground in the late eighteenth century but failed to do so (Chapter Three), and the demarcation point when the practice was firmly established (Chapter Four). A discussion then follows of ramifications when judicial review fails to recognize essential rights (Chapter Five), and an examination of the relationship between the Fourteenth Amendment and the role of the judiciary to safeguard rights (Chapter Six). This book also examines the influence of rights theory upon the American founding (Chapter Seven) and judicial review's role in the expansion of rights recognition in the twentieth and twenty-first centuries (Chapter Eight). The book concludes with a discussion concerning the ironic and precarious role of the Court (Conclusion), in which its power to act as a safeguard for individual rights against majority opinion and government overreach nevertheless requires a perception of legitimacy in the minds of the electorate. The Conclusion further emphasizes judicial review's historic role in American intellectual history and its influence upon the design of the American republic.

CHAPTER ONE

Primary Source Analysis: Philadelphia Convention, Ratification Debates, and Early Court Cases

A proper understanding of judicial review in the American system of governance requires an examination of the judiciary during the colonial era, the revolution, and the years preceding and following ratification of the United States Constitution. An inspection of primary sources related to the revolutionary and constitutional eras will reveal that judicial review was not an invention of the Marshall Court in the early nineteenth century. Rather, it was a power discussed and debated numerous times throughout the decades preceding the *Marbury* v. *Madison* decision in 1803, which ultimately enshrined the power in American jurisprudence. Furthermore, judicial review was exercised prior to the *Marbury* decision, by state courts in the 1780s and the federal Supreme Court in the 1790s. The common argument against judicial review as a novel invention made out of whole cloth in *Marbury* v. *Madison* is due to the absence of such a power expressed in Article III of the U.S. Constitution. However, this ignores the robust discourse involving judicial review at the Philadelphia Convention and the state ratification debates. It additionally overlooks the dialectical prose of Federalists and Antifederalists regarding judicial review, as well as numerous court decisions that exercised the power implicitly and explicitly. This chapter will thus establish, through primary source evidence, that a court's prerogative to rule a law void due to its unconstitutionality was seen by many as a legitimate function of the judiciary long before John Marshall gave his opinion asserting the power in 1803. Such evidence is crucial, because a thesis that emphasizes the legitimacy of judicial review as an instrument of rights theory must first demonstrate the legitimacy of judicial review itself.

In works such as this, a historiography is often provided in the first chapter. A survey of relevant judicial review scholarship will appear instead here in Chapter Two. The reason for this is a pragmatic one. Among scholars (both recent and from decades ago) who argue against the legitimacy of judicial review, is a subset who declare that it was a power unimaginable to those who created the United States Constitution and who facilitated the early years of the American republic. Many of the primary sources included in this chapter will make those arguments moot, as the history makes clear that a number of the most important figures involved in the design of the American constitutional system advocated for judicial review. Providing such evidence related to the early history of the republic will then allow for the remaining discussion regarding judicial review scholarship in Chapter Two to address other criticisms among judicial review skeptics. An additional reason for providing primary source evidence of judicial review in the late eighteenth century prior to any historiographical analysis is to reveal how fundamental the power was in the minds of many in earlier eras and to inform the reader of the relevant history prior to a scholarship-related discussion of such history. Demonstrating the history prior to a discussion of the scholarly debates thus provides the reader with an enlightened understanding of the topic at hand.

Colonial America

Americans during the colonial era did not enjoy the judicial independence of lifetime tenure for judges, unlike appointments to the courts in England. This was due to practical matters that nevertheless underscored the second-class status of the American colonies. Bernard Bailyn observes that "life tenure ... had been denied to the colonies, in part because properly trained lawyers were scarce in the colonies, especially in the early years, and appointments for life would prevent the replacement of ill-qualified judges by their betters."[1] Though lifetime appointments for judges became standard in England following the Glorious Revolution in the late seventeenth century, it would not be followed in the American colonies for almost another century and, when instituted by colonies themselves, was overruled by the monarch. Gordon Wood notes that prior to the eighteenth century, as "a consequence of the Glorious Revolution and the Act of Settlement of 1701 ... royally appointed judges in the mother country had won tenure during good behavior. But in most colonies judges had continued to hold office at the pleasure of the crown."[2] In the middle of the eighteenth century, the Pennsylvania and New York colonies sought to establish judicial independence through lifetime appointments, but their attempts were squelched. Bernard Bailyn remarks that in 1759 "the

Pennsylvania Assembly declared that the judges of that province would thereafter hold their offices by the same permanence of tenure that had been guaranteed English judges…. But the law was disallowed forthwith by the crown."[3] Bailyn also observes that New York's judiciary was able to secure lifetime tenure in 1750, but this was "interrupted by the death of George II in 1760 which required the reissuance of all crown commissions. An unpopular and politically weak lieutenant governor, determined to prevent his enemies from controlling the courts, refused to recommission the judges on life tenure."[4]

Despite the absence of tenure during good behavior for American judges, William E. Nelson has discovered that American courts exercised judicial review even prior to the revolution. He contends that "real power in colonial British North America lay mainly in the hands of local, usually county, courts…. When local judges and juries freely nullified the legislation and other commands of central authorities, weak governors and inactive legislatures."[5] It is thus useful to discover that as colonies sought to establish lifetime tenure for judges in order to mirror the appearance of judicial independence represented in England, they were exercising a far more extreme inclination toward independence through their exercise of judicial review. Colonies were denied judges who would serve during good behavior, yet they practiced a stronger form of judicial independence in their local courts than those in England. This may have influenced a particular worldview which posited the judiciary as a body more central to liberty than generally understood in the mother country.

The history of Colonial America and its formation played a decisive role in the judicial practice which would ultimately set the United States apart as an innovator of constitutional law. Among the earliest influences was the recognition of colonial charters as the standard to which other laws would be measured. As Mary Sarah Bilder observes, in her brief historiography of judicial review, it "developed from a long-standing English practice of reviewing the bylaws of corporations for repugnancy to the laws of England…. Because early colonial settlements were initially structured as corporations, this practice was extended to American colonies."[6] Keith Whittington's work has made a similar observation, recognizing that essentially "the colonial charters created legally enforceable limits on the power of local government officials."[7] Cases would be decided by comparing local and colonial legislation to the charters. This practice of review might be utilized by local courts or by the Privy Council in England. In another work by Mary Sarah Bilder, along with collaborator Sharon Hamby O'Connor, it is revealed that over a period of centuries, the English Privy Council had transformed from the "monarch's most trusted inner circle into a formal body of advisers, counseling the sovereign on administrative, legislative, and judicial matters. By the dawn of the eighteenth century, its power was waning as the power of Parliament ascended. Nonetheless, the Council and related subsidiary bodies continued to have responsibility for the administration of the growing number of English colonies."[8] Thus a form of review emerged in the American colonies in which a judicial body rendered verdicts based upon the fidelity of legislation to a higher, written law. These verdicts transpired both from the external force of the Privy Council in England as well as from local courts within the colonies.

By the late 1760s, when tensions between England and the colonies intensified, the role of the judiciary was again a point of contention when it was rumored that judges would no longer receive their pay from local jurisdictions but directly from the crown. According to Pauline Maier, in her examination of the history of the Declaration of Independence, *American Scripture* (1997), such fears that the king "sought to control the judiciary increased after the Townshend Act of 1767 suggested that it would soon begin paying the judges' salaries, as it did in Massachusetts six years later."[9] Colonists thus defied not only the idea of absolute authority of England's Parliament, which is generally provided as the essential motivator of resistance in the telling of the American Revolution, but also protested the subversion of their judiciary. Two years prior to the Townshend Act, the Stamp Act had already created strife when local courts contemplated closing their doors until they could operate legally with government-stamped documents. William E. Nelson observes, "The specific issue that confronted courts was whether to remain open and process pleas and other documents filed on unstamped paper or to close until stamps became available … the main argument in support of remaining open was the unconstitutionality of the Stamp Act."[10] When the Coercive Acts were imposed in 1774 (named the "Intolerable Acts" by colonists), the judicial power in the colonies was further weakened when one measure allowed for British agents accused of capital offenses in the course of their duties to be tried in England or a neighboring English colony. This act specifically undermined the authority of the Massachusetts colony to administer justice against officials they saw as abusing their positions of power. Resistance to the judicial reforms were deep and widespread. One instance was reported by *The Boston News-Letter* on September 1, 1774:

> that vast numbers of the people assembled to attend the last Session of the County Court in Great Barrington and, unarmed, filled the Court House and Avenues to the Seat of Justice, so full that no Passage could be found for the Justices to take their Places. The Sheriff commanded them to make way for the court, but they gave him to understand that they knew no court on any other establishment [legal basis] than the ancient laws and usages of their country, & to none other would they submit or give way on any terms.[11]

The erosion of colonial judicial power played a significant role in the resistance to the Coercive Acts and the ultimate revolution that followed. The debates over parliamentary authority versus local control during the imperial crisis has obscured the vital function the loss of the judiciary also played in the events leading up to the American Revolution. The creation of numerous independent states and their increased legislative authority as a result of the revolution further concealed the central role the judiciary had occupied in colonial life prior to the 1770s.

The Philadelphia Convention

When the Constitutional Convention in Philadelphia assembled in 1787, four years had passed since the end of the American War for Independence. With independence achieved, the weak character of the national government grew increasingly obvious, a fact known to some going back to the Revolutionary War itself. General of the revolution and convention attendee, George Washington, knew all too well of the ineffective and inefficient nature of the national government under the Articles of Confederation. He had seen plans, arms, and provisions constantly kept from his soldiers due to bureaucracy and a lack of authority on the part of the Confederation Congress. For others, the lack of an energetic national government became clearer in the years after the war was won. States struggled to suppress violent uprisings, the use of paper money wreaked havoc upon the national economy, and the anemic national government failed to satisfactorily address such matters. Under the Articles of Confederation, the national government was essentially a political body run by committee with little to no authority of its own to tax or impose significant and necessary reforms.

Out of the convention came a newly-drafted Constitution that would empower a new national government with considerable authority if ratified by a minimum of nine states. Unlike the model in operation under the Articles of Confederation, the new design would consist of a more powerful central body that nevertheless exhibited the ideal of balanced government. It was defined by a separation of legislative, executive, and judicial powers. The national authority was also to be tempered by powers reserved to the individual states.

The judiciary's status and powers were considered numerous times at the convention and these discussions shed light upon the role the framers anticipated for the Supreme Court. Rather than members of the Philadelphia Convention being incapable of imagining the Court possessing the power of judicial review, ancillary roles of the judiciary were clarified and rejected through such an understanding. It is somewhat surprising how the role of the judiciary was rarely discussed alone and was often couched in larger conversations regarding the executive veto power and other matters. Nevertheless, the power of the Court to review and reject legislation in their capacity as constitutional guardians was an idea alive and well in the spring and summer of 1787.

Among matters deliberated regarding the judicial power in the convention was a question over the efficacy and legitimacy of a federal Council of Revision: a body with the obligation to evaluate the constitutionality of legislation prior to it being given the force of law. A number of individual states utilized councils of revision in various forms at the time of the convention. In the scheme of the national government, the Council of Revision model that was proposed would have been a body made up of the President of the United States and members of the Supreme Court. This was included with an idea to enforce a *national veto* on behalf of the federal government. James Madison, in his original formulation of the new republic, wanted the federal legislature to wield a national veto power to nullify state laws. A Council of Revision would be utilized to ensure that appropriate national laws were designed which were not repugnant to the Constitution. The scheme to include a national legislative veto on state laws and a Council of Revision to examine federal legislation was presented by Edmund Randolph as part of the Virginia Plan of national governance. At the Philadelphia Convention, Randolph argued

> the National Legislature ought to be impowered … to negative all laws passed by the several States, contravening in the opinion of the National Legislature the articles of Union, and to call forth the force of the Union against any member the Union failing to fulfill its duty under the articles thereof … that the Executive and a convenient number of the National Judiciary, ought to compose a Council of revision with authority to examine every act of the National Legislature before it shall operate, & every act of a particular Legislature thereon shall be final.[12]

The national veto power and the Council of Revision were both ultimately rejected. Elbridge Gerry's observation of the matter is telling. In James Madison's notes of the Convention debates, he observed that "Mr. Gerry doubts whether the Judiciary ought to form a part of [a Council of Revision], as they will have a sufficient check against encroachments on their own department by their exposition of the laws, which involved a power of deciding on their Constitutionality."[13] Thus, Elbridge Gerry recognized the Court would itself have the authority to review and nullify unconstitutional legislation by dint of its inherent judicial power.

Rufus King agreed with Gerry's position that members of the judiciary should not be part of a Council of Revision but for a different, though equally sound, purpose: those who rule on matters of law should not be parties to the law's authorship. King expressed that "observing Judges ought to be able to expound the law as it should come before them, free from the bias of having participated in its formation."[14] King thus argued that members of the Court should not be part of a Council of Revision not only because it would be their duty to rule on the constitutionality of controversial legislation, but because their role in that duty was fundamental to their purpose. They should thus be insulated from the creation of the laws. In this instance Rufus King asserted the Court's power of judicial review and the critical importance of separation of powers simultaneously.

Elbridge Gerry proposed that instead of a Council of Revision, the Executive should have the power to exercise a veto "which shall not be afterwards passed by _____ parts of each branch of the national Legislature."[15] James Wilson argued that such a tempered executive veto power did not go far enough, believing the executive should have an absolute veto. Wilson "was for varying the position in such a manner as to give the Executive and Judiciary jointly an absolute negative."[16] Here, in Wilson's argument for an absolute veto for the President of the United States, he also advocated for the power of judicial review by the Court, though in a manner fitting a Council of Revision.

Wilson and Madison continued to raise the idea of a Council of Revision that would include the participation of members of the judiciary. Others, including Elbridge Gerry, Rufus King, and Charles Pinkney remained opposed. The discussion soon moved elsewhere, not to refining and defining the powers of the judiciary, but to the formation of the Supreme Court, additional inferior courts, and the process of judicial appointments. As mentioned previously, it appears that much of the time the role of the judiciary was debated it was often embedded in a larger conversation about an executive veto, representation in the Senate, and other issues. This fact obscures the many clear instances of judicial review advocacy during the convention.

When matters regarding judicial review were reintroduced at the convention it was in response to James Wilson once again reasserting the need for a Council of Revision. Wilson argued that judges "should have a share in the revisionary power, and they will have an opportunity of taking notice of these characters of law, and of counteracting, by the weight of their opinions the proper views of the Legislature."[17] Wilson's view was similar to that of Madison's reasoning for a Council of Revision, believing it to be better to clarify and repair unjust and unconstitutional legislation prior to it being given the force of law. Madison was particularly concerned about undue legislative power because of what he had seen the state legislatures allow, including the breaking of contracts, paper money, and what he feared was a dangerous democratic spirit.[18]

It may demand considerable effort to understand and appreciate the views of James Wilson and James Madison in 1787. This is in no small part due to the sophisticated aims of their constitutional project, which was a plan to create a substantially stronger national legislature, yet simultaneously bind this powerful entity with checks and balances to protect and secure the liberty of the people. The challenge to create a government with enough energy to effectuate its aims but with controls imposed upon it to ensure its legitimacy was an ambitious and burdensome undertaking. It can be understood, then, why they would desire a Council of Revision, even as the notion blurred separation of powers and would, according to framers like Elbridge Gerry, be unnecessary as the Court would itself possess the power to nullify unconstitutional laws.

The proposal for a Council of Revision was again rejected. Elbridge Gerry reiterated the argument made by Rufus King that such a council would establish "an improper coalition between the Executive and Judiciary departments.... It was making the Expositors of Laws, the Legislators which ought never be done."[19] Revealing further how the judiciary's role was often mixed with discussions regarding the other branches and the extent of their powers, Gerry admitted that he would "rather give the Executive an absolute negative for its own defense than thus to blend together the Judiciary and Executive departments."[20] For Gerry, a Council of Revision posed a greater threat to liberty than a President with absolute veto power. John Rutledge agreed with Gerry and King that a Council of Revision blurred the crucial separation of powers. He asserted that "judges ought never to give their opinion on a law till it comes before them."[21]

Madison's goal to establish a Council of Revision was introduced once again when he proposed that every "bill which shall have passed the two houses, shall, before it become a law, be severally presented to the President of the United States, and to the judges of the supreme court for the revision of each."[22] Wilson seconded the motion. Unsurprisingly, familiar objections were given in response. Charles Pinkney opposed "the interference of the Judges in the Legislative business: it will involve them in parties, and give a previous tincture to their opinions."[23] Such opinions, it may be surmised, regarded the role of the Court to rule on the constitutionality of those very laws.

John Francis Mercer, however, explicitly opposed judicial review and offered one of the few overt objections to it at the convention. Mercer "disapproved of the Doctrine that the Judges as expositors of the Constitution should have authority to declare a law void. He thought laws ought to be well and cautiously made, and then to be uncontrollable."[24] Legislation duly enacted which would have no recourse for review or removal thereafter was arguably antithetical to a young nation which had founded itself upon the rejection of unjust laws. Mercer, however, was not alone. John Dickinson "was strongly impressed with the remark of Mr. Mercer as to the power of the Judges to set aside law. He thought no such power ought to exist."[25] Revealingly, however, Dickinson was nevertheless "at the same time at a loss what expedient to substitute."[26]

A rejection of the power of judicial review does indeed beg the question: what check against unconstitutional laws could alternatively be offered? Some scholars and political theorists argue that no such check should exist at all and that the will of elected majorities is enough to legitimize legislation. The electoral process of citizens voting out those who go beyond their prescribed authority may be another argument. Such claims beg a further question, however, which is *why then have a constitution at all?* Advocates of this line of thought will be discussed further in Chapter Two.

It appears that figures like James Madison and James Wilson sought a Council of Revision because of fears that the other branches would not themselves sufficiently check the power of the legislative branch. Some recognized the power of the Court to exercise judicial review but feared it would not possess the will to do so. Others, including Wilson, feared that the executive would not exercise an adequate check on the legislative, and that there would be "a dissolution of Government from the legislature swallowing up all the other powers."[27] This explains why Wilson believed an absolute veto power for the President was essential. The framers struggled to negotiate exactly how to arm the other branches in order to act as proper checks against the legislative power. This reveals that the framers themselves rejected the notion of absolute legislative supremacy. They feared that even with such powers granted to them, the executive and the judiciary branches would nevertheless fail to exercise the will to counter undue legislative fiat. There existed a rational concern that the executive would fail to exercise its veto power and that the judiciary would anemically defer to Congress. Proposing a Council of Revision, with the executive and judiciary acting in concert to hedge against and revise legislation before it became law, was an understandable if ultimately flawed answer to such fears. The arguments against a Council of Revision won out because opponents recognized the danger in bringing the executive and judiciary into such close proximity. Assertions that the judiciary's role would include ruling on matters of constitutionality kept the branches satisfactorily separate and underscored an appreciation for judicial review at the convention.

The power of judicial review was thus acknowledged at the Philadelphia Convention. Advocated by some and opposed by others, it was not absent from the discussion. Instead, it informed and complicated

constitutional questions related to the presidential veto and a proposed
Council of Revision. It also played a part in a larger conversation regarding checks against a powerful legislative authority. A national veto, an
absolute executive veto, and a Council of Revision were ultimately unnecessary because the judiciary would exercise its power to rule on the constitutionality of laws.

Federalists, Antifederalists, and the State Ratification Debates

When the convention concluded and the Constitution was sent to
the individual states for ratification, some of the most essential debates
regarding the role of the judiciary transpired. Advocates of the proposal,
James Madison, Alexander Hamilton, and John Jay, writing collectively
under the name Publius, drafted a collection of essays known as *The Federalist.* Though James Madison's contribution to the collection may be most
exemplary for its arguments for balanced government, it is the essays of
Hamilton that speak most directly to matters regarding the judiciary.[28]
Federalist No.'s 22, 34, and 78 are especially revealing for their discussion
of the judiciary and constitutional legitimacy.

In "Federalist No. 22," Hamilton describes the judicial branch as a
body which gives clarity and legitimacy to the laws through interpretations and rulings. "Laws are a dead letter," he asserts, "without courts to
expound and define their true meaning and operation."[29] "Federalist No.
34" addresses concerns raised by opponents such as George Mason, who
feared the power of the Constitution's Supremacy Clause. "Hence we per-
ceive that the clause which declares the supremacy of the laws of the Union
... only declares a truth which flows immediately and necessarily from the
institution of a federal government. It will not, I presume, have escaped
observation that it expressly confines this supremacy to laws made pur-
suant to the Constitution."[30] Thus the supremacy of the national government over that of the states was limited to the express powers granted to
it by the Constitution. "Federalist No. 78" most strongly asserts the legal
philosophy judicial review and natural rights theory attend to: the nul-
lity of unjust, unconstitutional laws. "No legislative act ... contrary to the
Constitution, can be valid. To deny this would be to affirm that the deputy
is greater than his principal; that the servant is above his master; that the
representatives of the people are superior to the people themselves."[31] The
connection between judicial review, constitutional law, and rights theory
will be explored more deeply in Chapter Seven. It will suffice for now to
recognize Hamilton's assertion in "Federalist No. 78" that a law repugnant

to the Constitution possesses no legal force. It is an interpretation of law and legal legitimacy that informed the American Revolution and facilitated the American practice of judicial review.

Essays written expressing opposition to ratification of the proposed Constitution by various persons labelled "Antifederalists" emphasized an understanding of the power of the judiciary.[32] The writings of Centinel and Brutus argued against ratification because they explicitly feared that judicial review would be exercised. In Centinel XVI, the author clearly recognized

> the supreme court of the union, whose province it would be to determine the constitutionality of any law that may be controverted; and supposing no bribery or corrupt influence practised on the bench of judges, it would be their sworn duty to refuse their sanction to laws made in the face and contrary to the letter and spirit of the constitution, as any law to compel the settlement of accounts and payment of monies depending and due under the old confederation would be. The 1st section of 3d article gives the supreme court cognizance of not only the laws, but of all cases arising under the constitution, which empowers this tribunal to decide upon the construction of the constitution itself in the last resort.[33]

The Antifederalist writings of Brutus similarly recognized the Court's power of judicial review and warned of its consequences.[34] "It is to be observed that the supreme court has the power, in the last resort, to determine all questions that may arise in the course of legal discussion, on the meaning and construction of the constitution."[35] Brutus further warned that this was a power the Supreme Court "will hold under the constitution, and independent of the legislature."[36] In another essay, Brutus recognized the immense authority the Court was to have because of its power to rule on the constitutional legitimacy of legislation, observing that the Supreme Court would be "in many cases superior to that of the legislature ... this court will be authorized to decide upon the meaning of the constitution, and that, not only to the natural and obvious meaning of the words, but also according to the spirit and intention of it. In the exercise of this power they will not be subordinate to, but above the legislature."[37] For Brutus, judicial review was not a legal fiction but a constitutional reality under the proposed model of government. His arguments, like that of Centinel, confirm that the duty of the judiciary to rule on the constitutionality of laws was foreseen by both supporters and opponents of the Constitution prior to ratification.

Further confirmation of the recognition of judicial review can be found in the state ratification debates. At the Pennsylvania ratification convention, James Wilson defended the Constitution against Antifederalist William Findley specifically by casting the Court as a body which would rein in the powers of the national legislature:

I say, under this constitution, the legislature may be restrained, and kept within its prescribed bounds, by the interposition of the judicial department. This I hope, sir, to explain clearly and satisfactorily. I had occasion, on a former day, to state that the power of the constitution was paramount to the power of the legislature, acting under that constitution. For it is possible that the legislature, when acting in that capacity, may transgress the bounds assigned to it, and an act may pass in the usual *mode*, not withstanding that transgression; but when it comes to be discussed before the judges—when they consider its principles, and find it to be incompatible with the superior power of the constitution, it is their duty to pronounce it void.[38]

At the Connecticut ratification convention, Oliver Ellsworth asserted judicial review as a check against the national legislature as well as the individual states, claiming:

If the general legislature should at any time overleap their limits, the judicial department is a constitutional check. If the United States go beyond their powers, if they make a law which the constitution does not authorize, it is void; and the judicial power, the national judges, who to secure their impartiality are to be made independent, will declare it to be void.… On the other hand, if the states go beyond their limits, if they make a law which is an usurpation upon the general government, the law is void, and upright independent judges will declare it to be so.[39]

James Wilson, by James Barton Longacre, copied after a work by Jean Pierre Henri Elouis, c. 1825. Sepia ink wash with watercolor on paper (National Portrait Gallery).

It is advisable to recognize that both James Wilson and Oliver Ellsworth's defense of judicial review carry significant weight considering the two men would be among the earliest Justices on the United States Supreme Court. Wilson was appointed by President George Washington as part of the original six-member body in 1789 and Oliver Ellsworth was appointed as the third Chief Justice by Washington in 1796. Their legal acumen and judicial philosophy proved to be influential both at their respective state ratification conventions and on the Court itself.

Perhaps the most revealing admission of the judicial review power and its legitimacy was made at the Virginia ratification convention. Ardent Antifederalist and revolution icon, Patrick Henry, asserted judicial review during the Virginia debates. However, unlike Centinel and Brutus, his intention was not to warn against the judicial power under the proposed Constitution, but to question whether a national judiciary would have the fortitude to exercise its constitutional authority. Henry's criticism appeared to be that the power of judicial review had not been sufficiently underscored *enough*. Henry was thus not convinced federal judges would be the champions of republican liberty that jurists in Virginia had proved to be. In his debate with James Madison, Henry argued:

> The Honourable Gentleman did our Judiciary honour in saying, that they had firmness to counteract the Legislature in some cases. Yes, sir, our judges opposed the acts of the legislature. We have this land mark to guide us. They had fortitude to declare that they were the judiciary, and would oppose unconstitutional acts. Are you sure that your federal judiciary will act thus? Is that judiciary as well constructed, and as independent of the other branches, as our state judiciary? Where are your land-marks in this Government? I will be bold to say you cannot find any in it. I take it as the highest encomium on this country [Virginia], that the acts of the Legislature, if unconstitutional, are liable to be opposed by the Judiciary.[40]

The ratification debates and the writings of the Federalists and Antifederalists thus reveal the extent of understanding and appreciation for the exercise of judicial review in the late 1780s when the Constitution was being considered. An additional catalog of primary sources support the function's legitimacy and use further: state instances of judicial review in the 1780s and federal examples in the 1790s. State instances of judicial checks against the legislative power were referred to by Patrick Henry at the Virginia ratification convention. Henry clearly embraced the practice by Virginia courts with pride. At the Philadelphia Convention, Elbridge Gerry referenced state instances of judicial review. He observed that in "some States the Judges had actually set aside laws as being against the Constitution."[41] The following section will examine such instances of judicial review, beginning with state-level cases in the 1780s.

Judicial Review in Practice: Rutgers v. Waddington

In May 1783, the state of New York passed the Trespass Act, which established that Patriots who lost property due to occupation, destruction, and other acts of war on behalf of British Loyalists during the revolution, could sue for damages. Historian Peter Charles Hoffer observes that if "a Loyalist purchased or received any such property, or benefited from occupation of it, the Loyalist was not allowed to plead that the British made him do it (military necessity), or that he did not know that he was taking property that belonged to a Patriot."[42] A Patriot family in New York City were driven from their brewhouse in the late 1770s when British forces invaded and occupied the city. The family matriarch, widow Elizabeth Rutgers, and her sons, fled the brewhouse in the summer of 1776 and British soldiers then occupied the property before abandoning it in 1778. Later, commissary general David Weir licensed the building to merchants Benjamin Waddington and Evelyn Pierrepont through New York resident (and British Loyalist) Joshua Waddington. The tenants of the brewhouse paid rents for the next several years. They eventually departed the property in March of 1783. In November of that year, an unexplained fire destroyed the building's interior.

Elizabeth Rutgers's son, Anthony, brought suit against Joshua Waddington under the Trespass Act for damages and loss of revenue over the seven years the property had been denied them, as well as for damages to the property caused by the fire of unknown origin. The amount sought, £8,000, would be the equivalent of approximately $1 million today.[43] The case, *Rutgers* v. *Waddington*, transpired in an era when New York had become the center of politics for the young republic. The case proceeded where the Stamp Act Congress (precursor to the Continental Congress) had met, and as Peter Charles Hoffer observes, where, in 1776, the "Declaration of Independence was read to a crowd from the City Hall balcony... [Later, in 1788,] City Hall became Federal Hall, the first seat of the U.S. federal government."[44]

The Trespass Act was an ex post facto law, criminalizing behaviors retroactively. This was rationalized by supporters of the legislation as a remedial act. New York's constitution at the time utilized a council of revision, which endeavored to stop the Trespass Act from becoming law. The attempt failed and the law was passed. Critics of the act questioned its legitimacy, due to its ex post facto character, as well as possibly being in violation of the Treaty of Paris (the treaty of peace established with England that had officially ended the war). One such critic was New York lawyer Alexander Hamilton, who decided to join Waddington's legal defense team.

Hamilton indeed argued in *Rutgers* v. *Waddington* that the Trespass Act was void if it violated the law of nations or the provisions within the Treaty of Paris, which he asserted it did. In his legal arguments, Hamilton employed the philosophy of seventeenth-century English jurist Edward Coke, discussed in the introduction, that statutes against law and reason are void.[45] As he would argue a handful of years later in *The Federalist* essays, it was the duty of courts to give form and force to the law, and laws which violated the bounds of the body which enacted them were of no force.

The case's decision was delivered by magistrate James Duane. He ruled back rent was owed to the Rutgers family from 1778 to 1780, when the property was operated under a civil authority but that back rent was not owed from later in 1780 to 1783 when the property was under military authority. The larger relevance of the case was not the financial details of the decision but the aspect of the ruling that challenged the legitimacy of legislation which appeared to violate higher law. The New York Constitution of 1777 had incorporated the law of nations and thus the common law recognition of military necessity.[46] Considering this, the Trespass Act violated the principle of military necessity in times of war. Hoffer observes that Duane "had to assert or assume that the state constitution controlled legislation, that is, that the New York constitution was the fundamental law against which legislation had to be measured. This was a novel argument ... because after the 'Glorious Revolution' of 1689 Parliament was supreme. Its legislation was the constitution and it could say what that legislation meant."[47]

Duane, though asserting that the Trespass Act violated the New York Constitution, appears to have been unable to resolve the constitutional matter fully and stopped short of deeming the law void. Because of this, further suits were filed and more damage cases were dismissed. Alexander Hamilton kept himself occupied with such cases for months thereafter. *Rutgers* v. *Waddington* is thus an interesting case, like many in the 1780s, which asserted the unconstitutionality of a law but without the force of will to assert such legislation void.

Peter Charles Hoffer's analysis of the *Rutgers* case in his book, *Rutgers v. Waddington: Alexander Hamilton, the End of the War for Independence, and the Origins of Judicial Review* (2016), notes this phenomena in the 1780s. He observes that a number of cases cited as early instances of judicial review may have ruled in a way that recognized a law's unconstitutionality, but without actually nullifying the relevant law. The New Jersey case of *Holmes* v. *Walton* in 1780, for example, did not nullify the law in question but ruled that the specific case had not followed proper constitutional processes because the appellant had been tried by a jury of six rather than a prescribed jury of twelve.[48] The appellant was thus victorious but no law was nullified. Virginia's *Commonwealth* v. *Canton* (1782) is cited by the College of William and Mary's Law Library as "an early version of the doctrine of judicial review, holding that the highest court in the Commonwealth of Virginia had the power to invalidate laws that contravened the Virginia Constitution," but Hoffer argues that because the case was not widely known or discussed until decades afterward, that its

influence is suspect.[49] Under such a standard, however, Hoffer's own assertion of *Rutgers* v. *Waddington* as part of the origin of judicial review is
equally debatable. As previously stated and affirmed by Hoffer, *Rutgers* v.
Waddington did not ultimately nullify legislation, though it indeed recognized its unconstitutionality. Curiously missing from Hoffer's list are
the Massachusetts cases which arguably stand as better examples of early
judicial review than the *Rutgers* case. The Massachusetts cases, discussed
presently, ultimately led to the end of slavery in that state. *Brom and Bett*
v. *Ashley,* and a handful of cases collectively known as the *Quock Walker
cases*, underscore the larger connection made within this work: the relationship between judicial review and fundamental rights values in the
canon of American law.

Judicial Review in Practice: Massachusetts Cases of Brom and Bett *and* Quock Walker

Though practiced more substantially in the south, slavery existed in
every state during the revolutionary era and had been practiced in Massachusetts since the seventeenth century. One of the state's most celebrated cultural exports in the late eighteenth century was the poet Phillis
Wheatley, who had been a slave of the New England Wheatley family. She
was named after the slave vessel she arrived on as a child, *The Phillis*, and
educated by the Wheatley family. Her poems made her a cultural sensa-
tion. She travelled to England following the publication of her first book
of poetry and was celebrated as an American literary figure. She was eventually emancipated by the family that had both owned and educated her.

Phillis Wheatley's story highlights the awkward relationship between
New England Christians in the late eighteenth century and the practice of
slavery. The juxtaposition grew exceedingly stark as the American Revolution became equated with cries for freedom against arbitrary tyranny. The
Massachusetts Constitution of 1780, which asserted that all men were born
free and equal, with certain natural rights, further emphasized the visible
contradictions between the commonwealth's stated ideals and the inhu-
mane practice.

When the case of *Brom and Bett* v. *Ashley* was argued in 1781 in Berkshire County, the plaintiffs' attorney, Theodore Sedgwick (later a Massachusetts Congressman and Senator), asserted that slavery had been
implicitly abolished in Massachusetts as a consequence of its Constitution's Declaration of Rights. As a result Mum Bett (or Mumbet) and
another slave who had been under the ownership of John Ashley, known
only as Brom, were free. According to "Africans at the End of Slavery in

Phillis Wheatley, **unidentified artist, 1773. Engraving on paper (Library of Congress).**

Massachusetts," a project by the *Massachusetts Historical Society,* the jury in the case agreed "and both Mumbet and Brom were set free. John Ashley was also instructed to pay thirty shillings in damages plus trial costs."[50] Though little is known about the life of Brom thereafter, Mumbet assumed the name Elizabeth Freeman and became a paid servant for the Sedgwick family as a free citizen of Massachusetts for the next forty-eight years. Catharine Maria, the youngest daughter of Theodore Sedgwick, wrote an account of Freeman's life, published in *Bentley's Miscellany* under the title "Slavery in New England" in 1853. John Ashley endeavored to appeal some years after the decision, but a group of cases known as the Quock Walker cases appeared to convince him that attempts at retrieving his former slaves was a lost cause.

In 1783, three separate trials arose from an incident involving a runaway slave, Quock Walker, petitioning for his freedom on the grounds that his previous owner had promised his manumission. The man claiming to be his rightful and current owner, Nathaniel Jennison (who had married the previous master's widow), failed to fulfill the agreement. Walker sued Jennison for assault and battery in the first trial and demanded his freedom. The jury ruled Walker to be a free man and awarded him £50. The second trial ran simultaneous to the first and involved Jennison's suit against the Caldwell brothers, relatives of the deceased previous owner who had harbored Walker after he ran away. The jury found for Jennison in this case, ruling that his property had been disturbed. Jennison was awarded £25. The rulings of both cases were thus in conflict, where Walker was recognized as a free man in one case and as property in another. The third trial took place in April 1783 and unlike the previous two, was a criminal case that proceeded under the jurisdiction of the Supreme Judicial Court of Massachusetts. Jennison was ultimately convicted of criminal assault and battery and fined forty shillings in damages plus court costs. The more noteworthy outcome of the case was the legal establishment of Quock Walker's freedom and the unconstitutionality of slavery in Massachusetts as a result of the Declaration of Rights in its Constitution. Justice William Cushing's trial notes reveal both his view of the decision and the natural rights philosophy which underpinned it:

> As to ye. doctrine of Slavery & ye. right of Christians to holding Africans in perpetual servititude, & selling & treating them as we do our horses & Cattle, that, (it is true) has been heretofore countenanced by the province Laws formerly, but no where is it expressly enacted or established.—It has been a usage—a usage which took its origin, from ye practice of some of ye. European nations, & the regulations of british Govmt respecting the then Colonies, for ye. benefit of trade & Wealth. But whatever Sentiments have been formerly prevailed in this particular or slid in upon us by ye. Example of others, a different Idea has taken place with ye people of America more favorable to ye. natural rights of Mankind, & to that of and natural innate, desire of Liberty, with which Heaven (witht. regard to Colors, complexion or Shapes of noses features) has inspired all ye. human Race. And upon this Ground, our Constitution of Govmt, Sets out into by wch. ye people of this Commonwealth have solemnly bound themselves, Sets out with declaring that all men are born

free & equal—& yt. Every subject is intitled to Liberty, & to have it guarded by ye. Laws, as well as Life & property—& in short is totally repugnant to ye. Idea of being born Slaves. This being ye. Case I thinkye. Idea of Slavery is inconsistent with our own conduct & Constitution & there can be no such thing as perpetual servitude of a rational Creature, unless it his Liberty is forfeited by Some Criminal Conduct or given up by personal Consent or Contract.[51]

Elizabeth Freeman, **by Susan Anne Livingston Ridley Sedgwick, 1811. Oil pastel on ivory (Wikimedia Commons).**

Following this passage, Justice Cushing wrote, "The preceding Case was the One in which, by the foregoing Charge, Slavery in Massachusetts was forever abolished."[52] When John Ashley considered appealing the *Brom and Bett* v. *Ashley* decision, it was the news of the Massachusetts Supreme Court Quock Walker case that likely changed his mind. Slavery in Massachusetts was over, ruled unconstitutional as a violation of the rights values enshrined in the Massachusetts Constitution.

Some scholars have questioned whether the Massachusetts cases were in fact responsible for the end of slavery in the commonwealth. Articles by John Cushing in 1961 and Arthur Zilversmit in 1968 both highlight the difficulty in tracing an explicit cause-and-effect thread from the legal decisions to statewide emancipation. This is due to Justice Cushing being merely one of five judges who presided over the case and the fact that it was ultimately decided by a jury. Superior courts prior to the Marshall Court were not always decisive and clear in their rulings. This phenomenon of a diversity of legal opinions offered by justices rather than providing an unequivocal verdict was regularly practiced by state courts as well as the early federal court prior to the early nineteenth century. The judiciary, who were to give clarity to the law, thus often failed to do so in the late eighteenth century. Zilversmit notes that in the third and final Quock Walker case, the "Supreme Court was composed of five judges, each of whom could give an interpretation of the relevant law to the jury, perhaps disagreeing on fundamental points. It was the jury, and not the panel of judges, who delivered the verdict. This was not a system which lent itself to the establishment of clear rulings on difficult points of constitutional interpretation."[53] It could thus be argued that it was the character of the judicial power during the era, and its tendency to fall short of full elucidation, that is to blame for any ambiguity on the matter rather than the decisions themselves. Justice Cushing certainly believed that slavery had been nullified in Massachusetts. Nathaniel Jennison assumed slavery's unconstitutionality due to the *Brom and Bett* decision prior to his participation in the Quock Walker cases. In 1782, Jennison petitioned the Massachusetts General Court (the Massachusetts Legislature) to ask whether slavery had become unconstitutional:

> That by the Bill of Rights prefixed to the Constitution ... it is among other things declared "that all men are born free and equal"—which clause ... has been the subject of much altercation and dispute-that the Judges of the Supreme Judicial Court have so construed the same ... that by the Determination of the Supreme Judicial Court, the ... Bill of Rights is so to be construed, as to operate to the total discharge and manumission of all the Negro Slaves whatsoever.[54]

The practical result of the Massachusetts cases was the elimination of slavery within its borders. Though questions persist regarding how relevant the cases were to slavery's demise in Massachusetts, the fact remains that the institution of slavery disappeared from the commonwealth within the decade. There is also an absence of reliable alternatives to explain the phenomenon. The outcome of the relevant slave cases discussed above appears to have facilitated the eradication of slavery on constitutional grounds through assertions of natural rights. No alternative explanation with equal weight or evidence has ever been submitted.

The lack of any specific slave-related legislation to be nullified in the examples above may at first appear to undercut viewing the Massachusetts cases as instances of judicial review. It was the assertion of rights values, however, by a judicial body, which affirmed the freedom of plaintiffs against a practice that had actually been in existence longer than many statutes had been. Judicial review in Massachusetts thus transcended both written and unwritten law. Fidelity to the Massachusetts Constitution manifested the destruction of a practice anterior to and in violation of the Enlightenment-influenced rights values the new republic saw as its legitimate charter.

Judicial Review in Practice: Federal Supreme Court Cases in the 1790s

When the federal Supreme Court was created under the Judiciary Act of 1789 and began adjudicating cases soon after, it was not long before it too would begin practicing judicial review. The explicit character of Chief Justice John Marshall's ruling in *Marbury* v. *Madison* in 1803 that it is the role of the Court to say what the law is (discussed further in Chapter Four) obscures the historical reality that the Supreme Court had already ruled on the constitutionality of laws in cases preceding *Marbury*. Such examples provide the clear implication that the Court saw it as its duty to rule on the legitimacy of legislation and give form and force to the law prior to the nineteenth century and Marshall's tenure. The participation of figures like James Wilson and Oliver Ellsworth as early Justices of the Court, who had asserted the judicial power during the Pennsylvania and Connecticut ratification conventions, further supports this thesis.

In 1792, a matter known as the *Hayburn's Case* was deliberated by the Supreme Court. The case involved the federal Invalid Pensions Act, which sought to utilize a review process concerning names added to a list of military pensions for disabled veterans of the American Revolution. According to William Michael Treanor, at issue in the case was if the circuit court—charged with adopting the procedure—found someone on the list eligible, "it would inform the Secretary of War. The Secretary could then put the person on the pension list. But, if he decided that there was 'cause to suspect imposition or mistake,' he could decide not to put the person on the pension list and inform Congress of that action."[55] The law cast the Secretary of War into a legal authority, and one of higher status than the federal circuit court by giving the Secretary the final word on the matter. Treanor observes that before "any claimant came forward, the Circuit Court for New York ... concluded that, if read literally, the statute was unconstitutional."[56]

Justice James Wilson's written decision in *Hayburn's Case* also asserted that the law improperly assigned to the court non-judicial duties. It thus had not offered proper respect to constitutional principles of judicial independence and the separation of powers. "[N]either the legislative nor the executive branches can constitutionally assign to the judicial any duties, but such as are properly judicial, and to be performed in a judicial manner."[57] The duties assigned via the law were inherently nonjudicial "because it made their determinations subject to review by the Secretary of War and by Congress," thus failing to recognize the judiciary's role of being the last word on matters of law. "[B]y the constitution, neither the secretary at war, nor any other executive officer, nor even the legislature, are authorized to sit as a court of errors on the judicial acts or opinions of this court."[58]

William Michael Treanor notes that "the court, however, adopted a saving construction. The judges concluded that they could sit, in their individual capacity, as commissioners, rather than as judges. They proceeded to consider petitions in this capacity."[59] This saving construction may well be the reason why *Hayburn's Case* is not identified as the official origin of judicial review by the federal courts. It may also be due to the fact that the Justices did not deliver the decision *en banc* (from the Supreme Court bench with a unified voice), but through separate opinions delivered in their individual capacities as Circuit Court judges. It is a distinction without much difference, however, as they nevertheless rejected federal legislation (as it had been intended) on constitutional grounds. They would not be a party, in their official capacity, to a scheme that undermined their role as the last word on matters of law.

A year after the *Hayburn's Case*, *Chisholm v. Georgia* would act as an early example of judicial review by the federal courts against the power of the individual states. The outcome of *Chisholm* in 1793 also inspired the first amendment to be added to the United States Constitution following the adoption of the Bill of Rights. In 1792, Alexander Chisholm, a citizen of South Carolina, sued the state of Georgia to enforce a payment of claims. Georgia refused to appear in proceedings and maintained that the federal court had no such jurisdiction over it, asserting state sovereignty. The Supreme Court rejected Georgia's claim of sovereign immunity. Justice Iredell ruled that "unless the State of Georgia shall, after reasonable notice of this motion, cause an appearance to be entered on behalf of the said State on the fourth day of next Term, or show cause to the contrary, judgment shall be entered for the plaintiff, and a writ of enquiry shall be awarded."[60] The judicial opinion was informed by the relevant text in Article III of the U.S. Constitution, which provides for federal jurisdiction "wherein a State is a party in the following instances: 1st. Controversies between two or more States. 2nd. Controversies between a State and citizens of another State. 3rd. Controversies between a State, and foreign states, citizens, or subjects. And it also provides that, in all cases in which a State shall be a party, the Supreme Court shall have original jurisdiction."[61]

The reaction to *Chisholm* was quick and decisive. In response to the Court's rejection of state sovereignty, the Eleventh Amendment was soon drafted. Ratified in 1795, the amendment states, "The Judicial power of the United States shall not be construed to extend to any suit in law or equity, commenced or prosecuted against one of the United States by Citizens of another State, or by Citizens or Subjects of any Foreign State."[62] Thus the federal judiciary was not to have original jurisdiction in such matters thereafter.

Chisholm reflects the crucial aspect of judicial review that clarifies constitutional law, but it is also an important example of how the Court's power to interpret the Constitution and rule accordingly can inspire popular backlash and a change to the Constitution itself. *Chisholm* would not be the last Supreme Court decision to bring about an amendment, but it occupies an important place in being the first. It may be maintained, similar to the Massachusetts slave cases, that *Chisholm* is an inappropriate example of judicial review because there was no legislation nullified by the decision. That would be a limited and flawed interpretation of the judicial power, however. The Court's assertion of what the law was in *Chisholm* underscored the judiciary's authority to remind the state of Georgia that its assumption of sovereign immunity was not supported by the text of the Constitution. In response the Constitution was amended to comport with Georgia's position because it received popular support. Thus even in a case which inspired a change to the Constitution, the Court's role as defenders of the nation's charter proved to be critical.

In the year following *Chisholm*, the federal government enacted a tax "on carriages for the conveyance of persons, kept for the use of the owner."[63] The federal tax was challenged by Daniel Lawrence Hylton, who alleged "the said law was unconstitutional and void."[64] It is noteworthy that Hylton argued his case to the Court on grounds implying the power of judicial review, asserting that a duly-enacted law should be ruled void if it exceeds constitutional legitimacy.

The *Hylton* v. *United States* decision in 1796 upheld the constitutionality of the federal carriage tax but the deliberation of the case supports the view that the Court would have ruled the law void if it had found it unconstitutional. Keith Whittington observes that "the Court did not hesitate to side with Congress and uphold its taxation authority. Doing so strengthened the government's hand and its newly granted power to tax, and it kept the judiciary out of potential disputes over tax policy."[65] More than this, however, the relevance of the Hylton case was its deliberation regarding the constitutionality of a federal statute. Thus *Hylton* v. *United States* is an important example of judicial review more for the evidence of its consideration than for its ruling. The fact that the case centered on the constitutionality of federal legislation marks it as a forerunner to *Marbury* v. *Madison*.

A Historical Record of Judicial Review

The primary sources utilized and examined in the course of this chapter provide strong evidence for the existence of judicial review, both intellectually and in practice, long before the principle appeared in the Marshall Court in 1803. It was a practice informed by the utilization of charters as standards of law, as ruled by local courts as well as England's Privy Council in the colonial era. The constitutionality of acts of the

British Parliament were openly questioned by colonists during the imperial crisis, especially when the power and independence of the judiciary was threatened. Members of the Constitutional Convention asserted judicial review in 1787, its legitimate exercise was outlined in Federalist essays, and the concept was condemned and celebrated in tandem by Antifederalists in writings and at the state ratification conventions. Advocates for the Constitution at a number of those very ratification conventions, who later became Justices of the United States Supreme Court, championed the position that the judicial branch's duty was to nullify unconstitutional laws. Additionally, state courts prior to the Constitutional Convention and the federal Supreme Court prior to *Marbury* v. *Madison* expressed an inclination to rule that a law's legitimacy is to be measured against its relationship with the higher law of constitutionality. Opposition to judicial review cannot thus rest on any supposed innovation by Chief Justice John Marshall in *Marbury* v. *Madison*. Challenges to the practice must instead present sound political and philosophical critiques and must, most importantly, offer superior alternatives. The following chapter analyzes the history of judicial review scholarship. It addresses relevant arguments against the practice, particularly now that arguments asserting that judicial review advocacy did not exist during the founding era have been demonstrably disproven. Ultimately, the following chapter reveals how other arguments against the judicial power fail to offer a remedy equal to that of judicial review.

CHAPTER TWO

Survey of Judicial
Review Scholarship

Scholarship in the area of judicial review has developed for well over a century. Interdisciplinary at its core, the canon is made up of contributions by historians, political scientists, and legal scholars. Among the three, American historians have arguably paid least attention to the subject overall. This is to some degree understandable. Political scientists evaluate the political process, including acts of the judiciary. The political ramifications of an unelected, undemocratic body's actions upon the population plays a critical role and is thus crucial to apprehending the nuances and complexities of American governance. Legal scholars, naturally drawn to matters of law, precedence, and jurisprudence, study the practice of judicial review and debate its legitimacy precisely because of its function as the last word on what the law is. Historians have been, perhaps, the least comprehensive in their judicial review scholarship (with notable exceptions). As will be presented in the following pages, historians have often taken judicial review for granted, treated the practice as an inevitability, missed the range of debate regarding the process during the revolutionary and constitutional eras, or presumed the *Marbury* v. *Madison* decision in 1803 to be its historical starting point. It is important to note that historians have not been alone in making such errors, as will be seen. Considerable contemporary research has corrected much of what earlier scholars missed, whether by historians, political scientists, or students of law.

The aim of this chapter is to provide a history of the scholarship among some of the most influential members of the three fields. Though a comprehensive historiography is beyond the scope of this work, a considerable number of academics will be discussed ranging from the nineteenth century to the first two decades of the twenty-first century. Beyond the wide range of time examined, a diversity of views regarding the legitimacy of judicial review will also be explored. This chapter will thus attempt to disentangle previous errors which have at times informed a particular opinion about the role of the Court, and ultimately assert that alternatives to judicial review fail to satisfy protections of essential rights. It is necessary to analyze the judicial review-related work of intellectuals in the fields of law, political science, and American history in concert with one another to facilitate a proper understanding of the relevant discourses. This chapter is thus purely an assessment of judicial review scholarship. Analyses of judicial review in practice is examined in later chapters of this work.

Nineteenth Century

Of all the legal scholarship regarding American constitutionalism and the role of judicial review in the nineteenth century, the work of Justice Joseph Story is arguably the most noteworthy. Story is, to date, the youngest person ever appointed to the Court, nominated to the bench by President James Madison at the age of thirty-two in 1811. Justice Story had no previous judicial experience but was a strong supporter of the president's party as a Massachusetts state legislator and member of the United States Congress. Though Story's reputation as a loyal member of the Jeffersonian Republicans implied he would be an intellectual ballast to Chief Justice John Marshall's Federalist views (discussed further in Chapter Four), he instead proved to be quite aligned with Marshall's nationalist aims and judicial perspective.

Justice Story's *Commentaries on the Constitution of the United States: with a Preliminary Review of the Constitutional History of the Colonies and States Before the Adoption of the Constitution*, first published in 1833, remains one of the most important legal treatises on American constitutionalism ever written. Most relevant to the discussion within these pages, however, is Story's exposition on the proper role of judicial review, found in Book III, Chapter IV. Story discusses the rightful role of judicial review both as an exercise in the enforcement of the separation of powers among the federal branches, as well as to act as an arbiter of constitutionalism upon the separate states.

Regarding its role as a guardian of the separation of powers, Justice Story asserts the importance of the Court to honor the legitimate scope of powers held by the other federal branches. He observes that "in measures exclusively of a political, legislative, or executive character, it is plain that as the supreme authority, as to these questions, belongs to the legislative and executive departments, they cannot be re-examined elsewhere."[1] In cases where Congress or the Executive branches exceed their authority, however, Story is adamant that it is the role of the judiciary to intervene:

But where the question is of a different nature, and capable of judicial inquiry and decision, there it admits of a very different consideration. The decision then made, whether in favor or against the constitutionality of the act.... It is in such cases, as we conceive, that there is a final and common arbiter provided by the Constitution itself, to whose decisions all others are subordinate; and that arbiter is the supreme judicial authority of the courts of the Union.[2]

Story's support for the power of judicial review as a power exercised against the individual states is also resolute. He emphasizes that one of the most critical aspects of the United States Constitution is its power to bind states together through a universal standard of constitutional interpretation. In this regard, Story does not refute the role of federalism and the power of states and localities to exercise their recognized sovereign powers. Story does underscore, however, the role of the Court to apply the Constitution against the separate states and explicitly rejects the legitimacy of state nullification (a philosophy explored in more detail in Chapter Three). Story asserts the role of judicial review against the states, and does not merely recognize it as an instrument for protecting the separation of federal powers. This is because the federal Constitution was to be something that brought the states into a shared sphere of political philosophy. States may differ with each other regarding non-constitutional matters and may thus operate and enforce laws differently. When the Court provides a constitutional ruling, however, it is binding upon all of the states. Story observes that the alternative, which would allow for states to rule upon the constitutionality of matters for themselves, would descend into chaos and subvert the entire national agenda of possessing a national constitution:

Is the exposition of one State to be of authority there, and the reverse to be of authority in a neighboring State entertaining an opposite exposition? Then there would be at no time in the United States the same Constitution in operation over the whole people. Is a power which is doubted or denied by a single State to be suspended either wholly or in that State? Then the Constitution is practically gone, as a uniform system, or, indeed, as any system at all, at the pleasure of any State. If the power to nullify the Constitution exists in a single State, it may rightfully exercise it at its pleasure. Would not this be a far more dangerous and mischievous power than a power granted by all the States to the judiciary to construe the Constitution?[3]

Justice Story's *Commentaries* popularized and made explicable American constitutionalism and the power of judicial review for countless Americans (scholars and laypersons alike) in the nineteenth century and beyond. The Court explicitly asserted its role to say what the law is, in Chief Justice John Marshall's words, in *Marbury* v. *Madison* in 1803 (discussed in Chapter Four). Justice Story's *Commentaries*, however, provide a wealth of legal reasoning for the judicial power and articulate its value both as protector of the separation of powers and the importance of binding the individual states to a universal legal standard. In the late nineteenth century, however, the power of judicial review began to be openly challenged. Thus commenced an enduring legacy of scholars who sought to replace a philosophy of constitutional fidelity and counter-majoritarian principles with majoritarian fidelity and legislative supremacy.

Late Nineteenth/Early Twentieth Century

The power of the United States Supreme Court to nullify laws began to be a broader area of academic study and debate in the 1890s, roughly a century following ratification of the Federal Constitution. Among the first scholars to question the extent of the judicial power and to make a lasting influence, both on the academy and the Court, was James Bradley Thayer. Thayer's *Harvard Law Review* article, "The Origin and Scope of the American Doctrine of Constitutional Law" (1893), argued against a broad exercise of judicial review. Thayer asserted that the Court should generally employ a presumption of constitutionality regarding legislation enacted by the duly elected representatives of the American people. For Thayer, because there is no reference to a judicial review power in Article III of the Constitution nor in the confirmation oath of judges, the Court has no authority "reversing, displacing, or disregarding any action of the legislature or the executive which these departments are constitutionally authorized to take, or the determination of those departments that they are so authorized."[4] His arguments regarding the muddled history of judicial review in the founding era and the lack of such references to the power in Article III are compelling. He betrays the power of his own position, however, by providing an additional claim in the form of a logical fallacy. Thayer's bandwagon argument that "France, Germany, and Switzerland have written constitutions," and yet "such a power is not recognized there" is not convincing.[5] Using European states as an appeal to authority is unfit for a nation whose revolution and constitution explicitly rejected Old World models of government, including their reformed iterations of legislative supremacy. He also fails to address the important role that rights values played in the formation of the American republic and how the principle of limited government informed the project of the Constitution as supreme law. Possibly the weakest of Thayer's assertions, however, is the unquestionable wisdom he attaches to elected politicians. "It must be studiously remembered," he contends, "in judicially applying such a test as this of what a legislature may reasonably think, that virtue, sense, and competent knowledge are always to be attributed to that body."[6]

Concerns over subversion of the people's representatives by the Court in Thayer's work can be appreciated. A republic with the stated goal of accomplishing a more perfect union for We the People should be given some latitude in the enacting of legislation. It is certainly true that laws may be created that are unwise and ill-advised but not necessarily unconstitutional. In such cases, when unpopular or overly controversial legislation displeases the electorate, it is in their power to have themselves heard through the ballot box. The people, to some degree, legitimize or delegitimize legislation in the form of approval or disapproval through their vote. There is a danger in a judiciary nullifying laws which are seen as constitutional and legitimate by the people and the people's representatives. This form of overreach by the Court and against Congress is justifiably addressed in Thayer's article. A virtuous Congress which cannot attain its intended purpose is a threat to the health of the republic. As Thayer observes, the "checking and cutting down of legislative power ... cannot be accomplished without making the government petty and incompetent."[7]

Giving Thayer his due, this is an argument not unlike that of James Madison when he sought to design a more powerful and energetic legislative branch in the 1780s. The political body that is to represent the will of the people must indeed function, and function well. The trouble with Thayer's thesis is his assertion that the Constitution itself is a problem to be resolved rather than recognizing it as a limiting principle. When observing what he saw as a menace to the legislative power, he was arguing less against specific constitutional interpretation than against the Constitution itself. The problem, then, was not judicial review, but "numerous detailed prohibitions in the constitution."[8]

James Bradley Thayer's *Harvard Law Review* article in 1893 was enormously influential in academia and in the realm of jurisprudence. A student of Thayer, Oliver Wendell Holmes was appointed to the United States Supreme Court in 1902 by President Theodore Roosevelt. Holmes exercised the general presumption of constitutionality, sometimes referred to as judicial deference, that Thayer advocated. As will be seen in later chapters, other Justices, including Justice John Marshall Harlan—who preceded Holmes to the bench—shared this view. A number of subsequent Justices went on to express the same. Thayer's conviction in the reasonableness of legislative power has had lasting impact. The oft-used *rational basis test* in American jurisprudence can be traced back to Thayer and the arguments he outlined in 1893. Justice Holmes conveyed the concept of rational basis review in his dissent in *Lochner* v. *New York* in 1905. Rational basis soon became the Court's default position and would be articulated further in the 1930s (discussed more in Chapter Eight).

Thayer's work has seen considerable criticism by those possessing less faith in popular majorities and their representatives. His arguments for legislative supremacy, though generally well-reasoned in defense of Congress's role as the democratic voice of the people, nevertheless falls short of addressing the potential for legislative tyranny. The implication by Thayer appears to be that majoritarian tyranny is of little or no concern. How or why this could be is left unanswered. For Thayer, it appears that the popularity of legislation (and of the legislative power) is precisely the source of its legitimacy. This is not unlike his assertion that judicial review in the United States should not be employed because the practice is not employed in other countries. Such logic fails to address the rights of political, racial, and religious minorities, however, who in 1893 often endured discrimination and ill treatment under the law, as did women who possessed no national recognition of a right to vote. When judicial review is seen as an instrument of rights values, Thayerian assertions of judicial deference in the name of popular majorities fails to satisfy the larger matter of individual rights. Scholarship in the early twenty-first century critical of Thayer's presumption of constitutionality will be discussed presently.

In 1911, Louis B. Boudin's "Government by Judiciary," published in *Political Science Quarterly,* similarly argued against judicial review. Boudin claimed judicial review's lack of legitimacy was due to its ahistorical nature. The article asserts that "at the time of the American Revolution the power of the judiciary to annul legislation regularly enacted by the legislative department did not exist anywhere in the civilized world."[9] As was discussed in Chapter One, this claim is incorrect. Courts were nullifying legislation and customs at the state level in the 1780s when the Revolutionary War was still in progress, and historian William E. Nelson's work demonstrates that acts of judicial review had occurred during the colonial era. Boudin expresses another historical error when he claims "the Constitution was adopted by the Philadelphia Convention, and ratified by the people of the states, without any belief, without even a suspicion on the part of the great majority of those voting for it, whether in or out of the Constitutional Convention, that it contained any such [judicial review] implications."[10] Also discussed in Chapter One, the role of the judiciary to review and nullify unconstitutional laws was discussed by members of the Philadelphia Convention, in Antifederalist essays, and was asserted by both Federalists and Antifederalists during state ratification conventions. The matter was debated, and not all supported it, but it was not in absence during the crucial ratification period as Boudin's article suggests.

Boudin's article fostered claims that had been made even earlier in the new century by figures such as attorney Walter Clark and dean of the Dickinson School of Law, William Trickett, who alleged that the judiciary had usurped the power of the legislature. In response, historian Charles

Beard—whose 1913 work, *An Economic Interpretation of the Constitution of the United States*, would prove to be profoundly influential in the field of history—wrote an article in 1912 challenging the judicial usurpation thesis. In his article "The Supreme Court—Usurper or Grantee?" Beard maintained that the framers were not "among those who favored the assaults on vested rights which legislative majorities were making throughout the Union. On the contrary, they were, without exception, bitter opponents of such enterprises; and they regarded it as their chief duty ... to find a way of preventing the renewal of what they deemed 'legislative tyranny.'"[11] Though Beard's economic thesis of the Constitution is to some degree flawed, his article countering the usurpation thesis is correct. Those who drafted the Constitution, specifically the chief architect of the project, James Madison, was not in favor of absolute legislative power. As Beard observes, "No historical fact is more clearly established than the fact that the framers of the Constitution distrusted democracy and feared the rule of mere numbers."[12] Beard's assertion is important because his later work offers a sometimes scathing critique of the framers as a political minority who had used the Constitution as a vehicle to increase and protect their wealth. His critique of the usurpation argument, then, is not a defense of the framers or their motivations, but an admission that they did not see popular sentiment as a necessarily legitimizing force for government. Yes, the will of the people was a critical component, but it was not the only important feature, nor necessarily the most integral. Individual rights, including rights of private property, were also essential. Finally, the dearth of evidence among judicial review opponents, according to Beard, was itself telling. Beard maintained, "it certainly is incumbent upon those who say that judicial control was not within the purpose of the men who framed and enacted the federal Constitution to bring forward positive evidence, not arguments resting on silence."[13]

Lawyer and historian, William M. Meigs, published one of the first substantial examinations of what he called the judicial power in his book, *The Relation of the Judiciary to the Constitution*, in 1919. Meigs was motivated, in part, by progressive arguments against judicial review which had begun in the 1890s and continued through the early decades of the twentieth century. Arguing from a perspective poles apart from Thayer and Boudin, Meigs contended that those "who consider themselves 'Progressives' have, many of them, taken up the hue and cry, and to-day our ancient doctrine is traversed and certainly in danger of being rejected, or perhaps confessed and then avoided through some by-way."[14] Whereas Thayer and Boudin feared judicial usurpation of the legislature, Meigs worried that progressive aims to strip the Court of the power to nullify legislation was a threat to the Constitution and balanced government. He explicitly argued against mob rule and asserted that the rule of law is paramount. Treating the Court as subordinate to the legislature, according to Meigs, was a perilous enterprise. He contended that there "is the great danger that this noisy minority will lead the country largely, even entirely, to abandon its canons and laws and to launch out upon evil ways, much to its detriment, precisely as a street mob will often follow courses far worse than the average desire of its members."[15]

According to William Meigs, the historical evidence for the intention and appropriateness of judicial review was overwhelming. He believed "the evidence accessible to-day is a demonstration, only less certain than those of astronomy and mathematics, that the Judiciary was plainly pointed out by our history for the vast function it has exercised, and that it was expected and intended, both by the Federal Convention and the opinion of the publicists of the day, to exercise that function."[16] Primary sources included in Chapter One of this work, including the debates at the Philadelphia Convention and the Federalist essays, support this claim. Meigs maintained, however, that evidence went back farther than the Constitutional Convention or the Revolution. The seeds of judicial review were planted in Colonial America, with the reliance upon colonial charters, and especially the influence of England's Privy Council (also discussed in Chapter One). The Privy Council, a body within the King's Court that reviewed colonial legislation and possessed the power to nullify laws of the colonies repugnant to charters or fundamental English law, "was, beyond doubt, of great influence in leading to that judicial power."[17] Beyond mere inspiration, William Meigs's work contends that the role of the Privy Council acted essentially as an explicit precursor to the United States judiciary, observing that it is "remarkable how closely the action of the Privy Council ... resembled the action of our American courts in modern days in holding a statute unconstitutional, and hence refusing to carry it out."[18]

William M. Meigs's *The Relation of the Judiciary to the Constitution* thus asserted that the power of judicial review was supported by various instances of precedence going back to the colonial era, had been an intended power of the Court by the framers, and was—perhaps most importantly—grounded in fundamental principles of balanced government. Historical precedence, it could be argued, is not enough to legitimize a law or procedure. Indeed, some of the most critical moments of judicial review in the history of the United States were refutations of previous rulings, as will be explored in later chapters. The appropriateness of judicial review, for William Meigs and those who find affinity with his appraisals, is found in the combination of the exercise's long history *and* its pertinence for achieving separation of powers and limited government.

1950s and 1960s

In the middle of the twentieth century, notable scholars again expressed their views regarding the history and legitimacy of judicial review. Cecelia Kenyon's article, "Men of Little Faith: The Anti-Federalists on the Nature of Representative Government," published in the *William and Mary Quarterly* in 1955, was among the earliest works to provide a substantial analysis of the views of the opponents of the Constitution. Kenyon's scholarship informed the work of later Antifederalist scholars such as Herbert Storing, and her critique of Charles Beard's economic thesis paved the way for the next era of American historians who would revolutionize the field in the 1960s, including Bernard Bailyn and Gordon Wood. Though Kenyon's work is noteworthy for its influence upon later scholarship, her analysis of judicial review is astonishingly off the mark. For example, her observation that during the ratification era there was a "complete absence of debate over judicial review" is plainly wrong.[19] Additionally, her contention that "Anti-Federalists probed the Constitution for every conceivable threat," and that if "they had considered judicial review such a threat, they would surely have made the most of it" overlooks the concerns voiced by Brutus and Centinel that referenced the power of the judiciary explicitly.[20] Kenyon's scholarship marks an important moment when the influence of Charles Beard began to wane and Antifederalist intellectual history became more central to the discourse. That said, her limited and faulty analysis of the judicial review debate in the 1780s makes her an unsatisfactory source for understanding the subject.

Alexander Bickel's *The Least Dangerous Branch: The Supreme Court at the Bar of Politics* (1962) offered a more refined opposition to general judicial review, but did so with familiar arguments about judicial review's antidemocratic nature similar to those made by Thayer and Boudin decades earlier. Bickel famously labelled judicial review a "counter-majoritarian force in our system" and contended that when "the Supreme Court declares unconstitutional a legislative act ... it thwarts the will of representatives of the actual people of the here and now."[21] Bickel, however, was no progressive. His recognition of the tension between democracy and judicial review informed a view that narrower remedies should address the narrowest of controversies. Bickel should thus be seen as a conservative critic of broad judicial review rather than an opponent of the practice itself. His advocacy for judicial restraint proved to be influential upon twenty-first-century Justices, including Samuel Alito and Chief Justice John Roberts. Bickel's contention that "nothing in the further complexities and perplexities of the system ... nothing in these complexities can alter the essential reality that judicial review is a deviant institution in the American democracy"[22] reveals a conservative nod to judicial deference toward legislative power and popular will. Indeed, conservative criticism of judicial review is a critical aspect of American legal history. While concerns over judicial supremacy in both the early twentieth and twenty-first centuries were dominated by progressives, backlash to the judicial power arose among conservatives in the middle of the twentieth century. Bickel's advocacy for a more surgical approach to judicial review that doesn't needlessly nullify laws and practices a level of restraint played an important role in the growth of conservative jurisprudence. *The Least Dangerous Branch* provides a prescient recognition of the growing power of the court and possible ramifications judicial review can impose upon the democratic process, and does so from a decidedly conservative perspective of legal scholarship.

In 1963, political scientist Charles Hyneman published *The Supreme Court on Trial: How the American Justice System Sacrifices Innocent Defendants*. Hyneman asserted that the lack of reference to a judicial restraining power in the Constitution should be interpreted as the judicial branch having no significant restraint upon the executive or legislative branches. *The Supreme Court on Trial* argues that the Constitution "expressly endows the president with powers to restrain Congress and the judiciary" and "expressly endows Congress ... with powers enabling it to check the president and the judiciary." However, the Constitution "contains no provision which asserts that the Supreme Court or any other court may exercise a specific power which would restrain the president or Congress in the exercise of their powers."[23] Hyneman's analysis thus ignores crucial instances of judicial review during the colonial and constitutional eras and provides a limited understanding of the intellectual history that informed the practice prior to and following the revolution. Nevertheless, *The Supreme Court on Trial* proved to be influential, especially for scholarship dealing with the treatment of defendants by the courts, such as Erwin Chemerinky's *The Case Against the Supreme Court* (2014).

Historian Clinton Rossiter, in 1966, presented Chief Justice John Marshall's assertion of judicial review in the *Marbury v. Madison* decision in 1803 as the ultimate culmination of the framers' mission. According to Rossiter, judicial review was not only legitimate, but vital to the constitutional project, suggesting that when "Marshall had finished reading his opinion in *Marbury v. Madison* on February 24, 1803, the Grand Convention stood at last adjourned."[24] Rossiter saw the precursor to the Supreme Court not to be the British Privy Council of the colonial era but the Court of Appeals in Cases of Capture during the revolutionary era. The Court of Appeals in Cases of Capture operated under the Articles of Confederation and was the only federal judicial body in existence during the

Revolutionary War. Its primary function was to rule on matters of property and seizure regarding vessels taken captive during the war. Rossiter maintained that the "three-man Court of Appeals in Cases of Capture … did its restricted but useful judicial tasks in a manner reasonably worthy of the only plausible candidate for the title of 'direct ancestor' to the Supreme Court of the United States."[25]

Gordon S. Wood's *Creation of the American Republic*, published in 1969, is one of the most influential works of academic history of the twentieth century. Generally applauded for its contribution to the intellectual and cultural history of the American founding, its analysis of the legal history of Colonial America and the early national period is also noteworthy. Wood traces instances of judicial review by the individual states prior to 1787, further discounting claims that the practice was an invention of the Marshall Court. Furthermore, Wood reveals the organic process the growth of judicial review took in the individual states as a response to the expansion of legislative power that the revolution facilitated. Championing of the will of the people during the revolution in the 1770s became tempered by concerns over unlimited legislative power by the 1780s. Judicial review, along with a formalized constitutional convention process (discussed further in Chapter Seven), acted as a means to wrest some of that power back from the state legislatures. Wood recognized that by the 1780s "the judiciary in several states, New Jersey, Virginia, New York, Rhode Island, and North Carolina, was gingerly and often ambiguously moving in isolated but important cases to impose restraints on what the legislatures were enacting as law."[26] The expansion in acceptance and practice of judicial review was thus itself part of an ongoing revolutionary process that recognized the need for limited government, however local and representative.

1980s and 1990s

Forrest McDonald's *Novus Ordo Seclorum: The Intellectual Origins of the Constitution* (1985) does a capable job of presenting the major points of the intellectual history that informed the American founding, but does not demonstrate substantial analysis regarding the role of the judiciary. One assertion McDonald makes regarding judicial review in the late eighteenth century concerns the relatively wide acceptance of federal judicial review over the individual states, but strong disagreement regarding the power of the Court to nullify federal laws. McDonald contends that "the belief that the supreme-law clause established the power of judicial review over state laws but not over acts of Congress obviously had widespread currency, as is attested by the intensely hostile reaction in the Congress and in the press on the two occasions on which, before the Civil War, the Supreme Court dared to declare an act of Congress unconstitutional."[27] The claim that the judiciary only struck down two federal statutes prior to the Civil War is a common one. Recent scholarship, however, provides evidence counter to this. Keith Whittington's work, in particular, regarding this matter will be discussed at the end of this chapter. McDonald's allegation regarding the low number of instances of judicial review in the first half of the nineteenth century is thus incorrect. Furthermore, his observation of a relatively broad acceptance of the federal judiciary's power to nullify state laws is debatable, as other historians have made opposite claims. Even if McDonald is correct on this matter, however, the power of the Court to nullify state legislation also had limits, as will be seen in Chapter Four with an analysis of the *Barron* v. *Baltimore* decision.

Jack Rakove's examination of constitutional interpretation and intellectual history, *Original Meanings: Politics and Ideas in the Making of the Constitution* (1996), offered a counterpoint to McDonald's *Novus Ordo Seclorum*. Regarding debates about the role of the judiciary, Rakove offers a position opposite to that of McDonald, maintaining that judicial review was seen as a mechanism to secure separation of powers and that its role against the individual states was the larger controversy. Rakove also notes that both supporters and detractors of ratification recognized this feature. Referencing the Antifederalist who focused most on the power of the proposed federal judiciary, he observes that "Brutus [initially] treated judicial review as an aspect of separation of powers, but he soon indicated that its real force would lie along the axis of federalism."[28] As for the view among Federalists, it is here that *Original Meanings* contradicts *Novus Ordo Seclorum* when Rakove observes that "the framers did intend judicial review to apply to the realm of national legislation, where it would help maintain boundaries among the branches of national government.... [The controversy] would rise instead along the uncharted borders where the powers of state and national governments would overlap."[29] Despite their clear disagreement regarding the prevailing controversies of judicial review during the drafting and ratification of the Constitution, McDonald and Rakove nevertheless agree that it was a facet of the new constitutional system actively discussed and debated. Their assessments then are differences in matters of degrees. Both historians recognized that judicial review, as an instrument of federalism and as guardian of separation of powers, was a power scrutinized during the ratification period and beyond. A subsidiary debate thus continues among scholars regarding the primary intent of judicial review, to ensure separation of federal powers or to establish federal dominance over the individual states.

In 1999, Mark Tushnet published *Taking the Constitution Away from the Courts*. Championing something he calls populist constitutionalism, Tushnet refutes judicial review and argues that it has facilitated political apathy. He asserts that a populist constitutionalism, informed by the principles enshrined in the Declaration of Independence, would be a preferable model. "The populist constitutionalist," he affirms, "believes that the public generally should participate in shaping constitutional law more directly and openly."[30] Tushnet advocates for reining in the Court's power through several measures. "We can take the Constitution away from the courts in several ways," he argues. "We could deny them the final word about the Constitution's meaning … or we could deny them any role in Constitutional interpretation whatever."[31] He maintains that taking the Constitution away from the courts "need not occasion deep concern about the preservation of our liberties."[32] This is a bold claim, and one he attempts to support with historical examples that include egregious instances of judicial review and noble figures who advocated against it, including Abraham Lincoln. For example, he employs an appeal to authority when he observes that, "as Lincoln saw it, the Constitution should be interpreted to advance the Declaration's project, when its terms were fairly open to such an interpretation."[33]

It is an understatement to note that Lincoln's rationales in the 1860s were informed by precarious and unique circumstances. He was a president during a constitutional crisis in the form of the Civil War who asserted rather ill-defined war powers, suspended habeas corpus, jailed dissidents without trial, and ultimately freed African Americans in the South explicitly through his implied war powers, which left slaves in the border states (and isolated pockets in the North, including New Jersey) in bondage until ratification of the Thirteenth Amendment. To use Lincoln and the era of the Civil War as a model for populist constitutionalism is, at best, bizarre.

Tushnet's recognition of the Declaration of Independence as the guidepost for American ideals and his attention to the need for the protection of rights is to be lauded. His arguments and examples, however, are not convincing. Worse, his defense of legislative supremacy, or what he promotes as *self-reinforcing constitutionalism* in opposition to judicial review, is delivered in the form of a strawman argument. He claims the "conventional assumption is that of course we get a higher rate of compliance with constitutional values if the courts enforce the Constitution. That assumption often rests on the unstated, and largely indefensible, belief that the courts never make mistakes. But they do."[34] This is a plainly absurd assertion, and, more critically, does not address the threat of legislative tyranny. Anyone ready to defend judicial review must be willing to confront its worst examples, as this work will do in later chapters. Tushnet's evasion in addressing the potential harm of legislative overreach in *Taking the Constitution Away from the Courts* is telling. While accusing defenders of judicial review of holding faulty assumptions, he assumes that a self-reinforcing constitutionalism would be a superior alternative. Tushnet's form of constitutionalism would mean a substantial lack of external enforcement of the Constitution upon the legislative power. The problem with the self-reinforcing thesis, that the legislature can decide for itself the constitutionality of the laws it passes, is thus: when else are institutions trusted to police themselves? Quintessential principles of justice, including separation of powers and that one cannot be a judge in one's own case, contradict Tushnet's thesis as a realistic and workable model of constitutional governance.

Early Twenty-First Century

The first two decades of the twenty-first century have seen further discourse regarding judicial review among scholars in law, history, and political science. Larry Kramer's *The People Themselves: Popular Constitutionalism and Judicial Review*, published in 2004, is particularly noteworthy. Kramer's *The People Themselves* suggests that the Court has been allowed to grow in power needlessly and that there are remedies to bring it more into line with popular sentiment. Kramer thus supports an end to judicial review as it has been established and advocates the legislative and executive branches to exercise their power to weaken the judiciary. "The Constitution leaves room for countless political responses to an overly assertive Court," Kramer observes. "Justices can be impeached, the Court's budget can be slashed, the President can ignore its mandates, Congress can strip it of jurisdiction or shrink its size, or pack it with new members or give it burdensome new responsibilities or revise its procedures."[35] Despite Kramer's matter of fact tone, some of his proposed measures are radical. Court-packing is merely one controversial proposal. Offered by President Franklin Roosevelt in the 1930s due to resistance by the judiciary to accept aspects of his New Deal program, court-packing did not prove popular among the majority of even his own party. So unpopular was it that it would not be seriously proposed again until the Democratic Party primary season in 2019. The issue of packing the court will be discussed in the conclusion of this work. It is fair to say, however, that a number of Kramer's propositions may not see the popular support he assumes they would garner. Additionally, some of the measures, including assigning the Court extra and burdensome duties may itself see constitutional challenges. The *Hayburn's Case* of 1792, discussed in Chapter One, established the precedent that the Court could and would not be burdened with non-judicial obligations by Congress. Added judicial obligations intended merely to weaken the Court may itself prove unpopular as well. Advocating that the President of the United States should flout legal rulings is also something that could ultimately cause more strife than stability.

Legal scholar Akhil Reed Amar's *America's Constitution: A Biography* (2005), offers a thoughtful and nuanced perspective on judicial review, both as historical practice and as a legal philosophy. Amar is in agreement with Forrest McDonald (and implicitly in disagreement with Jack Rakove) that the initial intent of judicial review was to empower the new federal government over the states and that the power to review federal statute was a thornier matter. He asserts that the Federalists "could all agree upon the need for strong vertical federal judicial review over states while disagreeing about the optional scope of horizontal judicial review against Congress."[36] Amar ultimately defends the power of judicial review but contends that it has been exercised too often, leading by default to a weakening of the other branches, maintaining that as "the Court has asserted more power for itself, the other branches and the citizenry have frequently yielded."[37] The judicial power, according to Amar, is an essential function but one to be exercised rarely. The procedure has thus become too much of a common feature of the Court. He makes a valid argument that the presidential veto was assumed by the framers to be the power used most generously to check Congress. He observes that "the Constitution carefully specified the procedures to be followed whenever the president sought to negative a congressional bill. Yet the document failed to specify comparable procedures to be followed when judges sought to void Congress's output ... [the framers thus] did not anticipate that the judicial negative would one day surpass the executive negative as a check on Congress."[38] Though this is a critical observation, it may also be argued that the framers in the 1780s could not predict the role party politics would play in succeeding decades. Once the party system emerged and solidified with the election of 1800, where the President of the United States began to occupy the simultaneous position of leader of his party, the role of the President to check the power of Congress through veto was weakened. Presidents are not likely to challenge the constitutionality of legislation passed by a Congress whose majority is of the same party. It may well be then that judges, who are not elected and who operate in a space most removed from politics, began to exercise the role of constitutional custodians more explicitly as a consequence of the emergent party system.

One of the most vocal critics of judicial review in the early twenty-first century has been Jeremy Waldren. His 2006 *Yale Law Journal* article, "The

Core of the Case Against Judicial Review," articulates his assertion that judicial review is "democratically illegitimate" and that "there is no reason to suppose that rights are better protected by this practice than they would be by democratic legislatures."[39] Thus Waldren, like many before him, posits that judicial review's inherently undemocratic feature makes it suspect and that "it disenfranchises ordinary citizens and brushes aside cherished principles of representation and political equality in the final resolution of issues about rights."[40] Waldren's concern underscores a relationship between rights and judicial review, a position empathized with in this book. Rights, according to Waldren, however, can be better and more appropriately protected through democratic representation and legislative power.

His arguments echo those of James Bradley Thayer when he casts the United States in contrast with that of other nations. "Like their British counterparts, the New Zealand courts may not decline to apply legislation when it violates human rights (in New Zealand, the rights set out in the Bill of Rights Act of 1990); but they may strain to find interpretations that avoid the violation ... declarations [of unconstitutionality or violations of rights] in New Zealand do not have any legal effect on the legislative process."[41] Thus Waldren advocates for a legal approach, like that of Britain and New Zealand, that may strain to find constitutionality in a controversial statute, or decide that the statute does not apply to a specific case and rule it null in that particular instance, but may not rule in such a way that nullifies the entire law itself. How such a model is more conducive to rights protection is puzzling. If a law is unjust in one instance, it may well be in another. Certainly, in some cases, a law can be misapplied or improperly enforced. Judicial review does not remove the option of a court to rule that a certain statute does not apply in a specific instance. This is, in fact, a common feature of the judiciary. Laws may be upheld while found illegitimate and of no legal force when improperly executed. Waldren's thesis, however, advocates for potentially bad laws to live on. The American judiciary, according to Waldren, may possess the power to rule that a law does not apply in a particular case, but not to recognize unconstitutionality of a law and rule it void.

Waldren does underscore a crucial observation about the nature of the Court. Two of its features, the protection of individual rights and the protection of separation of powers, are at times in tension with each other.[42] This is not an insignificant point. He argues that when the two are in conflict, rights become "subordinate to a defense of the structural role the courts must play in upholding the rules of the Constitution."[43] It is indeed important to recognize that the Court has certainly ruled in favor of government authority and procedural necessity over the rights of individuals. Anytime rights are threatened by institutional power, the scope of such power and its rationale should be carefully examined. While Waldren's argument is an important one, it does not satisfy why an elected body, armed with the power to make laws, would be a better guardian of rights than one that rules only on those laws presented to it for review. The Supreme Court, at most, can kill legislation. Congress, however, if not challenged, can conceivably make any law it wants.

Jeremy Waldren's analysis is of particular value here because his position stands in stark contrast to that of this work. Waldren argues against rights-based reasoning for judicial review. He believes, instead, that because different individuals and different groups disagree on the premise of rights and their scope that it is an inherently political matter and thus to be mitigated through democratic representation. He contends that "rights based judicial review is inappropriate for reasonably democratic societies whose main problem is not that their legislative institutions are dysfunctional but that their members disagree about rights."[44] This assertion should be given particular attention, as it is self-contradicting. According to his thesis, people disagree about the nature and extent of rights. His answer to this issue is to let political representatives decide the nature and scope of rights through the democratic process. How is it that a political body representing constituencies, holding the same disagreements regarding the nature of rights as their voters do, would transcend this matter? This essential question is not satisfactorily answered.

Professor of legal theory at Georgetown University, Randy Barnett, presents an anti–Thayerian formulation of judicial review in *Our Republican Constitution: Securing the Liberty and Sovereignty of We the People* (2016). Barnett's scholarship rejects the judicial deference to legislative power and presumption of constitutionality offered in various forms by Thayer, Boudin, Kramer, Waldren, and others, for what he calls a *presumption of liberty*. The problem with Thayerian majority rule, according to Barnett, is that it conflates democratic representation with legislative license. The people, as an aggregate of individuals, are the sovereign, and thus supreme to the legislative power. Barnett asserts that the Thayerian view of American governance assumes a delegation of power from the people to their representatives which never occurred, and that "the servants of the sovereign people got to define the scope of the powers that had been delegated to them by their masters."[45] Such a formulation is antithetical to the natural rights-based constitutional system, which is based upon limited government and defined by expressly enumerated powers. Furthermore, Barnett maintains, majoritarian assumptions are in conflict with a system founded upon individual rights. We the People, then, is not a monolithic body made up of a popular majority, but a group of individuals who retain their inherent autonomy. Judicial deference to the legislature assumes the supreme authority to be the legislative power because it is elected, rather than the Constitution which represents the sovereign people. As Barnett suggests, the "Thayerian presumption that a law is constitutional leads to a grave problem…. While the courts are deferring to the legislature, the legislature in turn is deferring to the courts. By this ruse, any scrutiny of legislation to ensure it is within the just powers of a legislature is avoided."[46]

Barnett's work, including *Restoring the Lost Constitution* (2004), defends the power of judicial review precisely because of its relation to rights values and the principle of limited government. He maintains that one can either subscribe to the Thayerian presumption and empower an ever-growing state, or a presumption of liberty which constrains government powers and protects rights under the intended model of the framers. Rejection of or devotion to judicial review informs such a decision. "We either accept the presumption that in pursuing happiness persons may do whatever is not justly prohibited," he asserts, "or we are left with a presumption that the government may do whatever is not expressly prohibited."[47] For Barnett, judicial review is a necessary legal instrument to limit undue government power and protect individual rights.

William E. Nelson's scholarship has satisfied an often-lacking comprehensiveness regarding analysis of judicial review in the field of history. Though his work spans five decades, his *Marbury v. Madison: The Origins and Legacy of Judicial Review*, published in 2018, is particularly significant. As discussed in Chapter One, Nelson's work provides evidence that judicial review operated as an aspect of American legal culture long before the imperial crisis and the American Revolution. Nelson's analysis of the scope, intent, and effects of judicial review are similarly valuable. He posits that to argue against judicial review because of its policy-making implications, and (conversely) to assert that judicial review can be exercised without policy implications are both incorrect. Instead, Nelson suggests that policy-making is a natural byproduct of the process of determining what the law is. Moreover, the policy-making results of judicial review are beneficial particularly in the recognition and protection of minority rights.

Nelson expresses doubt that unpopular decisions and controversial rulings were unforeseen by the framers, especially when their own experience with subversion of their courts by the British in the 1760s and 1770s is taken into account. He further notes that state court decisions in the 1780s that yielded substantial policy-making results (discussed in Chapter One) must have informed the intended scope of the judiciary among the framers. Nelson suggests "it is impossible to conclude with confidence that the framers assumed that all judicial review cases would be purely legal in character, totally apolitical, and noncontroversial."[48] Nelson's *Marbury v.*

Madison: The Origins and Legacy of Judicial Review thus fulfills something otherwise lacking in the field of history. It presents the long history of the practice of judicial review but also articulates its usefulness in protecting minority rights and returning to the intentions of the framers and the spirit of the Constitution. It additionally asserts that the policy-making ramifications of the Supreme Court's decisions are not to be avoided or denounced, but celebrated as a benefit to the American republic.

Just as William E. Nelson's work disputes any need to deny that policy is reformulated as a result of judicial review, Keith Whittington's *Repugnant Laws: Judicial Review of Acts of Congress from the Founding to the Present* (2019), similarly examines how the Supreme Court fits into the larger political system of American governance. Perhaps more importantly, Whittington approaches the power of the Court to nullify legislation as a function that developed and strengthened over time, rather than as a seizure of power by the Marshall Court or as an expression of abstract legal philosophy. He observes that the "process of institutionalizing the power of judicial review could not be achieved in a day, and it could not be achieved by the unilateral dictate of the Court."[49]

Refuting assumptions made by many scholars, including some previously mentioned in this chapter, Whittington asserts that judicial review was practiced far more often in the first half of the nineteenth century than has been generally suggested. He maintains there has been a common misconception about judicial review in this era as being "exceptional and idiosyncratic."[50] Scholars have often mentioned *Marbury* v. *Madison* (1803) and *Dred Scott* v. *Sandford* (1857) as two rare moments of the judicial power being exercised in the antebellum era. In actuality, the "Supreme Court was more active in exercising its power to interpret the Constitution and limit legislative authority of Congress than is conventionally recognized."[51] According to Whittington, between 1789 and 1861, the Court "substantively evaluated the constitutionality of a federal statutory provision" in sixty-two cases. "The Court struck down or imposed constitutional limitations on the applicable scope of the federal law at issue in 32 percent of those cases."[52] Whittington's statistical analysis, which evaluates the entire history of judicial review in the United States, reveals a higher rate of it in practice during the first half of the nineteenth century than the overall historic average (26 percent).[53]

Repugnant Laws suggests that an essential facet of the nineteenth-century Court was the project of nation-building. Paradoxically, as the judiciary increasingly asserted its independence and its role to adjudicate matters of constitutionality, it strengthened the federal government as a whole. Thus, the process of reining in executive and especially legislative power counterintuitively legitimized and empowered the national government in general. Whittington observes that this process "reaffirmed national priorities and helped protect and sustain the institutions needed to advance those priorities. It projected national power—such as it was in these early days—into the international arena, into the states, and into the frontier."[54]

According to Whittington, because the historical growth of the nation itself is connected with the Court's role to say what the law is, judicial review should not be seen as a counter-majoritarian phenomenon. It is an intriguing thesis, and one with much merit. The Court's role in contributing to nineteenth-century America's culture of nationalism casts judicial review as an aspect of popular sovereignty rather than merely a feature of antidemocratic philosophy. It is a facet of the Court's history and its power that should be appreciated and understood. It is not necessary, however, to view the national populism informed by judicial review in the nineteenth century and the undemocratic nature of the judicial power as being mutually exclusive or contradictory. These are differing, but not precisely oppositional aspects of the Court. If anything, the fact that judicial review strengthened national bonds and informed a level of civic patriotism in the early decades of the republic supports the argument that it is an essential and legitimate facet of American constitutionalism.

As stated at the beginning of this chapter, a comprehensive analysis of judicial review scholarship is beyond the scope of this project. Nevertheless, by presenting the work of various legal scholars, political scientists, and historians from the nineteenth century to today, it is hoped that an understanding of the relevant debates regarding judicial review's history and legitimacy have been demonstrated. Various arguments in support as well as opposition to judicial review have relied on its historical origins, its role in the formation of the United States, its countervailing position against democratic rule, and its character as a manifestation of constitutional fidelity. This book aims to contribute to the world of judicial review scholarship by proposing that the judicial power is something which cannot be disconnected from the history of rights values fostered in Colonial America and, ultimately, the United States.

Despite critiques of the works of Thayer, Boudin, Waldren, and others in this chapter, a concern regarding undue judicial power is legitimate. A common criticism among scholars (judicial review critics and champions alike) is that the judicial power can be abused, has been misappropriated, and should be utilized with great care. The Court can only rule on the constitutional legitimacy of laws in question, however. The Court does not make law. That is the prerogative of the legislative power.

It is up to the people's representatives to make the laws. Without an independent body to rule on the legitimacy of legislation, however, and nullify laws which violate the Constitution, the legislative power would know no limits. Assumptions of a self-reinforcing, constitutionally-devoted Congress to rein in the limits of its own power strain credulity and is precisely what the Constitution was designed to prevent. The national project of 1787 was to facilitate a stronger federal government, but the aim was always informed by principles that one power should act as a check against another. A system of government premised on the existence of natural and civil rights, such as the United States, requires such checks.

Attacks upon judicial review for its undemocratic character are ultimately attacks upon the constitutional system itself. Something becomes clear when analyzing the anti-judicial review position of James Bradley Thayer, Jeremy Waldren, and others. The position necessitates the assumption that the Constitution is not the prevailing and supreme law. Furthermore, it seeks not merely to subjugate the law of the Constitution to the power of present-day elected legislators, but to pretend that the Constitution is not a work of law at all. To accept the Thayer/Waldren view is to accept that the Constitution is not a legal document, that the Supremacy Clause does not mean what it says, and that the only recourse against legislative overreach the people possess are biennial elections. Such a thesis is contradictory to the known history.

Chapter One presented evidence of the acceptance and practice of judicial review prior to *Marbury* v. *Madison*. This chapter demonstrated the prevailing arguments both in support of and in opposition to judicial review in the academic literature. It further asserted why the anti-judicial review thesis, premised on the will of democratic majorities through legislative supremacy, fails to give a suitable and superior alternative to the position that it is the role of the Court to state what the law is and to rule unconstitutional legislation null and void. Later chapters will explore further instances of judicial review in practice and Chapter Four will assess the *Marbury* v. *Madison* case in 1803. In the following chapter, an alternative to judicial review that ultimately failed but warrants some measure of scrutiny, championed by Thomas Jefferson and James Madison in the 1790s, is examined.

CHAPTER THREE

The Sedition Act of 1798 and Nullification, i.e., *State Review*

Before discussing the pertinent details regarding *Marbury* v. *Madison* (1803) in Chapter Four, it is worth asking what could have been an alternative to judicial review. This is especially relevant bearing in mind the political tumult in the United States during the late 1790s. In the years before the *Marbury* decision, a different approach to challenging unconstitutional legislation was offered by Thomas Jefferson and James Madison. This occurred in the wake of domestic and international crises which tested the stability of the new nation only a decade after ratification of its new constitution. Providing focus and context to events of the era is useful both to appreciating the political climate of the age and for examining how alternative interpretations regarding separation of powers and checks upon unconstitutional laws were addressed prior to John Marshall's ultimate assertion of the Supreme Court's power of judicial review.

This chapter will thus focus on Jefferson and Madison's arguments for state nullification of unconstitutional federal laws as a response to the Alien and Sedition Acts in 1798. It will also examine the often overlooked role of state nullification in the defense of rights values, the conflation of nullification controversies in the eighteenth and nineteenth centuries, and how historians have routinely neglected nullification's role as an alternative and precursor to the rise of judicial review. It is the aim of this chapter, then, to demonstrate the oft mischaracterized locus of nullification in American history and to place it in its appropriate context as a rights values-based substitute for judicial review preceding and following the *Marbury* decision, even as its failure as an applicable procedure is ultimately stressed. State nullification, or as this work will also refer to it—*state review*—shares a crucial and undervalued history with judicial review and the legacy of American rights values. This chapter will thus return nullification to its proper historical framework. Though it was ultimately an inadequate alternative to judicial review, it was nevertheless a critical mechanism of rights-defense against unconstitutional federal power prior to *Marbury*.

Turmoil in the Late 1790s

President John Adams's administration was plagued with domestic and foreign calamities in the late 1790s. An attempt at diplomacy stirred uproar when French officials sought a bribe from American ambassadors in what came to be known as the XYZ Affair. The French Revolution and France's wars with European powers divided American politicians upon simultaneously ideological and partisan grounds. Thomas Jefferson's Republicans supported Revolutionary France and Adams's Federalists generally favored Britain and its allies (though President George Washington had officially declared neutrality regarding the France/Britain conflict years earlier, Republicans saw this as a treacherous betrayal against the United States' most vital ally during the American Revolution). Both French and British vessels were capturing Americans on the high seas, essentially enslaving them in a practice known as *impressment*.

In response, the United States created its first navy and sought to build a new army, with former President George Washington as acting commander in chief and actual operations facilitated by Alexander Hamilton. French and Irish immigrants in the United States, and their supporters, employed mass protests against the policies of the Adams administration, including its militarization. Anti-Federalist newspapers, encouraged (and often funded) by the Republican opposition, added to a culture of division and discontent. The Federalists, in their position as the majority party in Congress and who constituted the Adams administration, sought to address both foreign and domestic subversion through new legislation which would stem foreign influence and stifle political dissent.

The Alien and Sedition Acts

The Alien and Sedition Acts were passed in the House of Representatives and the U.S. Senate and signed into law by President Adams in the summer of 1798. It was composed of four measures, the first three of which addressed issues regarding naturalization and resident aliens, the fourth measure dealing directly with acts of presumed sedition by American citizens. The first measure expanded the residency requirement for naturalization from five to fourteen years. The second measure gave the President of the United States the power to expel any alien judged "dangerous." The third measure outlined the permissible treatment of aliens during times of war. The fourth measure of the Alien and Sedition Acts criminalized (through a fine or imprisonment) the writing or publishing of "any false, scandalous, and malicious" statements aimed at the President of the United States or members of Congress, which would bring them into "contempt or disrepute," or which would provoke "sedition with the United States."[1]

For many Federalists, the Alien and Sedition Acts were an understandable measure against the encroachment of mob rule fueled in no small part by the influence of recently-transplanted foreigners. Asa Earl Martin observes in his *History of the United States*, the "affiliation of these [Irish and French] radicals with the Republican party, the leaders of which encouraged their activity, furnished the Federalists, in view of the possibility of a French war, with an excellent excuse for silencing them or harrying them out of the country."[2] Indeed, one facet of the Alien and Sedition Acts controversy that is often overlooked was its popularity among Federalists. Not only did its passage necessitate a majority vote in both the House of Representatives and the Senate prior to its signing into law by President Adams, but some of history's most revered Federalists supported the measure. Woody Holton's biography of Abigail Adams notes that she "added her voice to a growing clang of demands for a legal crackdown on the American Jacobins."[3] Holton contends that the "only justification that can be offered for [Abigail] Adams's enthusiasm for the Alien and Sedition Acts is that she sincerely believed that the French government had placed secret agents, men bent on destroying her husband, the American republic, and Christianity, throughout the United States."[4] Ron Chernow's biography of George Washington similarly reveals the first president's "quiet sympathy.... [Washington] endorsed a Sedition Act prosecution of William Duane of the *Aurora* [newspaper], who had accused the Adams administration of being corrupted by the British government."[5] Chernow further observes that "Washington often seemed blind to the perils of the Alien and Sedition Acts, arguing that Republican criticism was just another partisan maneuver to discredit the government."[6]

Some have sought to claim Alexander Hamilton's letter to Oliver Wolcott regarding the Alien and Sedition legislation as evidence of his opposition to the measure. At first glance this assumption is understandable, as Hamilton expresses:

> I have this moment seen a Bill brought into the Senate intitled a Bill to define more particularly the crime of Treason &c. There are provisions in this Bill which according to a cursory view appear to me highly exceptionable & such as more than any thing else may endanger civil War.... I hope sincerely the thing may not be hurried through. Let us not establish a tyranny. Energy is a

very different thing from violence. If we make no false step we shall be essentially united; but if we push things to an extreme we shall then give to faction body & solidarity.[7]

James Morton Smith has observed, however, that on June 27, two days before Hamilton wrote the letter to Wolcott, "the Senate recommitted the treason and sedition bill to committee where its sponsors removed the section prescribing the death penalty for Americans adhering to the government or the people of France, or giving them aid or comfort."[8] Thus Hamilton's opposition was to a more drastic draft which was not the one that became law. "He did not oppose a sedition law as such, nor did he urge the Federalists to kill their bill," Smith asserts, "[Hamilton] only hoped that they would not hurry it through in its original form."[9] Despite Hamilton's concerns outlined in his letter to Wolcott, there is no evidence he contributed to the tempered version which became legislation. Furthermore, once the less draconian version of the Alien and Sedition Acts were passed, there is no indication Hamilton opposed it. Smith suggests that when "the Senate reported this revised but still 'energetic' sedition bill, omitting any reference to treason and the death penalty, Hamilton did not register any complaint or advise any mitigating amendment."[10] For many Federalists, though certainly not all, the Alien and Sedition Acts were a rightful remedy to an encroaching and insidious menace.

Republicans, however, voiced their clear disdain and outrage over the blatantly unconstitutional legislation criminalizing political speech. New York Republican Congressman Edward Livingston asserted his opposition to the Alien and Sedition Acts on constitutional grounds and for their violation of essential values of free expression and inquiry:

> If we are to violate the Constitution, will the people submit to our unauthorized acts? Sir, they ought not to submit; they would deserve the chains that these measures are forging for them. The country will swarm with informers, spies, delators [from Roman criminal law; secret informants, spies] and all the odious reptile tribe that breed in the sunshine of a despotic power.... [T]he hours of the most unsuspected confidence, the intimacies of friendship, or the recesses of domestic retirement afford no security. The companion whom you most trust, the friend in whom you must confide, the domestic who waits in your chamber, all are tempted to betray your imprudent or unguarded follie; to misrepresent your words; to convey them, distorted by calumny, to the secret tribunal where jealousy presides—where fear officiates as accuser and suspicion is the only evidence that is heard.... Do not let us be told, Sir, that we excite a fervour against foreign aggression only to establish a tyranny at home; that ... we are absurd enough to call ourselves "free and enlightened" while we advocate principles that would have disgraced the age of Gothic barbarity and establish a code compared to which the ordeal is wise and the trial by battle is merciful and just.[11]

The unconstitutionality of the Alien and Sedition Acts is beyond dispute. Legal scholar Akhil Reed Amar, for example, acknowledges that the legislation simultaneously violated basic free speech rights outlined in Article I of the United States Constitution as well as the Free Speech Clause of the First Amendment. Article I, Section 6 of the U.S. Constitution protects House members and Senators "for any speech or debate in either House, they shall not be questioned in any other place."[12] Amar notes that "this privilege had roots in the language of the Articles of Confederation and, deeper still, in English practice" and that the "core privilege in both England and America aimed to ensure that legislatures remained forums for robust political discourse."[13] The privilege to speak freely as a member of the legislative power became a recognized right of the people in the American system and was thus included in the First Amendment. Amar observes that the First Amendment's "free-speech clause thus complemented the Article I free-speech clause so as to guarantee America's true sovereign—the people—the same broad right of political discourse traditionally enjoyed in England by the sovereign Parliament."[14] Federalists in 1798 ignored and evaded the constitutional ramifications of the sedition law and prioritized instead their need to curtail foreign and domestic insurgence.

Nullification as a Remedy

In the wake of the Alien and Sedition Acts, Thomas Jefferson and James Madison authored two resolutions arguing that state governments had the power, and indeed the constitutional duty, to nullify unconstitutional federal legislation within a state's territory. Jefferson and Madison were in agreement with Edward Livingston and the Republicans generally that the Alien and Sedition Acts were unconstitutional and thus void. In a letter to John Taylor in November 1798, Jefferson shared his concern both with the overreach of federal power the legislation symbolized and what it said of the national government that it would go to such means. He also questioned the political culture that allowed such a law to come into existence, pondering, "I know not which mortifies me most, that I should fear to write what I think or that my country bear such a state of things."[15]

The Kentucky Resolution, authored (anonymously) by Jefferson, and the Virginia Resolution, authored by James Madison, are crucial to understanding the state of American politics during the late 1790s, but they are additionally useful in apprehending the Republican view of separation of powers in the pre–*Marbury* era. Together, along with further resolutions and reports in succeeding years, they posit essential constitutional

Thomas Jefferson, **by Charles Balthazar Julien Févret de Saint-Mémin, 1804. Engraving on paper (National Portrait Gallery).**

arguments regarding the role of the federal government and the scope of legitimate authority it was to exercise.

Thomas Woods observes that the combination of the Virginia and Kentucky Resolutions of 1798, the Kentucky Resolutions of 1799, and the Virginia report of 1800 collectively asserted three aspects of constitutional interpretation. These included "(1) the federal government had been created when sovereign states granted it a few enumerated powers; (2) any powers not so delegated remained reserved to the states or the people [reasserting the Tenth Amendment] ... and (3) should the federal government exercise a power it had not been delegated, the states ought to interpose."[16] This position, that states were to reject and refuse to follow or enforce federal legislation they deemed unconstitutional appeared as extreme to Federalists then as it may to some Americans today. Jonathan Gienapp notes that to many, the Virginia and Kentucky Resolutions "seemed like sedition, to others outright treason."[17] That said, the resolutions contain reasoned arguments by Jefferson and Madison which ought to be seriously contemplated.

Jefferson's Kentucky Resolution is more forceful than Madison's Virginia Resolution. This is likely due to two factors. First, Jefferson was generally more direct, uncompromising, and cutting in his tone than was Madison. Second, Jefferson held a personal as well as political stake in the Alien and Sedition Acts controversy. In 1798, Thomas Jefferson was Vice President of the United States, and a Republican Vice President in a Federalist administration. Because the U.S. Constitution had not foreseen how partisan politics would complicate the election process, it had decreed the candidate who came in second in the presidential race to become Vice President (this was later changed with the Twelfth Amendment). This explains why Jefferson authored the Kentucky Resolution anonymously. He was an agent of the federal government promoting the flouting of a federal law. Furthermore, the wording of the sedition measure within the law was conspicuous as well, as it criminalized speech critical of the President of the United States and members of the Legislative Branch, but did not explicitly criminalize speech critical of the Vice President. The Federalist legislation had included a convenient loophole which assured that publications critical of the Republican Vice President could legally persist.

Jefferson's Kentucky Resolution asserted an interpretation of the constitutional union as a compact:

> *Resolved*, that the several states composing the United States of America, are not united on the principle of unlimited submission to their General Government; but that by compact under the style and title of a Constitution for the United States and of amendments thereto, they constituted a General Government for special purposes, delegated to that Government certain definite powers, reserving each state to itself, the residuary mass of right to their own self Government; and that whensoever the General Government assumes undelegated powers, its acts are unauthoritative, void, and of no force: That to this compact each state acceded as a state, and is an integral party, its co-states forming as to itself, the other party: That the Government created by this compact was not made the exclusive or final judge of the extent of the powers delegated to itself; since that would have made its discretion, and not the constitution, the measure of its powers; but that as in all other cases of compact among parties having no common Judge, each party has an equal right to judge for itself, as well of infractions as of the mode and measure of redress.[18]

James Madison's Virginia Resolution makes a similar argument in its assertion of the United States as a compact and equally expresses the nullification argument, though with a somewhat milder tone:

> That this Assembly doth explicitly and peremptorily declare, that it views the powers of the federal government, as resulting from the compact to which the states are parties; as limited by the plain sense and intention of the instrument constituting that compact; as no farther valid than they are authorised by the grants enumerated in that compact, and that in case of a deliberate, palpable and dangerous exercise of other powers not granted by the said compact, the states who are parties there-to have the right, and are in duty bound, to interpose for arresting the pro(gress) of the evil, and for maintaining within their respective limits, the authorities, rights and liberties appertaining to them.[19]

According to the compact interpretation, all parties engaged in such a compact are themselves arbiters of the facilitation of the agreement. Following this logic, the federal government's Alien and Sedition Acts were a violation of the compact made between the states as to what powers the federal government would possess and exercise. Because the act was a violation of the compact, it had no legal legitimacy and thus no legal force. It was not a law that obliged in conscience the states enjoined in the compact.

This nullification argument of Jefferson and Madison has endured criticism from scholars and statesmen alike over many years. One reason is for conflations with other acts of nullification which this chapter will attend to presently. Other criticisms have included what might be called Jefferson's *compact problem* and what some historians have referred to as the *Madison problem*. Prior to a discussion regarding nullification in its broader context in American history, these two matters should be addressed.

The Jefferson and Madison Problems

In his Kentucky Resolution, Thomas Jefferson had described his understanding of the United States as that of a compact between the separate states. Though this work fundamentally agrees that the compact interpretation is to some degree flawed, it is not for the reasons often cited by scholars. The limitations and fallibility of state review, especially when compared to judicial review, will be addressed in the final section of this chapter. Nevertheless, the deficiencies in popular counterarguments regarding nullification should also be recognized. The compact argument made by Jefferson (and, to a lesser degree, Madison) requires respect to two foundational principles: the Tenth Amendment and the limits of the Supremacy Clause of the U.S. Constitution. Legal scholars and political thinkers who disagree with nullification as a principle struggle with one or both of these precepts. For example, legal scholar and former law clerk to Supreme Court Justice Harry A. Blackmun, Edward Lazarus, has sought to remove the teeth from the Tenth Amendment, or perhaps more accurately assert that it was toothless to begin

James Madison, **unidentified artist, c. 1801–1810. Stipple engraving on paper (National Portrait Gallery).**

with. Lazarus argues the amendment "simply states that 'the powers not delegated to the United States by the Constitution, nor prohibited to it by the States, are reserved to the States respectively, or to the people.' Nowhere in this somewhat opaque text does the Constitution vest states with the right to unilaterally pick and choose what federal laws to obey based on their own conceptions of the Constitution."[20] Lazarus's sleight of hand is admirable but obvious. By arguing that the Constitution does not "vest states with the right" he is implicitly arguing the very positive law position that the principles of the American founding rejected. The American system was built upon government based on the consent of the governed, informed by natural rights theory, following a design of express limited powers where the people are sovereign and the state their servant. Lazarus frames the wording of the Tenth Amendment as opaque though its surface meaning is entirely coherent and intelligible. His claim is flawed for another reason as well. The Tenth Amendment is a reassertion of the limited powers provided for in the Constitution itself. Article I does not give Congress *all* powers. It explicitly refers to powers "herein granted."[21]

Critiques of nullification do not appear from merely one end of the spectrum and are not limited to rejections of the plain meaning of the Tenth Amendment. Former congressman and conservative Alan West argued against nullification because under "the Supremacy Clause of the Constitution, federal law is superior to state law."[22] West employs the same incomplete reading of the Constitution as Lazarus. The Supremacy Clause indeed asserts the supremacy of federal law over state law when they are in conflict but there is an essential detail missing in West's analysis. The Supremacy Clause states, "This Constitution, and the Laws of the United States which shall be made in Pursuance thereof; and all Treaties made, or which shall be made, under the Authority of the United States, shall be the supreme Law of the Land."[23] The clause states that federal laws made "in pursuance thereof" the Constitution are supreme. It is thus implicit within the Supremacy Clause itself that it is speaking only to those laws which abide by the nation's charter. Lazarus's rejection of the Tenth Amendment and West's evasion of the necessary "pursuance thereof" in the Supremacy Clause conveniently evade the very issue that nullification sought to address, which is the problem of unconstitutional legislation by the federal government. These arguments either overtly (Lazarus) or implicitly (West) counter Jefferson's vision of the United States as a compact between the individual states, but are mute to the larger matter Jefferson's vision grappled with. This is not to say that because Lazarus and West's arguments are flawed that nullification is the rightful remedy. It is to say, however, that their critiques ring hollow. Nullification and Jefferson's compact interpretation of the Union may be an imperfect solution to federal tyranny, but such attacks and misnomers regarding the Tenth Amendment and the Supremacy Clause obscure rather than elucidate the issue.

Gordon S. Wood and other historians have discussed something called the *Madison problem*. The problem is as follows: how is it that James Madison, who overcame enormous odds to establish a strong central government through a new United States Constitution in the 1780s would then become a champion of state power against a strong national government only a decade later? This presumed contradiction between Madison of the 1780s as nationalist and Madison of the 1790s as advocate of state power demonstrates a challenge to some scholars in resolving the two. Similarly, this apparent conflict raises doubt as to Madison's sincerity, whether it is as advocate for a strong central government or as a defender of state autonomy.

The difference between Madison's outlook in the 1780s versus the 1790s can be compared to the disparities between Madison and Jefferson regarding crucial aspects of political philosophy. Madison's habit of following Jefferson's lead as a politician and theorist, as well as Madison's general affability and ability to compromise, has obscured some glaring differences between the two Virginian statesmen. The most critical difference could well be their distinct views of democracy. Jefferson generally held faith in the people while Madison tended to exhibit skepticism toward them. Gordon Wood observes that although both men were suspicious of government, including an elected legislative power, "Jefferson's suspicions was based on his fear of the unrepresentative character of the elected officials, that they were too apt to drift away from the virtuous people.... Madison's suspicion ... was based on his fear that the elected officials were only too representative, only too expressive of the passions of the people."[24] Jack Rakove describes their differing assessments thusly: "Jefferson ... better grasped the habits of democracy, Madison ... better understood its perils."[25] Noting this difference is important because it underscores Madison's distrust of majoritarian rule and recognizing this aspect of his thinking reveals that the Madison of the 1780s and the Madison of the 1790s were not as far apart as they might initially appear.

The James Madison of the 1780s made his concern regarding majoritarian rule clear in his essay, "Vices of the Political System of the United States," where he warned against the growing democratic element among the individual states.[26] Furthermore, his goal for a new constitutional system, it must be remembered, was not the one that came into being in 1789. In fact, Madison's vision of a stronger central government had included a power for the federal government to nullify state laws. This fact appears to underscore the so-called Madison problem, for it casts the 1780s Madison as a nationalist seeking to disempower the states against the 1790s

Madison seeking to empower the states against the federal government. Looking at the issue through such a binary lens, however, is part of the problem, because Madison's concern was not national over state, or state over federal, as it was minority versus majority. Madison was distrustful of powerful majorities. He saw this threat more in the democratic impulses of the individual states in the 1780s. He later recognized it more in the federal legislature in the 1790s. This is not a contradiction, at least not as Madison appeared to see it. This shift in where he identified threats against liberty was due in no small part to the growing political division between Republicans and Federalists in the 1790s. These divisions were spurred by the different visions the two parties held toward the role of the federal government. As Gordon Wood suggests, when Madison "came to realize what kind of consolidated national government [Alexander] Hamilton was trying to create, he naturally went into opposition."[27] Jonathan Gienapp depicts Madison's transition from nationalist to tentative champion of state power as a constant rather than contradiction, describing it as a "lengthy, unresolved struggle to comprehend the critical matter of constitutional maintenance."[28] Thus there is no *Madison problem*, as the distinction between the *two Madisons* disappears when circumstances and motivations are appropriately identified.

Nullification Conflation

Though, as this work will emphasize, nullification was not a workable answer to the problem of federal overreach, it can nevertheless be understood why such a principle would be championed in the aftermath of the Alien and Sedition Acts. The problem, historically, however, with an analysis of the principles of state review over federal law, has been the conflation of the nullification arguments of Jefferson and Madison in 1798 with later instances of nullification, particularly with the defense of slavery. Edward Lazarus commits this act of conflation and a moving of the historical goal posts when he claims that nullification has "long and obvious historical roots—and shameful ones."[29] When he discusses the "historical roots," however, he does not begin with the earliest instances of nullification, that of Jefferson and Madison in their fight against the speech restrictions of the Alien and Sedition Acts. Instead, he jumps forward in time thirty years. "Back in 1828, then-Vice President John C. Calhoun gave voice to the doctrine of 'nullification' in his fury over the federal tariffs that were then being imposed on states by the federal government."[30] Lazarus then, using Calhoun as a useful beginning point because of his notorious defense of slavery, conflates the principle of nullification with a defense of human bondage. "The nullification doctrine did not die there, however. Nullification was born with the issue of slavery in mind. Southerners conceived of the doctrine as a potential tactic for fighting any federal attempts to abolish slavery—claiming that they could just refuse to enforce any such law."[31] Despite Thomas Jefferson and James Madison's participation in the ownership and driving of human beings, their nullification arguments had nothing to do with slavery. Lazarus's thesis of nullification as a philosophy "born with the issue of slavery in mind" only begins to work if the first instances of state review, those against the suppression of free speech in the late 1790s, are ignored. Lazarus is correct that defenders of slavery saw it as a practice beyond the authority of the federal government. This was indeed Chief Justice Roger Taney's argument in *Dred Scott* v. *Sanford* (1857), which will be discussed in more detail in Chapter Five. The problem with Lazarus's analysis, however, is that he avoids—or perhaps is simply unaware—of nullification's actual beginnings and the antislavery uses of nullification in the nineteenth century.

Thomas Woods documents the use of nullification by antislavery advocates and other Americans who refused to follow the federal fugitive slave law in the mid-nineteenth century. "In northern states, nullification took the form of doing everything officials could do to make enforcement of the [fugitive slave] act difficult if not impossible.... Federal officials were not allowed to use local jails to house accused fugitives. Slaveholders ... were required to go before federal fugitive-slave tribunals rather than simply snatching their slaves and absconding with them."[32] Using Wisconsin as one example, nullification can thus be appreciated historically, to some degree, as an antislavery position. In fact, nullification's relationship with antislavery in the mid-nineteenth century is more direct and less tenuous than that of John C. Calhoun's nullification advocacy and slavery in the 1820s and 1830s. Calhoun's nullification arguments were not tied to the defense of slavery any more than President Andrew Jackson's opposition to nullification was a denunciation of slavery. The two men were both slaveholders and their political disagreement involved tariffs and not slavery. Thomas Woods explains that "while Calhoun did support slavery, so did Andrew Jackson, the slaveholding southern President who opposed nullification and Calhoun himself."[33] Connecting nullification to slavery because John C. Calhoun was a slaver who promoted nullification is further academic sleight of hand.

In 1859, the state of Wisconsin asserted its nullification power in a joint resolution. Abolitionist newspaper editor Sherman Booth had been arrested twice for obstructing the re-enslavement of a runaway slave, Joshua Glover. Both times Booth was jailed the Wisconsin Supreme Court ordered his release. The U.S. Supreme Court ordered Booth to be turned over to the federal government for his obstruction of the federal fugitive slave act. Wisconsin's joint resolution of March 19, 1859, was its official refusal to do so. With words echoing the arguments of Jefferson and Madison against the Alien and Sedition Acts in 1798, the Wisconsin legislature's resolution asserted:

> *Resolved*, the Senate concurring, That we regard the action of the supreme court of the United States, in assuming jurisdiction in the case before mentioned, as an arbitrary act of power, unauthorized by the constitution, and virtually superseding the benefit of the writ of habeas corpus, and prostrating the rights and liberties of the people at the foot of unlimited power.
>
> *Resolved*, That this assumption of jurisdiction by the federal judiciary, in the said case, and without process, is an act of undelegated power, and therefore without authority, void, and of no force.
>
> *Resolved*, That the government formed by the constitution of the United States was not made the exclusive or final judge of the extent of the powers delegated to itself; but that, as in all other cases of compact among parties having no common judge, each party has an equal right to judge for itself, as well of infractions as of the mode and measure of redress.
>
> *Resolved*, That the principle and construction contended for by the party which now rules in the councils of the nation, that the general government is the exclusive judge of the extent of the powers delegated to it, stop nothing short of despotism, since the discretion of those who administer the government, and not the constitution, would be the measure of their powers; that the several states which formed that instrument, being sovereign and independent, have the unquestionable right to judge of its infraction; and that a positive defiance of those sovereignties, of all unauthorized acts done or attempted to be done under color of that instrument, is the rightful remedy.[34]

Wisconsin's assertion of nullification in 1859, employing words similar to the Kentucky and Virginia Resolutions of 1798, is a testament to the rights-oriented tradition of state review in American history. It was also a reiteration of Jefferson's compact thesis. An implied relationship between nullification and slavery has endured in historical scholarship despite the first assertion of nullification being in defense of free speech in 1798 and despite Northern nullification in the nineteenth century on behalf of abolitionists. Nullification is an inherently precarious proposition. Its ramifications and limitations are real and to be considered seriously. One need not, however, conflate the origin of nullification with slavery when its connections are tenuous at best. Doing so is a dishonest enterprise.

State Review versus Judicial Review

Though connections between the principle of state nullification and slavery have been demonstrated to be strained and historically dubious, the inefficacy of state review as a constitutional check against federal over-reach must be highlighted. It is Madison's view of nullification as an act of interposition rather than Jefferson's assessment of state review as a constitutional bulwark that appears more reasoned and sensible. Whereas Jefferson spoke of the practice as an end itself, Madison understood it as a tool to stimulate discussion and debate between state and federal powers. It is thus the Madisonian framing of nullification which has been most useful and instrumental in assertions of rights values in American history. Madison, who famously discussed the need for power to check power in "Federalist No. 51," appreciated state review as a tool for constitutional discourse and the defense of rights in a system where state and federal power would exist in persistent tension.[35] Nullification, as a final answer to federal tyranny, was not practicable because it defeated the very idea of a federal union. John Ferling observes, "nullification would have emasculated the national government and restored the states to the predominant position they had occupied under the Articles of Confederation."[36] The reason Jefferson's compact interpretation ultimately fails, and indeed why Madison may had been less forceful with the thesis, is not because the Tenth Amendment doesn't mean what it says or because the Supremacy Clause allows for any and all federal legislation. It fails because in the compact scheme there is no neutral arbiter to fairly resolve circumstances. If all parties are equal judges of the agreement, and no neutral arbiter exists outside of the compact, there is no unbiased party who can reasonably review the case. Nullification ultimately breeds disunity and contributes to a lack of constitutional consensus. This may explain to some extent why Madison and Jefferson would differ in later years regarding their views over judicial review, with Jefferson never overtly accepting the principle and Madison ultimately embracing it (discussed further in Chapter Four). The larger problem with nullification's compact thesis is that it stands on a foundation of sand, as the United States Constitution was ratified by the people of the states and not by their state legislatures. This is a significant detail, as it underscores that the Constitution was a culmination of the *sovereignty of the people* and not the result of an agreement between state governments.

The Alien and Sedition Acts presented the challenge of what to do in response to unconstitutional federal legislation. In an era where judicial review had been expressed as an abstract principle and had been used in isolated cases among state courts in the 1780s and the federal judiciary in the 1790s, it nevertheless had not yet disclosed its ultimate expression as it would with *Marbury* v. *Madison* in 1803 and after. As the nation stumbled through a perilous state of embryonic constitutional balance, groping its way forward, nullification was asserted by Republican leaders as an antidote to oppressive legislation imposed by a shaken federal government and its Federalist operatives. It was ultimately the wrong answer, and judicial review would prove (eventually) to be the superior solution. Nevertheless, it does no good to conflate state review with slavery or its defense. Doing so ignores nullification's role in the fight against slavery and its spread in the nineteenth century, and it also diminishes the rights values connected to nullification arguments going back to its first expression against the Alien and Sedition Acts in 1798.

1800 and Beyond

The election of 1800 saw a Republican sweep. Federalists not only became the minority but the political party's days were numbered. The first ruling party of the United States was in decline and would soon vanish. Republican opposition to the Alien and Sedition Acts and Jeffersonians' more egalitarian and democratic philosophy appealed to Americans at the turn of the century. Thomas Jefferson, after a contentious election ultimately decided by the House of Representatives, became the third President of the United States. He referred to his electoral victory and the triumph of his party as a new American revolution. President Jefferson allowed the Sedition Act to expire, leaving the controversy of nullification to rest, if only temporarily. Americans in the north as well as the south would reassert the principle in succeeding decades. President Adams sought to temper the Republican revolution during his final days in office by appointing as many Federalist judges to the bench as he could. This facilitated the collision between the Jefferson administration, including Secretary of State James Madison, and the Supreme Court with the *Marbury* case in 1803.

In the final days of the first nullification crisis, sparked by Jefferson and Madison's respective Kentucky and Virginia resolutions, other states voiced their opposition to the practice. Their contention is important to note, but one specific articulation of disagreement may be most significant. Some states never conveyed a position regarding nullification during the Alien and Sedition Acts controversy. Many, however, specified objections. Gordon Wood observes that although "four Southern states took no action at all, nine Northern states decisively rejected the [Virginia and Kentucky] resolutions, most of them declaring that the judiciary, and not the legislatures, was the proper body to determine the constitutionality of acts of Congress."[37] This is a critical point, as it reveals that although Kentucky and Virginia, by way of Jefferson and Madison, had asserted nullification as the proper check against undue federal power, other state legislatures instead argued in favor of judicial review.

In 1800, the Pennsylvania legislature, for example, made their support of judicial review explicitly clear, maintaining that "the people of the united states ... have committed to the supreme judiciary of the nation the high authority of ultimately and conclusively deciding upon the constitutionality of all legislative acts."[38] The objections of state legislatures to embrace nullification and in some cases to assert judicial review demonstrates further that the principle that the federal judicial branch was to decide constitutional matters was alive and well prior to *Marbury*. Additionally, it should be recognized that nullification was not an anomaly of constitutional thought but one which struggled for dominance in the earliest years of the republic and could well had been triumphant if the principle of judicial review had not already taken root. It is also critical to an understanding of the intellectual and legal history of the United States to avoid casual and specious claims which overstate and mischaracterize nullification's connection to slavery. The principle of state review, however flawed, was often championed in defense of fundamental rights values. It was not to become the prevailing practice of American law regarding the final word on constitutional matters because it disturbed the balance of union even as it sought to resolve it. Judicial review additionally proved to be a more stabilizing force, though not without considerable exceptions. To apprehend and appreciate the role of judicial review as an instrument of rights theory in the intellectual history of the United States, however, the role of nullification, its limits, and its often honorable aims, need also to be understood and appreciated.

CHAPTER FOUR

Marbury, Stuart, McCulloch, and Barron

John Marshall ran for Congress and was elected in 1799 as a critic of the Alien and Sedition Acts, though it was his party, the Federalists, who were responsible for their passage. Marshall's ability to build consensus while simultaneously clarifying his distinct point of view came to be an identifiable trait of his career and his personal disposition. He was offered a seat on the Supreme Court by President John Adams to replace Justice James Wilson in 1798 but Marshall was not interested. He was instead convinced by George Washington to run for Congress. In his biography of Washington, Ron Chernow recounts, "John Marshall and Bushrod Washington appeared at Mount Vernon for a three-day visit. Washington entreated both men to run for Congress from their Virginia districts, stressing the need to oust Republican incumbents during a national emergency."[1] The national emergency was the domestic and international turmoil recounted in Chapter Three, including the fear of foreign influence by the French and the political divisions that had facilitated the Alien and Sedition Acts, which Marshall didn't support. Bushrod Washington, George's nephew, instead replaced James Wilson on the Supreme Court while Marshall ran for Congress.

Despite their differing views regarding the Alien and Sedition Acts, Marshall respected George Washington greatly. Marshall's service in the American Revolution had put him under General Washington's authority and direction, and both men's political philosophies were influenced tremendously by their military experience. Like Washington, Marshall's concerns became more oriented to the nascent nation than to any particular state or region. William E. Nelson observes that, during the war, as Marshall "worked with men from various parts of the new United States, he lost whatever parochialism he may have had and grew in appreciating the common interests of all Americans."[2] His military service made him an acolyte of Washington and, as Nelson notes, Marshall "accepted political direction from Washington as long as the general lived."[3] The first president's influence was so significant, in fact, that Marshall later became America's first Washington biographer.

John Marshall's antagonism toward the Sedition Act was pragmatic as much as ideological, believing it to be a solution worse than the predicament it was intended to address. He also foresaw the legislation producing terrible political ramifications for Federalists. As Francis N. Stites observes, Marshall "perceived that the Sedition Act was a blunder more likely to consolidate than stifle opposition."[4] Though his negative response to the legislation frustrated other Federalists, it aided his reputation as a sensible moderate and someone willing to vocally disagree with facets of his own party. Marshall's reasonable temperament carried currency in an era defined by partisanship and warring ideologies.

The nationalism Marshall championed stood in stark contrast to the state autonomy argued by his cousin, Thomas Jefferson. Both men descended from the Randolph dynasty, one of the first families of wealth and influence in Virginia. As prominent men from a powerful family line, they each presented themselves with fashion and propriety characteristic of Virginia gentry. As Aaron Burr biographer, Nancy Isenberg, observes however, their shared bloodline and mode of dress and decorum was where resemblances ended. "They were fierce partisan opponents, and intensely disliked one another."[5] John Ferling's assessment is more harsh, and suggests that the two men's distinct backgrounds and experience during the revolution increased the tension between them, remarking that "Marshall ... not only despised Jefferson, who had lived sumptuously at Monticello while he had suffered with the Continental Army, but was contemptuous of his fellow Virginian's ideology of decentralization and greater state autonomy. Jefferson, in turn, thought Marshall had betrayed Virginia by embracing the Federalist Party."[6] In 1800, when Jefferson and his Republicans swept Congress and ultimately won the Presidency, Marshall's vision of the country, and his political party, was decidedly out of favor.

In response to his own presidential loss and the diminishment of his party, John Adams set out to assure the survival of Federalist power in the courts by signing the Judiciary Act of 1801 in the final weeks of his tenure. The act reduced the number of Supreme Court Justices from six to five (taking the opportunity away from incoming President Jefferson to appoint a new Justice), established the first circuit courts (ending the obligation of circuit-riding for Supreme Court Justices), and created a host of new court-related offices. The legislation allowed Adams to appoint sixteen new judges for the newly-established circuit courts and fill the new court-related posts. He was thus able to pack the growing judiciary with devoted Federalists just as he left office and just as his party had lost decidedly at the polls. This evoked the image of Adams signing the commissions late in the night, as the days and hours dwindled away, and branded those appointed under the act as *midnight judges*. Adams had, in fact, finished the paperwork for the appointments eight days prior to Jefferson's inauguration, but the late-stage characterization of the appointments persisted and not entirely unfairly.[7] With the loss of Federalist control of the executive and legislative branches, Adams sought to secure a foothold of Federalist power in the courts to hedge against the radical democratic tendencies and decentralization efforts of Jefferson's Republicans. Though Adams finished the paperwork for the new appointments, however, not all of the commissions were delivered, and this detail led to the *Marbury* v. *Madison* case in 1803.

John Marshall was appointed to the position of Secretary of State by President Adams in 1800 after Adams had fired Timothy Pickering (and Secretary of War James McHenry) over constant policy disputes. It was Marshall, then, in his capacity as Secretary of State for the Adams administration, who failed to deliver the entirety of the commissions in the final week of Adams's term. This important detail complicates the *Marbury* case and will be discussed presently.

After Marshall's brief stint as Secretary of State, John Adams appointed him to the Supreme Court as the new Chief Justice, replacing Oliver Ellsworth in 1801. It is noteworthy to remember Marshall's rejection to be appointed as an Associate Justice just a few years prior. Furthermore, it is significant that his appointments by President Adams, both to Secretary of State and Chief Justice, demonstrate that Marshall's opposition to the Alien and Sedition Acts did not put him out of favor with the president. Despite their difference of opinion

John Marshall, by Albert Newsam, copied after a work by Henry Inman, 1831. Lithograph on paper (National Portrait Gallery).

regarding the legislation, Adams respected Marshall as a statesman and legal scholar. Additionally, regardless of Marshall's loyalty to the Federalists, it may had been his legal and political independence that got him the position of Chief Justice. Marshall was of a different opinion on matters from Adams, but unlike Pickering and McHenry, he remained loyal and deferential to the president. John Adams had few political allies at the end of his presidency, and his appointment of John Marshall—who had campaigned for Congress on his opposition to Adams's Alien and Sedition Acts—underscores this point.

Marbury *v.* Madison *(1803)*

After Thomas Jefferson's inauguration, it was soon discovered that a number of the commissions intended to be distributed as a result of the Judiciary Act of 1801 were left undelivered. Jefferson, in one of his first acts as President of the United States, ordered his Secretary of State, James Madison, not to deliver the remaining commissions. President Jefferson saw it as his prerogative to annul such appointments, believing that despite having been signed by the previous president, they were of no legal force without being served to their intended recipients. Jefferson saw the Judiciary Act of 1801 and Adams's late judicial appointments as a personal and political affront to his ability to govern as he saw fit as the incoming president. In a letter to Abigail Adams in 1804, he expressed that he

> did consider [John Adams's] last appointments to office as personally unkind. They were from among my most ardent political enemies, from whom no faithful cooperation could ever be expected, and laid me under the embarrassment of acting thro' men whose views were to defeat mine; or to encounter the odium of putting others in their places. It seemed but common justice to leave a successor free to act by instruments of his own choice.[8]

William Marbury had been appointed to a Justice of the Peace position for the District of Columbia by President Adams and was among those who did not receive their commission. As a result, Marbury sued Secretary of State James Madison in the Supreme Court and requested a *writ of mandamus* from the Court. A writ of mandamus would compel the Jefferson administration to deliver the remaining commissions to the proper recipients. Marbury had not sued in a lower court first but directly through the Supreme Court under its original jurisdiction established and expanded in the Judiciary Act of 1789.

The legal questions the Marshall court needed to address in *Marbury v. Madison* was threefold: (1) was William Marbury due his commission? (2) Was the Supreme Court the proper course to seek remedy? (3) Does the

Court have the authority to issue a writ of mandamus against the executive branch to order delivery of commissions? The ruling had much wider repercussions than the seemingly trivial matter of appointments, signed commissions, and their delivery. *Marbury* v. *Madison* revealed that a case with relatively small stakes could have far-reaching implications.

Marshall's arguable conflict of interest complicates *Marbury*, as it had been his duty as Secretary of State under President Adams to deliver the commissions that resided at the center of the case. If a Justice presided over such an incident today, in which he or she had been directly involved in the background of the dispute, calls for recusal would be widespread. This was not an issue in 1803. It could be easily argued that Marshall himself should have recognized his uncomfortably intimate relationship with the matter, but he did not recuse himself. It appears that Marshall's real concern was instead the appearance of the Court as feeble and ineffectual. R.B. Bernstein observes that Marshall "faced a seeming no-win situation, born of his failure to deliver the commissions. If he issued the writ, he knew that Madison would ignore it, and he had no way to make Madison obey it, for federal courts rely on the executive branch to enforce their orders.... If he did not issue the writ, his failure would make him look weak."[9]

In the end, the Court ruled that Marbury would not receive his commission, but for reasons entirely separate from those argued by Secretary Madison and the Jefferson administration. Instead, Chief Justice Marshall asserted in the decision that the original jurisdiction Marbury had relied upon for the case—provided to the Court by the Judiciary Act of 1789— was unconstitutional, thus a writ of mandamus could not be enforced by the Court on behalf of Marbury. Because the legislature cannot create powers for themselves nor for other branches which go beyond those enumerated in the Constitution, the original jurisdiction created by the Judiciary Act of 1789 was void. The immediate result of the decision was Marbury's loss of the case. His suit was dismissed due to the absence of proper jurisdiction. The more significant implication was the affirmation of the power of judicial review by the Supreme Court.

Of course, as has been presented in previous chapters of this work, and as Bruce Ackerman has observed, "Marshall's arguments for judicial review were not particularly new."[10] Since the revolution, judicial review had been recognized by members of the Philadelphia Convention, attendees of the state ratification debates, and was used in state court decision in the 1780s and federal court decisions in the 1790s. The importance of *Marbury* was not that judicial review was novel in 1803, but that the decision underscored and affirmed once and for all the power of the judicial branch to nullify both state and federal unconstitutional laws. State sovereignty and sovereign immunity was rejected in the *Chisholm* case a decade earlier in 1793. Though the case led to the Eleventh Amendment, prohibiting a citizen of one state from suing another state, the *Chisholm* ruling nevertheless affirmed limits on state power, as ruled by the judiciary. *Marbury* affirmed the Court's role similarly in acting as a safeguard against the encroachment of unconstitutional federal power as well. Though even in this regard *Marbury* was not unique, nor the first. As referenced in Chapter One, *Hylton* v. *United States* (1796) ruled on the constitutionality of a carriage tax imposed by the federal government. Though in *Hylton* the legislative act was upheld, the principal matter at hand was the same: the Court's role in ruling on the constitutionality of legislation. The only relevant legal distinction between *Hylton* and *Marbury* was that one decision affirmed the constitutionality of a law while the other's was rejected.

When Marshall delivered the Court's ruling, he laid out the decision in reverse and, by doing so, put the executive (and legislative) branch, and Jefferson's Republicans, on notice while simultaneously giving them a legal victory. Francis N. Stites explains that "Marshall could have first denied the Court's jurisdiction. But reversing the order of questions enabled him to scold the president for disobeying the laws. Then, by denying Marbury the writ, he gave the Republicans what they wanted—but he did so through an assertion of judicial review. Jefferson could do nothing about a decision that in its outcome was favorable."[11] Marshall thus capitalized upon the opportunity to affirm that it "is emphatically the province and duty of the judicial department to say what the law is."[12]

Marbury resolutely asserted judicial review as a mechanism for the preservation of separation of powers. The ruling also acts as a reminder regarding the purpose of a written constitution, which is to establish as well as limit governmental authority:

> The powers of the legislature are defined and limited; and that those limits may not be mistaken, or forgotten, the constitution is written. To what purpose are powers limited, and to what purpose is that limitation committed to writing, if these limits may, at any time, be passed by those intended to be restrained?...
>
> It is a proposition too plain to be contested, that the constitution controls any legislative act repugnant to it; or, that the legislature may alter the constitution by an ordinary act.
>
> Between these alternatives there is no middle ground. The constitution is either a superior, paramount law, unchangeable by ordinary means, or it is on a level with ordinary legislative acts....
>
> If the former part of the alternative be true, then a legislative act contrary to the constitution is not law: if the latter part be true, then written constitutions are absurd attempts, on the part of the people, to limit a power in its own nature illimitable.[13]

The distinction between regularly drafted legislation and constitutional law is a critical facet of the American system and a peculiarity not seen in most other models of government. It is a crucial detail borne out of the drafting of state constitutions in the 1770s and 1780s which informed a uniquely American intellectual political perspective that refused to conflate the people with the people's representatives. The distinction Marshall points to in *Marbury*—between constitutional law and regular legislation—is the same tenet the American people asserted during the American Revolution and immediately afterward: that a Constitution is only legitimate when facilitated through a convention and/or ratification process and not through mere legislation. Considering this, Marshall underscored something in the American intellectual tradition that was already decades old and which separated the United States from all other governments in the world and all other republics in history. The significance of the discrepancy between the drafting of constitutions and general legislation, and this legal principle's relationship to rights values, will be explored further in Chapter Seven.

Marshall concludes the *Marbury* decision by upholding judicial review on established constitutional grounds:

> Certainly all those who have framed written constitutions contemplate them as forming the fundamental and paramount law of the nation, and consequently, the theory of every such government must be, that an act of the legislature, repugnant to the constitution, is void....
>
> Thus, the particular phraseology of the constitution of the United States confirms and strengthens the principle, supposed to be essential to all written constitutions, that a law repugnant to the constitution is void; and that courts, as well as other departments, are bound by that instrument.[14]

Jefferson and Madison on Judicial Review

Thomas Jefferson appeared to almost immediately lose sight of the fact he had won the *Marbury* case and instead expressed his profound displeasure with Marshall's assertion of judicial review. In another letter to Abigail Adams in 1804, Jefferson conveyed his condemnation of the practice. He also advocated a point of view not entirely dissimilar from his stance regarding the role of states to exercise nullification of unconstitutional federal laws. Asserting something quite similar to his compact theory from 1798 (see Chapter Three), he argued that all parties to an agreement are empowered with following their own interpretation of a compact. In the letter to Abigail Adams in September 1804, he claimed that "nothing in the constitution has given [the judiciary] a right to decide for the executive, more than to the executive to decide for them. Both magistracies are equally independent in the sphere of action assigned to them."[15] He warned what such a power held by the judiciary could portend, cautioning that "the opinion which gives to judges the right to decide what laws are constitutional, and what not, not only for themselves in their own sphere of action, but for the legislature and executive also in their spheres, would make the judiciary a despotic branch."[16] Jefferson, like some who reject judicial review today, saw it as a threat to balanced government.

Jefferson's earlier writings, however, suggest a rather different view. In his *Notes on the State of Virginia* from the early 1780s, he had warned against an unchecked legislative power when criticizing the constitutional model of his home state and warned against a feeble judicial branch which held no independence or authority. "An elective despotism was not the government we fought for.... The judiciary and executive members were left dependent on the legislative, for their subsistence in office.... [They have] decided rights which should have been left to judiciary controversy."[17] In a letter to James Madison in 1789, Jefferson again implied the judiciary's proper role to protect rights by binding the other branches to their strictly prescribed powers during a debate over whether to add a Bill of Rights to the Constitution. Jefferson explained to Madison that in "the arguments in favor of a declaration of rights, you omit one which has great weight with me, the legal check which it puts into the hands of the judiciary."[18] Although Jefferson specifies that such a power by the judiciary must be "kept strictly to their own department," the implication is clear that he saw the judicial branch as an entity which would safeguard liberties through its power to review and contemplate the legitimacy of legislation.[19]

The Jefferson prior to the nullification assertions of 1798 and the post–*Marbury* version are thus *two Jeffersons,* or perhaps he never recognized the inconsistency. Conceivably, and more probable, is that the Alien and Sedition Acts transformed Jefferson's thinking and shifted his fear regarding where he saw the greatest threat due to concentrations of power. In the same letter to Madison in 1789, Jefferson clearly articulated that he saw the legislative power as the most threatening institution to Americans' liberties (as he had done in his *Notes on Virginia*), claiming the "tyranny of the legislatures is the most formidable dread at present, and will be for long years. That of the executive will come in its turn, but it will be at a remote period."[20] Jefferson's work as minister to France through the second half of the 1780s informed his knowledge regarding the necessity of decisive executive action and military power on the high seas. During his tenure in France he came to recognize the threat that European and North African naval powers posed to American trade interests. At this time, Jefferson's concerns were both national and international, which required executive strength and efficiency (which were very much lacking under the Articles of Confederation). These apprehensions may have clouded his perception of executive power as not being an immediate threat under the new constitution when he returned to the United States, especially as he had already recognized undue legislative influence in his native Virginia. By 1798, the Alien and Sedition Acts, passed by the legislative branch but signed into law and enforced by the executive, may have been what aided in Jefferson's conception of the American republic as a compact. If so, his formulation was conceived as a method for (understandably) seeking to counter unconstitutional federal legislation.

Where Jefferson saw an imbalance of power in judicial review, others (prior to Marshall and after) have perceived judicial review itself as a guardian of balanced government and separation of powers. Just as Jefferson's state nullification assertions in 1798 were understandable though ultimately flawed for contributing to division rather than acting as a remedy, his argument that each branch of the federal government has equal authority to interpret the constitutionality of a law was similarly precarious. Both can be seen as variations of the compact scheme and neither provide a satisfying resolution for giving the final word on *what the law is*. Without a final and authoritative ruling on the legitimacy and constitutionality of a law, how could stability and progress be realized? More importantly, what is the legitimacy of a law, a constitution, or a government if its meaning, purpose, and enforcement are consistently reinterpreted and never settled into a form of legal canon that citizens of a republic can satisfactorily rely on? Without an authority which ultimately states what the law is, what obligations do citizens have to abide by it? As Randy Barnett contends, "[w]ithout judicial review to see that Congress stays within its powers and refrains from violating the rights retained by the people, there is little reason to believe that legislation is binding in conscience on the people."[21]

James Madison grew to feel differently than his friend and colleague regarding judicial review. Though he fought on behalf of President Jefferson and his administration as Secretary of State in the *Marbury* case, Madison would later reveal himself to be a supporter of the judicial power. Gordon S. Wood contends that this disagreement marks not only a schism between Madison's and Jefferson's political thinking, but also underscores an entrenched radicalization on Jefferson's part. Wood notes that Jefferson, after *Marbury*, "became parochial and alarmist … as even his sympathetic biographer Dumas Malone admits, [Jefferson's position] 'bordered on fanaticism.'"[22] This radicalism was not new for Jefferson, however, as he had once advocated for a new revolution every generation.[23] It nevertheless signifies a pivotal moment where Jefferson and Madison grew further apart politically and philosophically. They would never return to the intimacy of thought they shared during the late 1790s and the early years of the nineteenth century, and yet both grew to be nationalists of a sort over time.

Madison's support of judicial review is, upon inspection, less surprising. There is also more than a little irony that the result of *Marbury* was a fulfillment of national political prominence that the defendant of the case, Madison himself, had wanted to achieve back in 1787 at the Philadelphia Convention. Madison had been overruled on his desire for a national veto at the convention. Most believed a national veto in the power of the new federal legislature was too much power to be wielded by the law-making branch. Additionally, Madison's idea for a council of revision, made up of officials who would analyze the constitutionality of legislation, was rejected for its dangerous blending of the legislative, executive, and judicial branches. Madison thus gave up on a national veto (and a council of revision). Almost twenty years later, he was defendant in a case which ultimately affirmed a national power of reexamination, though in the hands of the judiciary instead.

After Marbury

It is only in combination with a lesser-known decision a week after *Marbury, Stuart* v. *Laird*, that judicial review's status in 1803 can be understood. The relevant facts of *Stuart* involved the Republican Congress and the Jefferson administration's passage of the Judiciary Act of 1802, which reimposed circuit-riding on Supreme Court Justices (though in a manner less demanding than the previous era). The act also dissolved some inferior courts and judgeships, and created a one-session-per-year schedule for the Court—thus keeping the Supreme Court out of session for the following ten months.[24] Federalists opposed the act and argued that the repeal of judgeships was unconstitutional due to their lifetime appointments. The Court nevertheless ruled in *Stuart* that Congress has the power to create and dissolve inferior courts. The decision was a retreat of judicial power asserted only a week prior in *Marbury*. If the Supreme Court had ruled the Judiciary Act of 1802 unconstitutional, which Marshall himself believed it was, it could have put at risk the Court's newfound legitimacy and authority. The *Stuart* case is thus noteworthy because it demonstrates the perilous position the Court would occupy going forward. It would continue, over time, to assert its judicial review power, but in the early decades it had to be careful not to overplay its hand and risk having its legitimacy questioned and authority challenged by the other branches.

Bruce Ackerman contends that the *Stuart* decision was a moment of judicial deference toward the legislative power that honored the duly elected Republican president and legislature who had enacted the Judiciary Act of 1802. Challenging the act, one week after *Marbury*, could have fomented animus toward the Court and undermined its established legitimacy. Ackerman suggests that "*Marbury* and *Stuart* together appear as a very preliminary effort at judicial synthesis—seeking to integrate the meaning of the revolution of 1800 [the Republican sweep and Jefferson's election] into the Court's interpretation of the Constitution of 1787."[25] This is a synthesis the Court would carefully navigate going forward, between deference to legislation passed by the people's elected representatives and recognizing the constitutional limitations of such legislation. The impact of *Marbury*'s judicial review assertion is complicated and tempered by the legislative deference of *Stuart* a week later. If judicial review was to be a power wielded by the Court, and if it was to retain its legitimacy, it would need to be a power used deftly in the early nineteenth century. By degrading themselves in *Stuart* and upholding the constitutionality of the Judiciary Act of 1802, the Court succeeded in not presenting itself as an enemy of Jeffersonian democracy, and thus lived to fight another day.

In the following decades, the Marshall Court established wide latitude of national power for the federal government. In 1819, the Court's ruling in *McCulloch* v. *Maryland* affirmed the supremacy of the national government over that of the individual states regarding its taxing power. The state of Maryland, in opposition to the existence of the Second Bank of the United States inside its borders, sought to tax the federal entity. The Marshall Court's decision implicitly upheld the legitimacy of the national bank and rejected the concept that an individual state could tax the federal government. In the ruling, Marshall stated, "the power to tax involves the power to destroy … the power to destroy may defeat and render useless the power to create; that there is a plain repugnance, in conferring on one government a power to control the constitutional measures of another."[26] *McCulloch* was a blow to supporters of states' rights and legitimized a loose construction interpretation of the Constitution, which asserted that some powers of the federal government may be found and exercised under the Necessary and Proper Clause, though much of Marshall's reasoning lay in the principle related to the sovereignty of the people as a national force. The constitutionality of a national bank was debated as far back as the Washington administration. The first bank bill was championed by Alexander Hamilton and other Federalists while Jefferson, Madison, and other Republicans generally believed the creation of a national bank to be unconstitutional. Hamilton and the Federalists won that battle and the first Bank of the United States was established with Washington's signing of the bank bill in 1791. The debate over its constitutionality persisted, however. By 1816, a second national bank was established and signed into law by President James Madison who, as he had in other matters, changed his view about the national bank controversy over the years. The *McCulloch* decision by the Marshall Court underscored and emphasized growing national power at the expense of the individual states and stretched the use of the Necessary and Proper Clause (and the principle of the sovereignty of the people) to new limits.

The expansion of federal power by Supreme Court rulings concerned many Republicans, but fourteen years after *McCulloch* the Marshall Court delivered a decision that empowered the individual states and substantially reasserted the limits of federal control over them. The *Barron* v. *Baltimore* decision in 1833 concerned plaintiff John Barron's suit against the city of Baltimore for damages to his wharf. He alleged that city construction had diverted water flow in the harbor, causing sediment accumulation which made his wharf inoperable. He sued for violation of the Fifth Amendment's Takings Clause in the U.S. Constitution, which states that no "private property [may] be taken for public use, without paying just compensation."[27] The Marshall Court's ruling was historically and legally correct but nevertheless created substantial repercussions for the country for decades to come. John Barron's suit against Baltimore was ultimately dismissed, with the Court ruling that the first eight amendments of the United States Constitution applied only to the federal government and not to the individual states. State and local governments could thus not be found in violation of these amendments because they were not designed to be enforced against them. Akhil Reed Amar observes that the *Barron* decision asserted "that if the First Congress had meant to apply the Bill of Rights to states, Congress would have used explicit words to that effect, just as the Philadelphia framers had used explicit words in Article I, section 10 when they imposed various limits on state governments."[28] Marshall stated that the case was "of great importance, but not of much difficulty," and the ruling was unanimous.[29] Marshall was correct. The history was clear that the Bill of Rights was not designed to be enforced against the individual states. The *Barron* decision empowered states and recognized limits on the federal government over them, a facet of jurisprudence not often seen during Marshall's tenure as Chief Justice.

The 1830s had already proved to be another precarious time for the Court, putting it in opposition with the Jackson administration, which will be explored further in Chapter Five. *Barron* v. *Baltimore* was a notable decision, however unremarkable it may have seemed at the time. It capped a long line of consequential rulings of the Marshall Court in the final years of its tenure. John Marshall died two years after the *Barron* decision in

1835. He shaped the role of the Court more than any other Chief Justice in history and filled the role longer than anyone else as well. Because *Barron* underscored the limits of federal power and emphasized crucial facets of state autonomy, however, it exacerbated the already complicated issue of slavery and clouded it further. *Barron*'s assertion of state immunity from the first eight amendments, though legally sound at the time, put the nation on a course of continued tension over the role of slavery in American society. It obscured rather than clarified questions over the authority the federal government and the individual states possessed regarding the peculiar institution. This matter ultimately culminated in the *Dred Scott* v. *Sanford* case in 1857, discussed further in Chapter Five.

John Marshall, in his role as Chief Justice of the Supreme Court from 1801 to 1835, provided wide latitude for federal power, influenced by a form of civic nationalism cultivated during the American Revolution under George Washington. Though Marshall was a champion of nationalism and found federal powers in the Constitution others (particularly Jeffersonian Republicans) did not, his greatest legacy is the assertion of the Court's power of judicial review. By affirming that it was the role of the judiciary branch to say what the law is, he crystalized and underscored a constitutional balance that other formulations failed to do. Madison's proposal of a council of revision at the Philadelphia Convention was rightly seen as a dangerous blending of legislative and judicial powers. Jefferson's compact theory suggested that each federal branch, as well as each individual state, could decide for itself what laws were constitutional. In Jefferson's compact theory one can see the democratic spirit in full force, seeking to give every party their due, but it also reveals the lack of unity and legal consistency that unchecked democracy also brings. Judicial review, by providing the last word regarding the constitutionality of executive decisions and enacted legislation, at both the state and federal levels, assures the judiciary's independence and keeps the branches to some degree separate.

The role of rights was implied in *Marbury*. William Marbury's right to a legal remedy for being denied his commission is referenced in Marshall's decision, though mostly to explain why the Court had no jurisdiction to provide such a remedy. Rights would not take center stage in Supreme Court matters for decades. Decisions would instead be characterized by their recognition of constitutional authority in matters involving federalism and separation of powers.

Stuart v. *Laird* demonstrated the limited capital the Court had in the wake of *Marbury* and revealed that the post–*Marbury* Court was not one with unlimited authority and legitimacy. The *McCulloch* v. *Maryland* decision affirmed vast federal authority over the states, one of the most remembered aspects of the Marshall Court, but *Barron* v. *Baltimore* underscored the legal purpose of the federal amendments and their lack of legal force against the states. Thus Chief Justice Marshall's secondary legacy, after that of judicial review, was in recognizing that the United States federal government held enormous power but that the individual states retained certain powers for themselves that were beyond the reach of the Bill of Rights. This combination of federal power and state immunity from significant federal amendments complicated questions regarding what authority federal and state powers possessed regarding the institution of slavery. While the Marshall era solidified the Supreme Court's power of judicial review, it also proved that such a power could harm its own validity. The Court's legitimacy informs its authority, thus requiring both sound constitutional judgments and the respect of the executive branch, which is charged with enforcing such decisions. The ramifications of bad rulings (i.e., rulings which violate fundamental rights values) and the consequences of an ineffectual judiciary are discussed in the following chapter.

CHAPTER FIVE

Indian Removal and Dred Scott

The American judiciary's power to nullify unconstitutional laws, and the affirmation of its legitimacy to do so, was not an entirely settled matter as the nineteenth century progressed. Two events which underscore the most egregious aspects of American history in that era are closely tied to the Supreme Court and its power to rule on the constitutionality of state and federal legislation. In one instance, concerning the policy of Indian removal, the Marshall Court ultimately ruled on the side of justice and Native American sovereignty but only after strengthening the federal government over a period of decades, which empowered the Executive Branch to flout the Court's decision in the 1830s. Twenty years later, the Court—under Chief Justice Roger Taney—exerted its most flagrant violation of both constitutional wisdom and human decency when it denied the citizenship status of free blacks and asserted that the federal government had no power to stem the institution of slavery in *Dred Scott* v. *Sandford* (1857). Indian removal and Dred Scott represent the two greatest weaknesses of the Court in the nineteenth century. In one case, a proper ruling was defied by the other branches, and in another the Court expressed the most unfortunate moral failings of the nation. For judicial review to be defended as an instrument of rights values, these cases cannot be ignored.

The legitimacy of the judicial branch has been understandably questioned due to its role in such matters. It was powerless to enforce the rights of the Cherokee, who were forcibly removed from their ancestral lands a handful of years after their sovereign rights had been affirmed by the Court. The Dred Scott decision, as this chapter will reveal, was both morally repugnant and constitutionally dubious. To understand the evolution of the American judiciary from a defender of separation of powers and constitutional fidelity to its later incarnation as a guardian of individual rights, its greatest failings must first be scrutinized. This chapter will demonstrate that the Cherokee case and the Dred Scott decision should not be taken as evidence of the Court's illegitimacy. Rather, they ought to be viewed as instances when the Court's rightful remedy was not respected by the other branches (in the case of the Cherokee) and when a ruling was motivated not by the constitution and the rights values that inform it but by personal prejudice and an evasion of historical precedence (as was the case with Dred Scott). The power of the Court in the late nineteenth century and the twentieth century can only be appreciated once its most blatant failings of enforcement and jurisprudence in the preceding eras are understood in their historical, political, and constitutional contexts.

Indian Removal

Indian policy in the early republican era was expressed through the encouragement of assimilation and the ratification of treaties. As Jason Edward Black explains, however, "assimilation policies still remained controlling; both Washington and Jefferson wished to augment Native character with American cultural mores and practices."[1] Black also notes that "following the American Revolution.... Picking up Britain's lead, the US government instituted a treaty system predicated on protectionism. The government promised security to American Indians in exchange for safe passage through Indian territory and the surrender of Native lands."[2] President Jefferson soon employed a more forceful method of obtaining Indian lands, sometimes through increased extortion, and at other times with more overtly militaristic practices. Roger G. Kennedy, author of *Mr. Jefferson's Lost Cause: Land, Farmers, Slavery, and the Louisiana Purchase* (2003), observes that after 1801, the federal government operated a "charter of amoebic imperialism: the master organism, the United States, sent forth a nucleus of colonists to cross a border into somebody else's territory. Most frequently, the unwilling 'host' was an Indian nation.... Once in a place, the nucleus formed a cell that then declared itself independent."[3] The newly *independent* body would then call upon the United States to secure its sovereignty and once this was done, the sovereign nation was suddenly declared U.S. territory.

Expansion intensified after the Louisiana Purchase in 1803. The purchase of Louisiana Territory from Napoleon was a boon for the United States federal government, but also promised further incursion into Indian lands and the spread of slavery in the American south. Louisiana Territory, which had changed hands between the Spanish and the French before being procured by the United States, did not recognize the sovereignty of the Native Americans living upon the territory's soil. Furthermore, Roger Kennedy observes that Article Three of the Louisiana Purchase secured for "Louisiana's slave owners and Virginia's slave sellers that those who possessed slaves in the region could retain them, and those who wished to market their human inventory there would not be impeded."[4] Thus the Louisiana Purchase, a selling of territory in North America by France motivated by slave insurrections and ultimate revolution in Haiti, empowered the nascent United States to spread its own practice of slavery and expansion further west. For Jefferson, the value of the Louisiana Territory was to "give establishments in it to the Indians on the east side of Mississippi, in exchange for their present country."[5] As Jefferey Ostler observes, the Louisiana Purchase meant "Jefferson could go beyond fantasizing about eliminating Indians from the eastern United States. He had a place to put them."[6] Indian removal was thus in the planning stages for decades.

Jefferson's vision of a republic of yeoman farmers depended on the displacement of Native Americans to ensure occupation and cultivation of land. Adding to this was the waning philosophy of civilizing Native Americans through the encouragement of assimilation. Paul Finkelman and Tim Garrison observe that support for a more passive form of assimilation decreased dramatically after the War of 1812, in which a high number of Indians chose to ally with the British against the United States. They further note that "the cultural conservatism of most Woodland Indians—who sometimes adopted weaving or stock-raising but would not give up their languages or customs—suggested that the United States could not hope to assimilate its Native American population."[7] Furthermore, a nascent form of scientific racism which would emerge more fully in the United States and Europe in the later nineteenth and early twentieth centuries also had an impact on Native American relations. Finkelman and Garrison explain that some Americans believed "that Indians might therefore be inherently unfit for civilized life ... [some] philanthropists argued that proximity to white American society was actually harmful to Native Americans ... and that the eastern Indians must either emigrate across the Mississippi or become extinct."[8] The fact that the remedy to the eastern Indians' plight was exactly the prescription offered by Jefferson years earlier was a convenient one. By 1830, under the presidency of Andrew Jackson, the policy of Indian removal became explicit. Among the rationales for the policy was the need to facilitate the survival of those who were to be removed. The Indian Removal Act was approved on May 28, 1830. In a message to Congress in December of that year, President Jackson celebrated the legislation. Jackson's message asserted that the removal of Indians from the southeast to west of the Mississippi would be beneficial not merely to the federal and state governments but to the Native Americans themselves:

> The consequences of a speedy removal will be important to the United States, to individual States, and to the Indians themselves. The pecuniary advantages which it promises to the Government are the least of its recommendations. It

puts an end to all possible danger of collision between the authorities of the General and State Governments on account of the Indians. It will place a dense and civilized population in large tracts of country now occupied by a few savage hunters. By opening the whole territory between Tennessee on the north and Louisiana on the south to the settlement of the whites it will incalculably strengthen the southwestern frontier and render the adjacent States strong enough to repel future invasions without remote aid. It will relieve the whole State of Mississippi and the western part of Alabama of Indian occupancy, and enable those States to advance rapidly in population, wealth, and power. It will separate the Indians from immediate contact with settlements of whites; free them from the power of the States; enable them to pursue happiness in their own way and under their own rude institutions; will retard the progress of decay, which is lessening their numbers, and perhaps cause them gradually, under the protection of the Government and through the influence of good counsels, to cast off their savage habits and become an interesting, civilized, and Christian community.[9]

If the Indians were to perish, they would do so in lands separated from whites. The declining numbers of Native Americans according to Jackson was not due to war, disease, and displacement by Euro-Americans but because their savage ways facilitated their "progress of decay." Forced removal may actually save them. Later in the address, Jackson argues "the General Government kindly offers [the Native American] a new home, and proposes to pay the whole expense of his removal and settlement."[10] Such rationalizations were secondary to the primary reasoning for removal, however. The objective was ultimately to make lands available for occupation and cultivation by whites. The project would not only empower the Jacksonian *common man* but would also temper the growing tensions manifesting between state and federal powers. In the process of taking lands from Native Americans, the federal government secured more territory for itself and state governments benefited from agricultural and industrial development. An important feature of such development was the use of slaves. As Jefferey Ostler acknowledges in his book, *Surviving Genocide* (2019), lands freed from the occupation of Native Americans "would allow planters to use enslaved people to produce cotton for global markets. The policy would also expand markets for slave owners on the eastern seaboard to sell slaves (often their most valuable form of property) to labor on new plantations in Alabama and Mississippi."[11]

The idea that Native Americans were unfit as either American citizens or as sovereign property holders because of their savagery and uncivilized ways was betrayed by the efforts of some, most notably the Cherokee, to adopt both Euro-American and republican practices and mores. Following the encouragement of British and then American officials for several generations, going back to the earliest days of the republic and before, the Cherokee had embraced Euro-American forms of dress, marriage ceremonies, schools, and a written language. Politically, they had adopted a republican model of governance. Historian Tim Alan Garrison, author of *Legal Ideology of Removal: The Southern Judiciary and the Sovereignty of Native American Nations* (2002), observes, "The Cherokees had been remarkably successful in adapting to dramatic changes in their economic, political, and diplomatic situation over the previous century and a half."[12] In the late 1820s the state of Georgia sought to annex Cherokee land, abolish its government, and redistribute lands to white citizens of the state. When threatened with removal from their ancestral home, the Cherokee similarly demonstrated their adept adaptability and determination, through the American courts.

Cherokee Nation *v.* Georgia *(1831), George Corn Tassel, and* Worcester *v.* Georgia *(1832)*

In response to the Indian Removal Act and the acts of the state government of Georgia, the Cherokee, seeking to live under its own sovereignty sought legal recourse by retaining attorney William Wirt. Wirt believed the wisest course was to request a legal injunction against Georgia by appealing through the original jurisdiction of the Supreme Court. The Cherokee had been encouraged in this direction by opponents of President Jackson in response to the Indian Removal Act. John Marshall biographer, Francis N. Stites, notes the political calculations made by Jackson's opponents, including Daniel Webster. Stites remarks that within days of the enactment of the Removal Bill, "the anti–Jackson forces, loudest in opposition to removal, began laying out plans to capture the presidency in 1832. Webster and others who hoped to use the Court as a forum for discrediting Jackson urged the Cherokees to hire eminent counsel to test their rights."[13] On the last day of the 1831 term, the Marshall Court issued its opinion regarding *Cherokee Nation* v. *Georgia*. The Chief Justice announced dismissal of the case due to the Court's lack of jurisdiction, effectively handing the Cherokee a legal defeat. Marshall further articulated the growing paternalistic sentiment of the United States government against Native Americans by describing them as domestic dependent nations. By denying the Court's original jurisdiction in the matter and by asserting the ward-like status of all Native American tribes—declaring them to be under the care and authority of the United States federal government—Marshall denied the Cherokee their full sovereignty. The move appears to have been a political one, as it tabled any possible conflict between the state of Georgia and the Federal government. Marshall's assertion of Indians as wards of the United States government followed his decades of jurisprudence which had generally solidified the authority of the federal government over that of the states. This is an important aspect of Marshall's influence which will be scrutinized more closely following a discussion of *Worcester* v. *Georgia* and Andrew Jackson's response to it. Marshall's history of observing the authority of the United States government over that of the states culminated in the *Cherokee Nation* v. *Georgia* decision through his denial of Indian sovereignty. Jason Edward Black posits that in the *Cherokee Nation* v. *Georgia* case "Marshall argued that the Cherokee Nation was neither a foreign entity nor a sovereign state, but rather a domestic 'case of people' that the United States watched over. He denied the injunction against Georgia not based on the Cherokee claim to sovereignty; rather, he saw it fit that the Court protect indigenous populations from states that could not care for 'our red children.' The possessive *our* referred to the federal government's identity, not that of the individual states."[14] Thus, in his denial of sovereignty of the Cherokee, Marshall simultaneously outlined the limits of Georgia's sovereignty and indeed the limits of all of the individual states. Indian relations was exclusively a matter for the federal government because it acted as a paternalistic force over the child-like and uncivilized Native American people. The limits of individual state power were defined in part by the need for the federal government to be condescending to the Cherokee and other Indians.

When the standard of judicial precedence is examined, the *Cherokee Nation* v. *Georgia* decision becomes easier to comprehend, as it simply echoes a decision made the decade prior. In 1823, the Court had ruled in *Johnson* v. *McIntosh* that the federal government held exclusive negotiation rights with Native Americans and that Indians did not possess the right to sell their lands to individuals. The decision came out of an inheritance dispute which originated from a case earlier in the century, but the relevance of the decision was in officially making void the rights of Indians to sell their own property to whomever they chose. Their status was one of *diminished sovereignty*, according to the Marshall Court. While *Cherokee Nation* v. *Georgia* reinforced this idea, as well as that of the United States federal government having sole powers to negotiate with the Native Americans, the denial of essential private property rights in the *Johnson* v. *McIntosh* decision reveals the lack of equal treatment of Indians in the realm of American law well before the cases of the 1830s. The United States government routinely bemoaned that Native Americans supposedly did not respect or understand principles of private property and then would use this same reasoning to argue why they should not hold those very property rights. It was a form of circular legal logic that benefited the taking of lands away from those who allegedly did not understand what they had and, therefore, were not fit to possess them. It was also a vehicle for the federal government to protect the Indians from exploitation by the separate states, but was executed through paternalistic rationalizations that ultimately undermined native sovereignty.

The desire of the state of Georgia to rid the Cherokee from within its borders and the aspiration of the United States to implement Indian removal on a grand scale meant the two parties possessed the same ultimate goals, even as southern states consistently challenged the authority of the United States over them during the era. Georgia had a long history of denying the authority of the United States federal government. As discussed in Chapter One, the impetus of the Eleventh Amendment was the *Chisolm* case in the 1790s in which Georgia denied the Supreme Court to have original jurisdiction in cases where the citizen of one state sued the government of another state. Georgia's claim of state sovereignty was denied in *Chisolm* but Georgia's stance was popular enough that the Eleventh Amendment was ratified in 1795 to align the U.S. Constitution with Georgia's position. Georgia thus had an established history already in the 1830s of asserting its sovereignty and ultimately winning on such grounds. Georgia exercised the flouting of federal authority again in *Worcester* v. *Georgia* the following year when the state refused to send counsel to offer opening arguments. It was Georgia's defiance toward federal authority and the directives of the United Supreme Court that had also facilitated the *Worcester* case.

Despite the dismissal of *Cherokee Nation* v. *Georgia*, and despite the condescending portrait of Native Americans in Marshall's decision, Francis Stites explains that the Chief Justice apparently held more concern for the plight of the Cherokee than his ruling had let on. Important to the decision were the dissents of Associate Justices Joseph Story and Smith Thompson, both of whom believed the Cherokee to have sovereign rights. Stites reveals that Marshall encouraged the two Justices to write their dissents in such a way as to be informative in how a similar case might be positively received by the Court. He explains that Marshall "encouraged Story and Thompson to write opinions explaining their dissent after the Court had risen. This unusual step revealed Marshall's eagerness for a correct decision, and Thompsons's dissenting opinion went into great detail suggesting the manner in which another case might come before the Court."[15]

In December of 1830, Georgia executed a Cherokee Indian by the name of George "Corn" Tassel. Tassel had been convicted for the murder of another Cherokee man. His appeal was denied by Georgia's highest court. Cherokee Chief John Ross convinced U.S. Attorney General William Wirt (the same William Wirt who took up the legal cause of the Cherokee in 1831 in *Cherokee Nation* v. *Georgia*) to appeal Tassel's case to the

United States Supreme Court. The Court prohibited the execution of Tassel, requested all relevant Georgia court documents in his case, and called for the state's governor, George Gilmer, to appear before the Court in January 1831. In response, in late December 1830 the state of Georgia refused to offer court records, passed laws nullifying all contracts between whites and the Cherokee people, hanged Tassel, and passed legislation requiring white Cherokee to pledge loyalty to the State of Georgia and requiring all whites entering Indian territory working for the Cherokee to first obtain a license. In the final weeks of the year of 1830, Georgia thus defied demands of the federal judiciary, illegally hanged a man officially given legal protection from execution, erased any legal relationship between citizens of Georgia and the Cherokee, and demanded loyalty oaths and arbitrary licenses from those within their own borders.

Though the incident regarding Tassel's case, his illegal execution, and the relationship between Georgia and the Supreme Court (as well as relations between Georgia and the Cherokee) preceded the *Cherokee Nation v. Georgia* case in 1831, its influence upon the *Worcester v. Georgia* case in 1832 is more significant. As a consequence of Georgia's requirement for whites to obtain a license prior to entering and working in Cherokee territory, a group of missionaries friendly with the Cherokee who advocated their sovereign rights, which included Samuel Worcester, were arrested and convicted for violating the law. Worcester was initially given reprieve because his work was officially for the United States federal government as a postmaster. Worcester nevertheless refused to leave the territory and was ultimately convicted of violating the law and sentenced to four years of hard labor. Worcester appealed his conviction to the United States Supreme Court.

The United States Supreme Court ruled in 1832 that Georgia held no authority to enact laws relating to Indians, as it was a power possessed exclusively by the federal government of the United States. Treaties with Indians and other matters of law relevant to the issue was beyond the scope of Georgia's powers. As a result, Georgia's laws related to relations with the Cherokee were unconstitutional. Samuel Worcester thus violated no just law and was to be freed. The Marshall Court asserted that "treaties and laws of the United States contemplate the Indian territory as completely separated from that of the states.... The Cherokee nation, then, is a distinct community occupying its own territory in which the laws of Georgia can have no force."[16] Tim Garrison observes that Marshall was reportedly "disturbed by his conscience and disappointed with the waffling obfuscation of his opinion" in *Cherokee Nation v. Georgia* and that the *Worcester* decision, informed by the legal reasoning of William Wirt and the judicial dissent of Justice Thompson, "abandoned [Marshall's] reliance on the doctrine of discovery and embraced a natural rights theory of inherent Native American sovereignty."[17] The principle of natural rights of sovereignty and self-governance thus informed the Court to rule on behalf of Worcester in the case and, more significantly, on behalf of the Cherokee in their struggle to maintain their lands and way of life.

The *Worcester* decision gave the Cherokee hope that the United States government may mediate any further efforts by Georgia to remove them from their lands. The Jackson administration did nothing of the sort and the federal policy of Indian removal did not change. Samuel Worcester was not immediately freed. He later received a pardon from Georgia's subsequent governor. Worcester's work related to Indians continued, as he ultimately wrote a Cherokee translation of the Bible and continued missioning to Native Americans.

A small faction of Cherokee signed a removal treaty in 1835, called the New Echota Treaty, against the wishes of the majority of the Indian nation including Chief John Ross who had been a fervent opponent of removal. Jeffrey Ostler explains, "Because the majority of Cherokees regarded the treaty as illegitimate, U.S. officials anticipated the possibility of mass resistance and so issued preemptive threats.... General John Wool announced to Cherokees that they must prepare to depart."[18] Ostler also notes that many Cherokee during removal fled to the woods where many died and others subsisted off of berries and roots, and that a "few hundred survivors eventually joined a small group of Cherokees whose homes were in the mountains of southwestern North Carolina and who were exempt from the Treaty of New Echota's removal requirements."[19] Thousands were ultimately removed to the Oklahoma region west of the Mississippi, and more than four thousand men, women, and children died in the process. The lack of enforcement of the *Worcester* decision regarding Native American sovereignty by the

John Ross—A Cherokee Chief, by Alfred M. Hoffy, copied after a work by Charles Bird King, 1843. Hand-colored lithograph on paper (National Portrait Gallery).

federal government, both during Jackson's tenure and after, empowered state courts to ignore the intent of the Marshall Court in *Worcester*. Tim Garrison suggests that events like the removal of the Cherokee, known to history as The Trail of Tears, cannot be reduced to mere numbers of those who died as a result. The impact upon the Cherokee culture, economics, and psyche was immeasurable. As Garrison argues, "The removers not only took Native American real property and improvements, they eliminated the potential competition of a rising class of Indian planters and merchants and allowed whites to take over their homes, farms, and businesses." Removal allowed "southern politicians to capitalize on the prejudices and material desires of their constituents."[20] The displacement of the Cherokee facilitated not merely, then, the gutting of their forward progress but also the growth and strengthening of white southern economic and political power.

Looking at Indian removal, and the case of *Worcester* v. *Georgia* specifically, may bring one to question what role the Supreme Court occupied in such atrocities. On one hand, the Marshall Court defended the sovereignty of the Cherokee Nation though only doing so after repeatedly asserting the secondary and ward-like status of Native Americans in regard to their relationship with the United States. It can be reasonably argued that *Worcester*, in reality as well as in intention, was more about once again asserting federal dominance over the individual states than it was about Native American empowerment. This is the position of Jason Edward Black, who contends that "Worcester was simply a channel for a case that can be understood as a defense of federal power over state rights and of US governmental paternal control over American Indian nations."[21] If true, however, then why Marshall's desire to further articulate the rights of Native Americans referenced by Stites and Garrison? Was Marshall's aim simply to underscore the authority of the federal government over the states because Georgia had prevailed in the previous 1831 case through its dismissal? If so, then why formulate jurisprudence around the dissents of Justices Story and especially Thompson who defended the rights of the Cherokee?

If Marshall is to be condemned for his part in the plight of Native Americans in the nineteenth century it cannot be for his ruling in *Worcester*. The fate of the Cherokee evidently motivated him to allow for a case which would see a legal victory for them. The Marshall Court ultimately ruled in favor of Indian sovereignty, however couched in federal power. The fate of the Cherokee in this regard does not rest with Marshall but with President Andrew Jackson and those who followed who saw no obligation to obey the dictates of the Court. In this way, Jackson and others violated not only the spirit of the *Worcester* decision, but also breached essential aspects of separation of powers. Advocates of legislative and executive authority should use the fate of the Cherokee as a lesson for what can happen when these branches do not respect their constitutional limits as prescribed by the Court.

Rather than condemning Marshall for Indian removal due to the *Worcester* decision, it is more sensible to criticize his role more broadly in the facilitation of federal power which allowed the Executive branch to ignore the *Worcester* ruling. Though a strong advocate for the rule of law and a champion of judicial review as a central facet of that principle, Marshall also spent thirty years generally empowering the national government. Rather than acting as an enemy to the powers of the federal government, as a surface reading of the 1803 *Marbury* v. *Madison* decision might suggest (see Chapter Four), John Marshall most often acted as a supporter in the growth of national power. The role of nationalism in the nineteenth century was a substantial one. It informed westward expansion and the growth of industry, which was the kind of future that the Chief Justice wanted for the country. Marshall thus facilitated the enormous power of the national government. He did so in decisions such as *Johnson* v. *McIntosh* (1823) which deprived Native Americans of their property rights as he did with *McCulloch* v. *Maryland* (1819), which denied states the power to tax the federal government and which asserted the constitutionality of the Bank of the United States. When states and the other federal branches ignored the Supreme Court's decree in 1832, Marshall had to some degree become a victim of his own success. He had empowered the government to a level where it felt confident in being able to defy the Court's decision. *Worcester* v. *Georgia* is, if anything, evidence of the dangers of administrations, legislatures, and states that give no respect to the rule of law. If it is a failure of judicial review, it is a failure of judicial review to be followed by those obligated to honor it. *Worcester* is thus not so much a lesson in judicial review but in Marshall's legacy as one who empowered government to the point that Marshall himself could no longer restrain it. For this reason, Marshall's reputation as a constitutional guardian due to his assertion of the Court's power to nullify laws is to be tempered with his equally enduring legacy as a champion of national legislative and executive power.

Indian removal was among the most egregious acts of government power, at both the state and federal level, in the nineteenth century. The Supreme Court was powerless to stop it and had in fact facilitated the practice through rulings that denied Native Americans their inherent rights. The inability, or outright refusal, of the Court to recognize the rights values inherent in the American project, as articulated in the Declaration of Independence and given political form in the United States Constitution, made such atrocities possible. The Supreme Court's complicity in denying the property rights of Native Americans years before the *Worcester* decision gave precedence and legal legitimacy to Indian removal. Individual states and the other federal branches later eluded the dictates of the Court when Marshall and others began to recognize the rights of the Cherokee. This was because rulings like *Worcester* were a threat to imperial power and expansion. If a failure of judicial review is to be highlighted, it is not *Worcester* v. *Georgia* or *Cherokee Nation* v. *Georgia*, but *Johnson* v. *McIntosh*. Judicial review's legitimacy rests upon a fidelity to not only constitutional principles but the rights values which inform them. *Johnson* v. *McIntosh* violated such principles. In the mid-nineteenth century, another decision would do the same: *Dred Scott* v. *Sandford* in 1857.

Southern Politics of the Court and Slave Politics of Statehood

Just as the property rights of Native Americans were denied through a rejection of their basic humanity, Dred Scott and indeed all African Americans were denied their right of citizenship and freedom under similar assumptions. The treatment of Native Americans and the treatment of African Americans in the history of the United States contain respective, discrete traits because of the unique experiences each group endured. The fact remains, however, that because westward expansion in the nineteenth century exacerbated both Indian removal and the practice of slavery, the history of Native Americans and African Americans are inextricably tied. There was a reciprocal nature to the ill treatment of both. Indian removal facilitated the growth and spread of slavery, which fostered desire for still more lands to be taken. More land meant more agriculture and industry, which again meant more slavery, and the cycle would repeat.

No small part of the encouragement of assimilation for Native Americans in the antebellum South was adopting the practice of slavery for themselves. This is seen, as merely one example, among the Cherokee who were removed from their lands in the 1830s. Among those removed were the Cherokee's slaves, who they had acquired over generations in their attempt to practice a way of life that reflected Euro-American customs. Contextualizing nineteenth-century political and legal history through an analysis of the treatment of Indians and African Americans, and recognizing their connections, provides for a better understanding of the history of the Supreme Court and the United States generally. Indeed, an understanding of the 1850s is likely not possible without some knowledge of the events of the 1830s. Historical events do not occur in a vacuum, and historical actors generally transcend a single time and place.

One figure who connects the Jacksonian era of Indian removal with the late antebellum era of the 1850s, and contributed substantially to the politics and policies of both, was Roger Taney. Taney had been a devoted member of the Jackson administration, facilitating the shuttering of the Bank of the United States when others refused. A southern slave-owner like Jackson, Taney was ultimately appointed to the position of Chief Justice of the Supreme Court upon the death of John Marshall. Taney's personal loyalty and political affinity with Jackson made him a suitable choice for Chief Justice. His appointment also followed the trend of an empowered southern constituency on the Court. The power of the South in the federal legislative branch was significant due to the Constitution's Three-Fifths Clause. This remained true of the Court in the mid-nineteenth century because of slavery's connection to southern political influence. Akhil Reed Amar observes that "the South won a far larger share of judicial posts than its underlying free population [represented]."[22] Keith Whittington similarly notes that the reorganization of the judiciary with the Judiciary Act of 1837 allowed an exacerbation of this southern bent and empowered Jackson to appoint two new Justices to the Court during his final year in office. "The Judiciary Act of 1837 redrew circuit boundaries and expanded and reorganized the Court. Andrew Jackson had two new seats to fill on the Court, and the western states were organized into three new circuits, with the states created from the antislavery Northwest Territory making up only a single circuit."[23] When the Dred Scott case was presented to the Taney Court in the late 1850s, the Court was decidedly southern in its politics and antislavery sentiment was considerably underrepresented.

The politics of slavery played a significant role. Upon the election of James Buchanan in 1856, some Democrats took his victory as approval of slave policy. Whittington remarks that Buchanan's election "was taken by some, including the president and president-elect, as a mandate of the pro-slavery position."[24] Furthermore, Buchanan privately shared his desire for the Supreme Court to settle the matter constitutionally. The Dred Scott case, discussed presently, was in deliberations at the moment of Buchanan's inauguration. Buchanan received word, according to Whittington, "that the opinions being written in the Dred Scott case would in fact address 'the powers of Congress' to regulate slavery in the territories."[25] The new president used the opportunity in his inaugural address to promote deference to the Court, having prior knowledge that it would likely decide in a manner friendly to the pro-slavery position. Paul Finkelman, in his essay "James Buchanan, Dred Scott, and the Whisper of Conspiracy," published in *James Buchanan and the Coming of the Civil War* (2013), contends that "until Buchanan's inaugural address, no one had imagined that the issue of slavery in the territories was 'a judicial question, which legitimately belongs to the Supreme Court of the United States.' On the contrary, it had always been a political question for the Congress and the president to solve."[26] Finkelman's assertion, however, is incorrect. The idea of having the Supreme Court ultimately rule on the constitutionality of slavery was not new or exclusive to James Buchanan. In 1850, prominent Kentucky Senator Henry Clay promoted the idea, saying "what ought to be done more satisfactory to both sides of the question, to the free States and to the slaveholding States … to leave the question of slavery or no slavery to be decided by the only competent authority that can definitely settle it forever, the authority of the Supreme Court of the United States?"[27] Finkelman is correct, however, that the Court's role in taking on the slavery matter was new in the 1850s and that it had historically been handled through legislative operation.

The politics of slavery had grown over time due to the introduction of new states into the Union. In 1819, just before both Missouri and Maine achieved statehood, twenty-two states made up the country, half of which were free. Maine entered the Union as a free state while Missouri entered without any prohibitions against slavery. Included in the legislation known as the Missouri Compromise was an amendment which thereafter forbade slave states from being formed north of Missouri's southern border, at latitude 36°30.' For the next few decades, northern states entered the Union as free states while those admitted in the south held no restrictions on the practice of slavery. The Kansas-Nebraska Act of 1854 disturbed this practice and overturned the policy in favor of so-called *popular sovereignty,* allowing any state to decide for itself whether or not it would be a free or slave state upon joining the Union. Though the abolition movement was growing significantly at the time, much of the criticism against the notion of popular sovereignty was not the evil of slavery itself but its potential spread westward. Thus, the Dred Scott case took on increasing importance due to its involvement concerning questions of African American freedom as well as the debate over popular sovereignty.

Dred Scott *v.* Sandford *(1857)*

Dred Scott was born into slavery in Virginia in approximately 1799. He was ultimately under the legal ownership of a number of different masters and was relocated several times across different regions of the United States. While under the ownership of an army surgeon named John Emerson and living in slavery with Emerson in the free Wisconsin Territory, Scott met and married Harriet Robinson. Robinson was soon sold to Emerson. Emerson eventually relocated to Louisiana, married Eliza Irene

Sanford, and called for his slaves to join him at his new location. Masters and slaves later resettled once again in Missouri. Emerson participated in the Seminole War in Florida and then rejoined the family in St. Louis. He died in 1843 and left his estate, including his slaves, to his widow.

Dred Scott soon appealed to Mrs. Emerson to sell him his freedom but she refused. Upon the urging of his wife, Scott eventually sought freedom from the Missouri state court due to having lived on free soil when in the Wisconsin Territory. They initially won their freedom because Missouri law maintained that slaves were emancipated upon reaching free soil. The Missouri Supreme Court, however, reversed the decision of the lower court. Scott took his case to federal court and sued John Sanford, brother of Eliza Irene, who had since become his owner. The Scotts lost again in a lower federal court. Dred Scott then appealed his case to the United States Supreme Court.

The *Dred Scott* v. *Sandford* decision (Sanford was misspelled *Sandford* during earlier proceedings and thus became part of the official name of the case), decided in 1857, is the single most heinous judgment in the long and sordid history of the Court. The Chief Justice's reasoning and articulation of the decision underscore the personal prejudice, ahistorical assertions, and constitutionally dubious rationalizations of the Taney Court. The decision made white supremacy a matter of official United States policy and judicial philosophy. The decision asserted:

> The question is simply this: Can a negro, whose ancestors were imported into this country, and sold as slaves, become a member of the political community formed and brought into existence by the Constitution of the United States, and as such become entitled to all the rights and privileges, and immunities, guaranteed by that instrument to the citizen? One of which rights is the privilege of suing in a court of the United States in the cases specified in the Constitution.... The only matter in issue before the court, therefore, is, whether descendants of such slaves, when they shall be emancipated, or who are born of parents who had become free before their birth, are citizens of a state, in the sense in which the word citizen is used in the Constitution of the United States.... We think they are not, and that they are not included, and were not intended to be included, under the word "citizens" in the Constitution, and can therefore claim none of the rights and privileges which that instrument provides for and secures to citizens of the United States. On the contrary, they were at that time considered as a subordinate and inferior class of beings, who had been subjugated by the dominant race, and, had no rights or privileges but such as those who held the power and the Government might choose to grant them.[28]

The Taney Court denied Dred Scott, and indeed all African Americans—free or slave—not merely any semblance of legal status but also any sense of their humanity. Furthermore, Taney's reasoning, informed by a notion of Euro-Americans as "the dominant race," did not merely assert the most race-based reasoning for slavery and African American subjugation in United States legal history, but also betrayed the natural rights-based philosophy of the American founding. Taney's claim that Africans and their American descendants "had no rights but such as those who held the power and the Government might choose to grant them" stands in contrast to the natural rights-informed view that rights precede government and that respect to individual rights is the source of a government's legitimacy. Taney's formulation of government is one of arbitrary rule where its existence precedes the existence of rights, rather than the reverse.

In seeking to settle the slavery matter once and for all, the Court offered audacious assertions which defied the nation's own history and policy regarding the practice. The Court tied the right of private property, as a constitutional matter, with a right to own human beings, and claimed that such a right is beyond the reach of the United States government. By providing this argument, Taney not only maintained that slavery was permissible, but that it could not be regulated or limited through federal legislation. By connecting the practice of slavery with the natural right of private ownership and the role of the Constitution in recognizing the rights of American citizens, the Taney Court simultaneously ignored the humanity of African Americans, ignored the well-established powers of the federal government to regulate slavery, and made a mockery of the natural right of private property. Taney reasoned thusly:

> [T]he Federal Government can exercise no power over [a citizen's] person or property, beyond what that instrument [the Constitution] confers, nor lawfully deny any right which it has reserved.... For example, no one, we presume,

***Dred Scott. Harriet, wife of Dred Scott,* c. 1887. Wood engraving on paper (Library of Congress).**

will contend that Congress can make any law in a Territory respecting the establishment of religion, or the free exercise thereof, or abridging the freedom of speech or of the press, or the right of the people of the Territory peaceably to assemble, and to petition the Government for the redress of grievances.[29]

According to the Taney Court, the right to own and transport human beings was a right no different from the freedoms of religion, speech, and assembly. Because of this, slavery was a constitutionally protected right and thus could not be reined in through legislative power. Ignoring, for a moment, the inhumanity and absurdity of the argument, Taney's reasoning fails to satisfy a historical analysis of slavery and black citizenship in the United States. Regarding free blacks, the life and career of African American figures like the scientist Benjamin Banneker in the early republic complicates Taney's claim. His argument against the legitimacy of legislative power to regulate slavery is similarly flawed. Akhil Reed Amar contends, "However slanted toward slaveholders the original Constitution may have been, it offered little support for Chief Justice Roger Taney's extremist Dred Scott opinion, which claimed Congress was constitutionally required to allow slavery in the territories."[30] Paul Finkelman offers a similar point, observing that in "Article 6 of the [Northwest] ordinance the Congress banned all slavery in the territories north and west of the Ohio River.... The reenactment of the Northwest Ordinance illustrates that no one in the first Congress, dominated by the men who had written and ratified the Constitution, doubted the power of Congress to regulate slavery in the territories."[31]

Among the reasons James Wilson celebrated the proposed Constitution at the Pennsylvania ratification convention in December 1787 was precisely because it would be capable of regulating and perhaps ultimately eradicating slavery. Under the Articles of Confederation, no federal regulation of the slave trade or of slave practice within the nation existed. Wilson noted that the future of slavery in the United States could be put on a path toward abolition under the new Constitution, highlighting the end of the slave trade in 1808 as one of the document's most salient clauses:

> Under the present Confederation, the states may admit the importation of slaves as long as they please; but by this article after the year 1808, the Congress will have power to prohibit such importation, notwithstanding the disposition of any state to the contrary. I consider this as laying the foundation for banishing slavery out of this country; and though the period is more distant than I could wish, yet it will produce the same kind, gradual change, which was pursued in Pennsylvania.[32]

By the time of the Pennsylvania ratification debates, Pennsylvania had begun a policy of gradual abolition and Wilson looked forward to the federal Constitution facilitating the possibility of gradual emancipation throughout the United States. This, of course, was not to happen, but

Wilson's vision was not necessarily misguided. States in the north were ridding themselves of slavery since the Revolution and the aforementioned Northwest Territory clearly indicated the belief that the federal government would have the power to regulate slavery in the territories, including banning it outright if it so chose. The possibility of a United States without slavery, according to Wilson, was very real. He celebrated that the day would come when "the rights of all mankind will be acknowledged and established throughout the union" and that soon "congress will have power to exterminate slavery from within our borders."[33]

The Taney Court's assertion, then, that the federal government possessed no power to regulate, limit, or end slavery ignored the well-established history which contradicted such a claim. Taney had to ignore essentially the entire history of the United States federal government to make this allegation. Or, perhaps, deciphering through judicial review, none of the previous federal acts had been legitimate. This was certainly an aspect of Taney's argument. The Missouri Compromise, for example, limited slavery to the inclusion of new southern states. For this reason, it was unconstitutional—as was the free soil provision of the Northwest Ordinance—because it denied American citizens of their constitutional right to own human beings. The weight of Taney's claim rested on the notion that whites possessed a natural right to violate the natural rights of blacks. The Taney Court thus chose to defy precedence that limited slavery and embraced the most outlandish and incoherent interpretation of private property rights to support its decision.

Mark A. Graber, in his book *Dred Scott and the Problem of Constitutional Evil* (2006), claims that the Dred Scott decision, when studied in purely legal and constitutional terms and devoid of moral implications, was correct. His thesis is that evil existed within the constitutional system itself and it should thus be the Constitution and not the Taney Court that is ultimately worthy of blame. He contends that the lesson of Dred Scott is that "constitutional theory cannot mitigate or eradicate constitutional evil. Constitutional evils exist because, at crucial constitutional moments, citizens agree to accommodate a practice many think or come to think a substantial injustice. The reasons that originally suffice for accommodation become legitimate constitutional arguments for ongoing accommodation."[34] Graber's point is compelling. An imperfect, and indeed a malevolent feature of a system should be given the focus of critique rather than an ancillary byproduct of it. Unquestionably, the compromise over slavery in the constitutional era was a devil's bargain that culminated many decades later in the Dred Scott case and the Civil War. Also, Graber is certainly correct that "Taney's constitutional claims in Dred Scott were well within the mainstream of antebellum constitutional thought" and that the "judicial denial of black citizenship reflected beliefs held by the overwhelming majority of antebellum jurists in both the North and the South."[35] The popularity of opinion in the United States that the Dred Scott decision reflected, however, is less a sign of the Constitution's fallibility (even in its pre–Fourteenth Amendment design) than it is evidence that popular opinion is often the enemy of justice. It has already been established that the Taney Court's assertion that the federal government had no power to regulate slavery was in contradiction to the acts and statements of the framers. In this way alone it is recognized that the Taney Court was plainly wrong. Graber's claim that the Taney Court's decision was understandable given the context of popular sentiment at the time ignores the antimajoritarian impulse the judiciary and the rule of law is intended to express. Rationalizing the position of the Taney Court (though Graber certainly does not defend it) is similar to the arguments by champions of popular sovereignty in the nineteenth century. Its source of legitimacy was not rooted in human ethics or natural rights, but in local control and popular opinion. Though both local self-government and popular sentiment are quintessentially important American values, they do not supersede the ultimate constitutional project of recognizing and protecting the rights of individuals. The Taney Court may well have reflected public opinion, and understanding this is an important political point. It is not, however, a legitimate legal point. The Court is not designed to reflect public opinion but instead to interpret the law according to constitutional principles informed by rights values and an interest in establishing justice. The Taney Court's decision was wrong by virtually every metric: historically, constitutionally, and morally.

Though Dred Scott was denied his freedom as a result of the case, he and his wife were soon freed by the family who came to be their final owners. The family that freed Dred and Harriet Scott were descendants of those who had owned Dred upon his birth in 1799, the Blow family. Dred Scott's newfound freedom in the material world would not last long, however, as he died of tuberculosis the following year. Harriet Scott survived much longer. She lived to witness the American Civil War, as well as the ratification of the Thirteenth, Fourteenth, and Fifteenth Amendments. These amendments decreed the end of slavery, the citizenship of African Americans, and the right to vote for African American men. Harriet Scott died in the centennial year of American independence, on June 17, 1876.

The Role of the Court Versus the Role of Judicial Review

Regarding both Indian removal and slavery, the Supreme Court participated considerably in the development and facilitation of each. The failures of the Court in these matters are crucial to observe as they connect to the two great atrocities of nineteenth-century America. Concerning Indian removal, the Court sought to defend the sovereign right of the Cherokee to maintain their ancestral home, but did so belatedly. By contributing to and legitimizing the power of the federal government, particularly the executive branch, over a period of decades, John Marshall helped create a federal executive which could defy his orders and treat the judicial branch as inferior. The state of Georgia benefited from the flouting of the *Worcester* decision as a result of the President and others not enforcing the judgment of the Court. In its final years, the Marshall Court was pushed to the margins and relegated to being a political afterthought. It sought to defend the rights of the Cherokee from the state of Georgia and the federal government but only after ruling a decade earlier that Native Americans were not to have their property rights respected. The Marshall Court thus failed Native Americans long before the 1830s and endured a crisis of conscience too late to remedy that which it had been party to.

The Taney Court's Dred Scott decision was emblematic of the worst aspects of nineteenth-century cultural and political thought. It asserted the natural dominance of the white population and decreed that the inferior status of African Americans, both free and slave, was legitimate. The Court also maintained that the ownership of human beings was a constitutionally protected right and the federal government of the United States had no power to regulate or limit the practice. Though such claims were morally repugnant and constitutionally dubious, it reflected some level of popular sentiment in the middle of the nineteenth century. Taney betrayed the idealistic vision of the Declaration of Independence and the natural rights theory that informed it and chose instead to protect and empower an evil institution he and many other political figures from the South participated in. Roger Taney championed the worst aspects of American culture and sought to ignore the historical facts that contradicted his assertions, including the existence of free blacks in the founding era, the banning of slavery in the Northwest Ordinance, and the hopes of framers like James Wilson to implement a gradual end to the practice nationwide.

The atrocities of Indian removal and slavery in the history of the United States do not, however, support any reasonable critique of judicial review. The lesson of *Worcester* v. *Georgia* is not the failure of the Court to provide a just decision, but a federal government failing to respect that it is the Court's role to say what the law is, and to do so with constant recognition of rights values. In the case where the Court truly violated the rights of Native Americans, the *Johnson* v. *McIntosh* decision, it was the same circumvention to principles of natural rights seen against African Americans in *Dred Scott* that should be condemned rather than the power of judicial review itself. Though it is important to note that the federal government's treatment of Native Americans was on the whole better than that of the individual states in this era, and recognizing that the federal government faced a no-win situation regarding the matter in the nineteenth century (the decisions of state courts were the only real alternative, and a decidedly inferior one), that fact does not absolve the Marshall Court for asserting the diminished sovereignty of Indians in *McIntosh*. It can certainly be argued that keeping Native Americans from selling their lands was a means of protecting them from exploitation by the separate states, but such an argument at its core is a defense of robbing the Cherokee and other Indians of their natural right to dispose of their property as they saw fit. It was assuredly a crisis with no good answers, but the flouting of the property rights of Native Americans is not something to be overlooked. In the case of *Dred Scott*, which was an unquestionably immoral and legally improper opinion, the Court failed to provide a view which conformed with constitutional fidelity. The decision may have sought to utilize judicial review to remove the legislative power from regulating slavery but it did so in a way which reflected much of the country's ambivalent feelings toward the practice, both in the north and the south.

Using Dred Scott as an example for refuting judicial review is a misguided endeavor. For all of the championing of legislative power among many in academia, the fact remains that the people's representatives had decades to stem the tide of slavery and often instead went in the direction of slavery-appeasing popular sovereignty. By couching the debate increasingly in matters of local self-governance and popular opinion, the moral depravity of the slavery issue was obfuscated. Those arguing for legislative supremacy in the American system have as much to account for regarding the concessions to slavery among the people's representatives, if not more so, than those who defend the Court's power of judicial review.

The popular sovereignty position was a convenient one for defenders of slavery to champion. It demonstrates the dangers of defending policies and practices through their reputation rather than their ethical merit. If anything, the Dred Scott decision is more emblematic of a Court too interested in attaching itself to popular sentiment than in declaring the constitutionality of laws. The decision may have been an attack upon legislative power, but it was also to some degree a position which favored populism and the will of the people.

When the will of the people is not tempered with constitutional principles, informed by a philosophy of inherent individual rights, a republic—and its governmental organizations, including its judiciary—prioritizes popular opinion over that of moral judgment and the rule of law. The champions of legislative supremacy who criticize judicial review may want to return to the American founding when deliberating their position. After all, the great compromise that allowed slavery to exist and fester in the republic was facilitated by a body of delegates acting on behalf of the American people, as was the ratification process in each state. Thus, it was the people's representatives, and not any judiciary, that initially compromised on the issue of slavery. If the Supreme Court's Dred Scott decision was the culmination of the complexities and contradictions of a federal republic wrestling with the institution of slavery while espousing the principles of freedom, then the compromise over slavery by the people's representatives in the 1780s is also to be held responsible, and arguably more so.

Judicial review cannot be convincingly refuted through a critique of the United States Supreme Court's most significant failings. If this were true, some strange comfort could be found in Indian removal and slavery existing as unfortunate but inevitable byproducts of an ineffectual and morally repugnant Court. The reality is a much more difficult one to face: Indian removal and slavery were popular policies, made manifest by political representatives and supported by the people themselves. If no Supreme Court had existed in nineteenth-century America, or if its power of judicial review had not in any way been present, there would nevertheless have been no prevention of Indian removal and African American slavery. The reality is that American empire and the means of achieving it were far more powerful and popular than the American judiciary. As much as the Court's failings should be scrutinized, as this chapter has endeavored to do, this fact remains.

In the years following the *Dred Scott* decision, the country fell into civil war. On January 1, 1863, President Abraham Lincoln issued the Emancipation Proclamation, freeing slaves in the rebel South and changing the narrative of the war from one of preserving the Union to one of ending slavery. It was not the Emancipation Proclamation that ultimately ended the institution in the United States, however. Slavery's abolition was achieved through the Thirteenth Amendment. It is the amendment process, and not the dictates of the Commander in Chief nor the rulings of the Supreme Court, that act as the genuine final word regarding the Constitution. It was with the ratification of the following amendment, the Fourteenth in 1868, discussed in the following chapter, that the Court would begin in earnest to operate as an instrument of rights values and significantly transform the role of the judiciary in the American republic. The Court would not immediately follow the wishes of the framers of the Fourteenth Amendment, however, and stalled the overt recognition of rights values to a significant degree in the immediate decades following the amendment's ratification.

Chapter Six

Privileges or Immunities and the Fourteenth Amendment

Near the conclusion of the Civil War, the United States Congress passed the Thirteenth Amendment in January 1865. It was ratified when the required twenty-seven of the thirty-six states voted in favor of the amendment by the close of that year. Arguably, 1865 was the most turbulent and revolutionary year in the history of the United States since the founding. The Confederate States of America agreed to a ceasefire in early April, Abraham Lincoln was assassinated less than a week later on April 14, the South officially surrendered in November, and the Thirteenth Amendment constitutionally ended human bondage in December. Ending the practice of chattel slavery and freeing all African Americans still in servitude who had not been freed through President Lincoln's Emancipation Proclamation in 1863, the Thirteenth Amendment nevertheless did not explicitly recognize the citizenship status of former slaves. Many Republicans believed the spoils of war implied it, but enough were concerned with the amendment's absence of citizenship recognition for blacks that the Civil Rights Act of 1866 was written. As will be seen, however, the Civil Rights Act was simply legislation promoting the notion of African American citizenship without the constitutional foundation required to assert or enforce the principle. Some Republicans in the House of Representatives and the Senate realized that a subsequent constitutional amendment was necessary to give the principle the force of law and the power of constitutional credibility. The Fourteenth Amendment thus became, among other things, a vehicle for recognizing the citizenship of African Americans and a means for broadening the standard of rights values in American constitutional law.

The Fourteenth Amendment proved to be one of the most important evolutions in the history of American political thought. It reworked the concept of constitutional jurisdiction and—over time—advanced the Supreme Court's relationship with the recognition and protection of individual rights. In the process it reversed Justice Taney's assertion in *Dred Scott* v. *Sandford* (1857) that African Americans could never be citizens of the United States and ultimately overturned *Barron* v. *Baltimore* (1833) that had asserted that the Bill of Rights did not apply to the individual states. The amendment thus armed the Court with a more substantial form of judicial review to scrutinize the constitutionality of state laws more closely, in addition to reviewing the legitimacy of federal legislation.

The Fourteenth Amendment's scope and impact is simply too vast to discuss in its entirety in a single chapter. With this in mind, the most relevant aspects of the amendment in relation to its intent and the Court's interpretation in the aftermath of ratification and Reconstruction will remain the focus of this chapter's analysis. The Fourteenth Amendment included numerous ambitious aims. Unlike most other amendments, it sought to accomplish many objectives at once, including citizenship for African Americans and a widening of the rights recognized under citizenship, but also due process guarantees, equal protection of the laws, and other measures. Most important to the discussion in this chapter, however, is the drafting of the first section of the amendment—specifically, the Privileges or Immunities Clause—and its author's stated objective. Following this will be an examination of the Court's interpretation of the Privileges or Immunities Clause and how it contributed to a constitutional retreat of sorts before reversing its course once again in the twentieth century.

Congressman John Bingham of Ohio

The author of what became the first section of the Fourteenth Amendment was Ohio Congressman John Bingham. Bingham wrote the entirety of the first section himself, save for the first sentence which was added later during revisions. Bingham is lost to the larger culture of popular history today but his accomplishments belong in the American canon of revolutionary constitutionalist innovators along with that of James Madison and George Mason. It was Bingham who most ardently disagreed that the Thirteenth Amendment implied African American citizenship. The absence of any such language contributing to that principle, Bingham argued, would act as an obstacle to the citizenship of freed slaves being realized. When his fellow Republicans countered with legislation to recognize African American citizenship with the 1866 Civil Rights Act, Bingham argued that such legislation was meaningless without a constitutional amendment clearly articulating that freed slaves were citizens of the United States. So principled was Bingham regarding this that he voted against the Civil Rights Act, seeing it as a dead letter. As writer Damon

Root observes in *Overruled: The Long War for Control of the U.S. Supreme Court* (2014), "Congressional Republicans divided unevenly over the question, with most believing they did enjoy the power to enforce the Civil Rights Act (particularly given the outcome of the late war), while a few prominent skeptics argued otherwise. Foremost among the skeptics was Ohio Representative John Bingham."[1] Historian Eric Foner, in *The Second Founding: How the Civil War and Reconstruction Remade the Constitution* (2019), suggests that although the Civil Rights Act was historic in that it "severed citizenship from race, as abolitionists had long demanded, and abrogated the *Dred Scott* decision," and although Bingham supported the principle the legislation offered, he nevertheless "deemed another amendment necessary to give it constitutional authority."[2] The Civil Rights Act was soon passed by both houses of Congress but President Andrew Johnson vetoed it on March 27, 1866. Two weeks later it was passed through a congressional override. Foner notes that the legislation "became the first important statute in American history to become law over the president's objections."[3] Though the Civil Rights Act passed historic legislation recognizing African American citizenship and asserting citizenship of all persons born or naturalized in the United states (subject to its jurisdiction), as well as outlining certain protections including the right of property, the law nevertheless lacked reliance on a constitutional foundation. Without an amendment giving it such legitimacy, John Bingham doubted it would ultimately possess the force of law or survive constitutional scrutiny. Bingham thus sought to create an amendment which would make the Civil Rights Act and its aims more than an empty promise. His goals were substantially more ambitious than simply giving constitutional credibility to the Civil Rights Act, however, important as that was. He also sought to apply a new standard of rights values in the American system by writing an amendment that would apply the same fidelity to the Bill of Rights that had been imposed against the federal government in 1791 against the individual states.

The Bill of Rights, Universally Applied

Congressman Bingham's view of the Bill of Rights was outside the norm compared to conventional legal wisdom of the time, though there were other Republicans who shared his perspective. He rejected the idea that the Bill of Rights did not apply to the individual states. Bingham seemed incapable of philosophically accepting this premise, consistently contending that the Bill of Rights *should* apply to the states. This was reflected in his congressional voting record as well as what he sought to accomplish with the Fourteenth Amendment. His interpretation was generally unpopular prior to the Reconstruction era and the passing of the Civil Rights Act, but the need to hold individual states to a standard of rights values became substantially more prescient in the aftermath of the Civil War.

Legal scholar Randy Barnett articulates the principle of applying the Bill of Rights to the states, and using the judiciary to arbitrate such matters, in *Restoring the Lost Constitution: A Presumption of Liberty* (2004). He suggests that when "state legislatures restrict the liberties of the people, they are no more entitled to be the judge in their own case than is Congress. The exercise of liberty by the citizen should not be restricted unless the state can show, to the satisfaction of an independent tribunal of justice, that such a restriction is both necessary and proper."[4] Powerful forces among states in the South had routinely violated essential rights to protect the institution of slavery in the first half of the nineteenth century.

Beyond the most abominable practice of human bondage itself, southern states actively passed laws in the early to mid-nineteenth century that suppressed free speech and a free press, especially that which was critical of slavery. Michael Kent Curtis, in his historical analysis of the Fourteenth Amendment, *No State Shall Abridge: The Fourteenth Amendment and the Bill of Rights* (1986), highlights some examples. "In 1836, Virginia made it a serious crime for a member of an 'abolition' society to enter the state and 'advocate or advise the abolition of slavery.'" Laws were also passed "making it a felony to circulate books that denied the master's right to property in his slaves. A Louisiana statute imposed harsh penalties on anyone who spoke or published language that had a tendency to produce discontent among free blacks or excite insubordination among slaves."[5] Curtis notes that similar laws existed in other southern states and that Amos Kendall, President Andrew Jackson's postmaster general, had asserted in the 1830s that individual state governments had the power to legally ban abolitionist publications. Curtis further observes that southern states "passed laws requiring postmasters to rifle the mail and to notify justices of the peace if they found publications 'denying the right of masters in their slaves and inculcating the duty of resistance to such right.' Under such a law the *New York Tribune* was banned by a Virginia postmaster in 1859."[6]

Bingham's insistence upon the states abiding by principles enshrined in the Bill of Rights can be found in congressional testimony prior to the Civil War. His refusal to vote in favor of statehood for Oregon in 1859 was premised on its proposed constitution which aimed to deny free blacks the ability to enter and reside within the state, among other repugnant measures. The language of the state constitution also asserted that free blacks would not possess rights to own real estate, sue in court, or make contracts.

Bingham, in solidarity with the vast majority of congressional Republicans, thus voted against granting statehood to Oregon. Oregon achieved statehood due to support from Democrats in the years immediately preceding secession and the Civil War. Congressman Bingham registered his animosity toward admitting a supposedly free state that openly denied blacks rights of citizenship and flouted the values enshrined in the Bill of Rights:

> In my judgment, sir, this constitution framed by the people of Oregon is
> repugnant to the Federal Constitution, and violative of the rights of citizens
> of the United States. I know, sir, that some gentlemen have a short and easy
> method of disposing of such objections as these, by assuming that the peo-
> ple of the State, after admission, may, by changing their constitution, insert
> therein every objectionable feature which, before admission, they were con-
> strained to omit in order to secure the favorable action of Congress.[7]

As Michael Kent Curtis explains, "Bingham denied that states had the right to infringe rights of citizens of the United States, but admitted they might arrogate to themselves the power to do so."[8] Contrary to the *Dred Scott* decision, Bingham believed free blacks to be American citizens, even prior to the Thirteenth and Fourteenth Amendments. The matter at hand in the aftermath of the Civil War and in the spirit of Reconstruction was to make that principle a constitutional reality and to design an amendment that would compel state governments to abide by the Bill of Rights.

Though Bingham's position was somewhat unique in his assertion that states ought to be held to abide by the rights enshrined in the first eight amendments of the United States Constitution (amendments Nine and Ten concern unenumerated rights and reassert the role of federalism in the constitutional system, respectively), he was not alone nor was he the first.[9] Congressman James F. Wilson of Iowa stated in 1864 that freedom "of religious opinion, freedom of speech and press, and the right of assemblage for the purpose of petition belong to every American citizen, high or low, rich or poor, wherever he may be within the jurisdiction of the United States. With these rights no State may interfere without breach of the bond which holds the Union together."[10] Not only was Bingham not alone among Republicans who believed states ought to be held to the same rights standards as the federal government, but abolitionists had been making similar claims for decades. As Randy Barnett explains, "Prior to the Civil War, some abolitionists like Alvan Stewart and Joel Tiffany insisted that the Bill of Rights applied to the states, notwithstanding *Barron* v. *Baltimore*."[11] Stewart had argued for the immediate end to slavery in New Jersey in 1845 and Tiffany published a book in 1849 called *A Treatise on the Unconstitutionality of Slavery*.

The libertarian writer Lysander Spooner wrote a pamphlet in two parts, the first published in 1845 and the second in 1847, also titled *The Unconstitutionality of Slavery*. The 1860 edition contained both parts and additional essays, including a critique of the 1850 Fugitive Slave Act called "A Defence of the Fugitive Slaves," originally written the year the act was passed. Spooner's position, among other abolitionists, was that the United States Constitution was not a document upholding slavery, but "on the contrary, it presumes men to be free."[12] This view by Spooner and other antislavery advocates stood in stark contradiction to the views of leading abolitionist William Lloyd Garrison, who held that the Constitution was a pro-slavery document. The antislavery Constitution thesis among certain abolitionists had a profound impact on Garrison's colleague, Frederick Douglass. Douglass eventually distanced himself from Garrison and his perspective and embraced

Frederick Douglass, **by unidentified artist, 1856. Quarter-plate ambrotype (National Portrait Gallery).**

the vision that the United States Constitution was a "glorious liberty document."[13] He also accused Garrison of ironically sharing too much of a worldview with defenders of slavery. Douglass asserted that Garrison saw in "the Constitution precisely what John C. Calhoun sees there."[14] Douglass's schism from Garrison is noteworthy because it moved him toward seeing the Constitution not as an obstacle to African American freedom but as the means for accomplishing it. John Bingham was similar regarding his vision of what the Thirteenth and the Fourteenth Amendments would accomplish. The Thirteenth Amendment rid slavery from the United States and the Fourteenth Amendment would firmly establish citizenship for African Americans and provide a new rights standard against the states.

Second Amendment Rights

It was not merely abolitionists who made rights claims against state power in the antebellum era. A case in 1846 that was decided in Georgia's

Supreme Court centered on a contested law forbidding citizens of the state from carrying weapons. Although the case was decided over a decade following *Barron* v. *Baltimore*, Georgia's Supreme Court nevertheless nullified the law for its violation of the essential right of self-protection. Georgia did not rely on its own state constitution, because as Michael Kent Curtis observes, the "Georgia constitution seems to have lacked any protection for the right of bearing arms." Despite the lack of such an enumerated right in the state's charter, and despite the Bill of Rights not being binding upon the states during the era, "the Georgia court relied on the Second Amendment of the United States Constitution."[15] This begs the question as to why the Georgia Supreme Court would assert the federal Second Amendment when it had no legal obligation to do so. Articulated in the *Nunn* v. *Georgia* decision, the state Court referred to unalienable rights:

> does it follow that because the people refused to delegate to the general government the power to take from them the right to keep and bear arms that they designed to rest it in the State governments? Is it a right reserved to the States or to themselves? Is it not an unalienable right, which lies at the bottom of every free government? We do not believe that, because the people withheld this arbitrary power of disfranchisement from Congress, they ever intended to confer it on the local legislatures. This is a right too dear to be confided to a republican legislature.[16]

Nunn v. *Georgia* demonstrated that a court of law weighing constitutional issues may uphold fundamental rights, including rights not explicitly asserted in a government's charter. It is within this intellectual space that the Ninth Amendment of the United States Constitution resides, as it asserts the existence of unenumerated rights. This is a topic that will be explored further in Chapter Eight. *Nunn* v. *Georgia* was also important because it underscored self-protection as both an unalienable and individual right.[17] Those skeptical toward a fundamental right of gun ownership may feel compelled to couch this decision in the culture of a southern slave state that relied on arms to keep human beings enslaved and to protect their power as masters. If true, then the belief that keeping and bearing arms was an unalienable right should have been the exclusive feature of southern slave culture in the nineteenth century. If politicians in the North, especially those who wrote the Reconstruction amendments and the Civil Rights Act, offered no support for this political philosophy then it can be reasonably argued that the Georgia Supreme Court position was due primarily or exclusively to its existence as a slave society. Investigating the views of Republican framers of the Fourteenth Amendment, the Civil Rights Act, and other legislation is valuable, therefore, because it can be apprehended whether they believed individual gun rights to be fundamental to citizenship and liberty. Such an investigation is valuable also because it returns the focus of the discussion back to the aim of Congressman John Bingham and others who sought to use the Fourteenth Amendment to apply the Bill of Rights against the states.

Stephen P. Halbrook's analysis of gun rights and Reconstruction, *Freedmen, the Fourteenth Amendment, and the Right to Bear Arms 1866–1876* (1998), offers some understanding into what the framers of the Civil Rights Act and the Fourteenth Amendment thought about gun ownership. Halbrook suggests that the evidence for Republican politicians recognizing the right of former slaves to keep and bear arms is overwhelming. Considering that many of the legislators sought to establish equal rights of citizenship for freed slaves, this clearly indicates that any rights they advocated for on behalf of African Americans—and particularly those referenced in the Bill of Rights—were by implication the rights of all Americans.

Beyond the Civil Rights Act and the Fourteenth Amendment, however, Halbrook references legislation related to the Freedmen's Bureau, an agency created to assist newly freed slaves at the end of the Civil War. The first Freedmen's Bureau bills were enacted initially in 1865 and then in 1866 through congressional override of President Johnson's veto. The legislation included the recognition of former slaves to the right of gun ownership, stating that the "*constitutional right to bear arms, shall be secured to and enjoyed by all the citizens* of such State or district without respect to race or color or previous condition of slavery."[18] Halbrook observes that the same members of Congress supported the Freedmen's Bureau legislation as those who voted in favor of the Fourteenth Amendment. "[T]o a man, the same two-thirds-plus members of Congress who voted for the proposed Fourteenth Amendment also voted for the proposition contained in both Freedman's Bureau bills that the constitutional right to bear arms is included in the rights of personal liberty and personal security."[19] He also observes that no other "guarantee in the Bill of Rights was the subject of this official approval by the same Congress that passed the Fourteenth Amendment."[20] Those who supported the Fourteenth Amendment thus believed at least some of the liberties recognized in the Bill of Rights, such as the Second Amendment, should be a standard applied to the separate states as well as the federal government. How can it be known, however, that the intention was to apply *all* of the first eight amendments against the states? To answer this question, it is necessary to return to the statements of the author of the first section of the Fourteenth Amendment, Congressman John Bingham.

The Privileges or Immunities Clause

The primary author of the Fourteenth Amendment's first section was Congressman John Bingham from Ohio. He wrote every word of the first section save for the first sentence, which was added during a revising process. The first sentence explicitly establishes the citizenship status of all persons born or naturalized in the United States, subject to its jurisdiction, henceforth. The remainder of the section asserts rights values Bingham and others believed the individual states, as well as the federal government, were to abide by. The entire first section of the Fourteenth Amendment reads:

> All persons born or naturalized in the United States, and subject to the jurisdiction thereof, are citizens of the United States and of the state wherein they reside. No state shall make or enforce any law which shall abridge the privileges or immunities of citizens of the United States; nor shall any state deprive any person of life, liberty, or property, without due process of law; nor deny to any person within its jurisdiction the equal protection of the laws.[21]

Perhaps most critical to an understanding of the relevant intellectual history is to apprehend what exactly Bingham meant by asserting that the separate states could not abridge *the privileges or immunities* of United States citizens. An understanding of this phrase is important both for identifying the intent of the framer who wrote it, but also for evaluating the Supreme Court's interpretation of the clause in subsequent years.

Privileges and immunities can be thought of as twin pillars of fundamental rights values, differentiated between *rights to* and *rights from*. Some scholars have referred to these as positive rights and negative rights. Legal privileges guarantee rights to a jury of one's peers in a criminal proceeding, for example, or legal counsel, whereas legal immunities include one's right to speech without prior restraint. The combination of *rights to* and *rights from* in the modern American legal system have become so vast and so common to the culture that a distinction between the two is rarely discussed outside of academic circles or rights-oriented judicial decisions. Damon Root describes privileges and immunities with the following economy of words: "immunities are natural rights while privileges are civil rights."[22] The philosophy and history of American rights values, both natural and civil, are discussed further in Chapter Seven.

Congressman Bingham, then, sought to create a standard of *rights to* and *rights from*, or natural rights and civil rights, against the separate states through enforcement of the Fourteenth Amendment. It has already been established that among such rights, Bingham and the Republicans believed that the bearing of arms was a right to be protected from federal and state encroachment. The Freedmen's Bureau legislation, which advocated for the protection of Second Amendment rights for freed slaves, makes this clear. That legislation, much like the Civil Rights Act, was thus legitimated and strengthened with the Fourteenth Amendment. But what of the other amendments in the Bill of Rights? Were they also to be included as part of the new standard of privileges or immunities which the separate states were not to abridge? John Bingham declared explicitly on the House floor that the Fourteenth Amendment would "remedy this defect of the Constitution" that had not applied this standard against the states and that the amendment would "arm Congress of the United States ... with the power to enforce the bill of rights."[23] As Eric Foner observes, "Thus, the Privileges or Immunities Clause of the Fourteenth Amendment applied not only to racial discrimination but to any state actions that deprived citizens of essential rights such as freedom of speech and the press, which many Republicans pointed out had long been abridged in the South."[24]

This view of the Privileges or Immunities Clause of the Fourteenth Amendment and the Bill of Rights was not a position held exclusively by Congressman Bingham. Senator Jacob Howard of Michigan, who presented the amendment to the United States Senate, asserted that "the personal rights guaranteed and secured by the first eight amendments" would be applied to the state governments, because the "great object of the first section of the amendment is ... to restrain the power of the states and compel them at all times to respect these great fundamental guarantees."[25] Congressman Thaddeus Stevens argued that the Fourteenth Amendment's provisions expanded the original role of the Constitution as a check against only the federal government into one also against "the unjust legislation of the States."[26] Stevens articulated the federal Congress's role going forward as having more authority over the states than it did previously. This somewhat echoed James Madison's original vision of the federal government holding veto power over state legislation (see Chapter One). This did not come to pass, even in the aftermath of the Civil War, but individual state power was certainly diminished as a result. Though Stevens was emphasizing the role the federal Congress would possess over the states, especially those having been in rebellion, he nevertheless underscored the principle that the Bill of Rights was going to be the new standard by which state legislation would be judged.

In 1868, the year of the Fourteenth Amendment's ratification, the dean of the University of New York's law school, John Pomeroy, published *An Introduction to the Constitutional Law of the United States*. Pomeroy advocated and corroborated the premise that the Fourteenth Amendment now held state governments to the rights standards outlined in the first eight amendments of the United States Constitution. Stephen Halbrook observes that Pomeroy's book emphasized that "the Fourteenth Amendment would make the Bill of Rights applicable to the states. The work was favorably cited in Congressional debates and was used as a textbook at various law schools."[27]

Fourteenth Amendment scholar Michael Kent Curtis explains, "John Bingham, the author of the amendment, [and] Senator Howard, who

John A. Bingham, Representative from Ohio, Thirty-fifth Congress, **by Julian Vannerson, 1859. Photograph on salted paper (Library of Congress).**

managed it for the Joint Committee in the Senate, clearly said that the amendment would require the states to obey the Bill of Rights. *Not a single senator or congressman contradicted them* [emphasis in the original]."[28] Historian Eric Foner observes that on "more than a dozen occasions in 1866, and many times subsequently, Bingham described the Privileges or Immunities Clause as encompassing the Bill of Rights."[29] Legal scholar Akhil Reed Amar has similarly remarked that "Bingham's public explanations of his proposed amendment repeatedly linked the phrase 'privileges or immunities' to 'the bill of rights.'"[30]

Interpretation by the Court

It was not merely Republicans and constitutional scholars who understood the first section of the Fourteenth Amendment to now apply the Bill of Rights as a standard against the states through the Privileges or Immunities Clause. In 1871, a lower federal court ruled in *United States* v. *Hall* that the Bill of Rights applied to the states through the recently ratified Fourteenth Amendment. The defendants in the *Hall* case had been accused of denying the free speech and free assembly rights of fellow citizens. They denied the legitimacy of the charges, reasoning that freedom of speech and assembly were not rights standards imposed on the individual states. Judge William B. Woods (later a Justice) offered the court's rejection of this defense. Woods's historical and legal analysis reasoned that while the Bill of Rights had not applied to the states prior to 1868, the Fourteenth Amendment altered this due to a multitude of factors, including the Privileges or Immunities Clause and the redefinition of citizenship:

> The debates in the communities of the several states upon the adoption of the constitution and bill of rights proposed, especially in Massachusetts, New Hampshire, and New York, show that the purpose of the people in the

adoption of the first eight amendments was to limit, and not enlarge the powers of congress. See 1 Elliott's Debates, pp. 322, 326, 328. We are of opinion, therefore, that under the original constitution and the first eight articles of amendment, congress had not the power to protect by law the people of a state in the freedom of speech and of the press, in the free exercise of religion, or in the right peaceably to assemble. Jealousy of the power conferred on the congress by the original constitution suggested and accomplished the adoption of the first ten amendments to the constitution, and we entirely agree with counsel for defendants that it was the purpose of the people by these amendments to reserve to themselves and the states the power to secure the rights enumerated therein against the action of congress, and not give congress power to enforce them as against the states.

We have thus far considered this demurrer, and it seems to have been argued for the defense, without reference to the recent amendments to the constitution. As we are of opinion that the fourteenth amendment has a vital bearing upon the question raised, it is well that we should look to its provisions. It declares that "all persons, born or naturalized in the United States, and subject to the jurisdiction thereof, are citizens of the United States and the state wherein they reside." By the original constitution citizenship in the United States was a consequence of citizenship in a state. By this clause this order of things is reversed. Citizenship in the United States is defined; it is made independent of citizenship in a state, and citizenship in a state is a result of citizenship in the United States. So that a person born or naturalized in the United States, and subject to its jurisdiction, is, without reference to state constitutions or laws, entitled to all the privileges and immunities secured by the constitution of the United States to citizens thereof. The amendment proceeds: "No state shall make or enforce any law which shall abridge the privileges and immunities of citizens of the United States." What are the privileges and immunities of citizens of the United States here referred to? They are undoubtedly those which may be denominated fundamental; which belong of right to the citizens of all free states, and which have at all times been enjoyed by the citizens of the several states which compose this Union from the time of their becoming free, independent and sovereign…. Among these we are safe in including those which in the constitution are expressly secured to the people, either as against the action of the federal or state governments. Included in these are the right of freedom of speech, and the right peaceably to assemble.[31]

The lower federal court thus accepted the premise that the Fourteenth Amendment applied a new rights standard upon the separate states through the Privileges or Immunities Clause as well as other aspects of the first section of the amendment. The court's ruling followed the intent of the framers of the amendment and those who championed its passage, including Congressman John Bingham and Senator Jacob Howard. The privileges and immunities, or the civil and natural rights, of citizens of the United States were to be respected by individual states as well as the federal government. *United States* v. *Hall* signified a moment when the

federal judiciary recognized this principle and entered it into the realm
of American jurisprudence. In only two years, however, the United States
Supreme Court abandoned the ideals the Privileges or Immunities Clause
was intended to enforce—and with it—abandoned the mission to apply the
entirety of the Bill of Rights against the states.

In 1873, the United States Supreme Court decided the *Slaughter-House
Cases*. The matter originated in Louisiana, whose legislature in 1869
granted the entire slaughtering business in the state to a single corporation. A number of competing butchers challenged the state-sanctioned
monopoly, asserting it to be an infringement of their fundamental rights.
They claimed it to be a violation of their privileges and immunities and
a seizure that violated their due process guarantee of property rights. As
Randy Barnett explains, the argument was that they had been "abridged
the right to pursue the lawful occupation of butcher by depriving butchers of the requisite of maintaining a slaughter-house."[32] In a five to four
decision, the Supreme Court upheld the corporate monopoly and rejected
the premise that the Privileges or Immunities Clause of the Fourteenth
amendment made the Bill of Rights enforceable against the states. The
decision also denied the legitimacy of the due process and equal protection arguments of the plaintiffs.

The decision, delivered by Justice Samuel Freeman Miller, offered the
narrowest of interpretations of the intent of the Fourteenth Amendment.
Justice Miller asserted that the relevant clauses were applicable to recognize the rights of citizenship of freed slaves. As for the Privileges or Immunities Clause specifically, Justice Miller distinguished between citizenship
under a state and citizenship under the United States. His reasoning
appeared to directly contradict the reason the Fourteenth Amendment's
framers sought to redefine citizenship and underscore the role of privileges and immunities. Justice Miller declared:

> when the effect is to fetter and degrade the State governments by subjecting
> them to the control of Congress, in the exercise of powers heretofore univer-
> sally conceded to them of the most ordinary and fundamental character; when
> in fact it radically changes the whole theory of the relations of the State and
> Federal governments to each other and of both these governments to the peo-
> ple; the argument has a force that is irresistible, in the absence of language
> which expresses such a purpose too clearly to admit of doubt.
>
> We are convinced that no such results were intended by the Congress which
> proposed these amendments, nor by the legislatures of the States which rati-
> fied them.[33]

Eric Foner observes that "Miller narrowed the meaning of the Fourteenth Amendment's Privileges or Immunities Clause so dramatically as
to make it all but meaningless." He further notes that Miller "insisted that

the 'history' that produced the Fourteenth Amendment was 'fresh in the memory of us all.' Yet his account certainly departed from what most congressmen in 1866 thought they were accomplishing."[34] Michael Kent Curtis highlights that the Court ignored one of the most salient arguments made by the plaintiffs. "[I]n one of their briefs to the court," they "cited the congressional legislative history of the amendment, including statements by Bingham and Senator Howard indicating an intent to apply the Bill of Rights to the states."[35]

After the Slaughter-House Cases, *Application of the Due Process Clause*

The result of the *Slaughter-House Cases* was a retreat by the Court to apply the Bill of Rights in their totality against the states. Application of the Bill of Rights against the states was not to be comprehensive nor immediate. Instead, legal decisions over the following century would establish the application of specific rights enshrined in the first eight amendments through a process known as *gradual incorporation* or *selective incorporation*. This would not be accomplished through assertions of privileges or immunities but instead to due process and equal protection. Randy Barnett explains, "Although the Privileges or Immunities Clause was largely gutted by the conventional interpretation of *The Slaughter-House Cases* ... the courts began using the Due Process and Equal Protection Clauses to provide much the same constraint on state power that was originally intended to result from the Privileges or Immunities Clause, albeit with less textual justification."[36] The result, over subsequent decades, were assertions of the Due Process Clause of the Fourteenth Amendment, and the Court implementing incremental incorporation of specific aspects of the Bill of Rights against the states. The application of rights standards against the states was thus not entirely defeated by the *Slaughter-House Cases* decision, but they were stalled and significantly weakened. Over time, the Due Process Clause came to be the common tool for incorporating key Bill of Rights protections against the states. Eric Foner observes the awkwardness of applying due process language to recognize fundamental rights of life, liberty, and property, remarking that due process "suggests procedural fairness, not substantive rights."[37] The practice of recognizing substantive rights and implementing selective incorporation through the Due Process Clause of the Fourteenth Amendment later became known as *substantive due process*. This was an inelegant application and utilization of the clause that nevertheless succeeded over time in applying much of the Bill of Rights against the states after the Supreme Court had rejected full and immediate incorporation in the *Slaughter-House Cases*. The Due Process Clause thus went on to do much of the heavy lifting that the Privileges or Immunities Clause was intended to accomplish by the Fourteenth Amendment's framers. The clumsiness of application of the Due Process Clause to recognize substantive rights, enshrined in the Bill of Rights and beyond, is further evident when the history reveals that unlike the Privileges or Immunities Clause, according to Eric Foner, the Due Process Clause "was barely discussed in Congress or the press in 1866."[38]

It is worth considering for a moment how different the path of history might have been if the Court had honored the principle of full and immediate application of the Bill of Rights against the states. Though it is an alternate history unknowable to us, it is nevertheless worth contemplating how the Court might have considered issues regarding *separate but equal* legislation, the implementation of Jim Crow laws in the South, and other forms of discrimination and rights-violations. It should not be assumed, however, that a faithful reading and application of the Fourteenth Amendment's Privileges or Immunities Clause by the Court would have been a silver bullet. There is often a chasm between principles enshrined in founding documents and how a culture chooses to enforce its supposed ideals. The Fourteenth Amendment itself represents a seismic constitutional shift when the United States sought to implement policies and procedures that would more explicitly underscore and reiterate the values espoused in the Declaration of Independence. The principle of human equality championed in the Declaration was given legal weight and constitutional authority truly for the first time in the Fourteenth Amendment. The Privileges or Immunities Clause was to provide the remedy to the historic lack of enforcement power and provide a standard of universal rights by applying the Bill of Rights against the individual states. Though the Court ignored the intent of the framers of the Fourteenth Amendment to apply the entire Bill of Rights against the states through the Privileges or Immunities Clause, it would apply specific aspects of the Bill of Rights and other substantive rights incrementally over time. This process became one of the most common characteristics of the Court in the twentieth and early twenty-first centuries, which will be discussed further in Chapter Eight. Prior to this, however, the time has come to center the discussion upon the topic of American rights values. The following chapter demonstrates that the constitutional design of the United States, including its utilization of judicial review, was informed by a unique intellectual history that unfolded prior to and during the American Revolution.

CHAPTER SEVEN

Rights

The Reality of Rights in the Natural Rights Thesis

Are rights *real*?

The American framers certainly believed so. Nevertheless, some of the criticisms of natural rights theory has come in two distinct forms. The first is an assertion that natural rights theory is a theological claim and thus inappropriate for a secular society such as the United States. The second is that rights are not, in any genuine sense, real. These arguments are sometimes offered in tandem, though not always. It is essential to address these controversies and lay them to rest in order to then proceed with a discussion of how rights theory, in both its classical republican and liberal configurations, informed both the American Revolution and the creation of the American constitutional republic. This chapter will thus address these critiques of natural rights theory and offer problems with such assessments (and the schools of thought which generally espouse them) before proceeding to examine the intellectual history of rights theory upon the American founding and demonstrating its connection to judicial review. Along the way, a discussion of rights theory, including the subtle but crucial distinctions between natural rights and civil rights, will be provided. The aim of the chapter, ultimately, is to reveal that judicial review is an essential aspect of American law because of the rights theory that informed the design of the United States Constitution and the individual state constitutions. Without a history of rights theory during the constitutional era, the Revolution, and the colonial period before it, judicial review would never have asserted itself as an aspect of the American system.

Prior to addressing critiques of natural rights theory, however, an explanation of its fundamental tenet is required. Natural rights theory asserts an *a priori* philosophy that human beings are born with certain inalienable rights, thus there are certain powers no person, and indeed no institution, is allowed to exercise if such powers violate natural rights. This is known as natural law. Thomas Aquinas formulated the notion of just versus unjust laws in his *Summa Theologica*, written in the thirteenth century and first widely published in the fifteenth-century. Aquinas's thesis was influenced greatly by fifth-century philosopher St. Aurelius Augustine's work, *City of God*, which asserted "an unjust law is no law at all."[1] Aquinas's *Summa Theologica* advanced aspects of natural law in Catholic teachings and borrowed liberally from Aristotelian philosophy. Aquinas asserted, "Laws framed by man are either just or unjust. If they are just they have the power of binding in conscience."[2] He also argued that natural law obliged the legislative power to not exceed its law-making limits. He asserted, "Now laws are said to be just both from *the end*, when, that is, they are ordered to the common good, and from *their author*, that is to say, when the law that is made does not exceed the power of the lawgiver; and from *their form*, when, that is, burdens are laid on the subjects according to an equality of proportion and with a view to the common good."[3] Richard Tuck has observed that "despite his use of the idea of natural dominium, [Aquinas's] general theory … was not a genuine natural rights theory" as it came to be known.[4] While true in the strictest sense of its intellectual history, Aquinas's assertion of just and unjust laws (and how unjust laws were not binding in conscience) played a substantial role in the formulation of natural rights theory and the development of the rule of law. As legal scholar Randy Barnett explains, "for Aquinas … the force of a law depends on the extent of its justice."[5] This principle was utilized especially by seventeenth-century natural rights theorists who would prove to be profoundly influential upon the American framers.

Rights Critics

Some of the critiques of natural rights theory are due to its metaphysical nature. Professor of Philosophy and Ethics Keith Burgess-Jackson has noted agnostic and atheist objections to natural rights theory for its presupposition of divinely-conceived rights. At first glance, this criticism is convincing, especially considering the context of the United States as a secular government with a celebrated design based on the separation of church and state. Postmodernist historian Thaddeus Russell, for example, has labelled the natural law claims of classical liberals as "one of the weirdest superstitions."[6] Natural rights theory posits a metanarrative that postmodernists, among others, find uncomfortable, even as they reap the fruits of living under a rights-based model of law. The supposedly religious (or as Russell claims, superstitious) framing of natural rights, however, is misguided. Burgess-Jackson observes that although there is a long history of natural law connections to religious thought, such as Augustine and Aquinas, there have been secular champions of natural rights theory as well. The thesis of inherent rights serves a specific philosophical and social purpose, which is to maximize individual freedom and minimize arbitrary institutional power. American founders, most notably Thomas Jefferson, perceived no contradiction in secular government based on the concept of natural rights. Indeed, it was Jefferson's letter to the Danbury Baptists in 1802 which first gave life to the phrase "separation of Church and State."[7] Jefferson was arguably the most focused among the framers for ensuring the United States, and his state of Virginia, operated as secular governments. He maintained the primacy of natural rights in the Declaration of Independence in 1776 but also asserted the need for secular governance in his Virginia Statute for Religious Freedom in 1779.[8] Jefferson recognized that the assertion of natural rights was not a religious enterprise.

Materialist arguments against rights theory are, put mildly, complicated. Though many modern Marxists tout the need for the recognition of human rights around the world, they are contradicting much of their own ideology and betraying the arguments of their own ideological hero. Marxism is contrary to rights theory and its modern adherents sometimes fail to recognize this. Because of the Marxist belief in economic and political equality, self-proclaimed adherents will use the language of rights theory even though their own philosophy rejects it. Marx made clear his rejection of rights theory in his essay "The Jewish Question" in 1843:

> None of the so-called rights of man, therefore, go beyond egoistic man, beyond man as a member of civil society—that is, an individual withdrawn into himself, into the confines of his private interests and private caprice, and separated from the community. In the rights of man, he is far from being conceived as a species-being; on the contrary, species-like itself, society, appears as a framework external to the individuals, as a restriction of their original independence. The sole bond holding them together is natural necessity, need and private interest, the preservation of their property and their egoistic selves.[9]

Marx's rejection of rights theory was connected to the same rationalizations for why champions of rights theory advocated for it: the philosophy of private ownership. Indeed, the very idea of individual rights is premised upon the concept of ownership. What, after all, is the celebrated principle of bodily autonomy but the recognition that one owns (and thus exercises all right) over one's body? From the simple and essential natural right supposition of self-ownership derives the natural law to not harm another person because it is a violation of another's property. It is thus the domain of ownership, by way of rights recognition, which manifests just law in the natural rights thesis. This is in opposition to the Marxist notion of collective ownership manifesting from an arrangement of socialized animals. For natural rights theorists, rights come first. For the Marxist and other materialist schools of thought, the recognition of rights (collective or individual), if rights exist in the scheme at all, arrive as a mechanism informed by the needs for people to peacefully live together. They exist and operate as an afterthought and/or a function of practical social governance. Rights are not inherent in the Marxist scheme and, according to Marx himself, are not natural (and are actually unnecessary). Many modern thinkers would not dispute that bodily autonomy is a right, including Marxists, even though bodily autonomy is premised on property ownership and despite the fact that Marx rejected the notion of rights. This reveals the limitations of materialist political thought. Abstract concepts like rights are disputed in no small part because they are not part of the material world. Following such logic, are we to accept that bodily autonomy is not *real* because it is an abstract notion that exists metaphysically in the mind? Few, if any, would accept such a claim.

Marx was in no way the only critic of rights theory. Two important critics in the nineteenth and twentieth centuries, respectively, were Jeremy Bentham and Oliver Wendell Holmes. Jeremy Bentham's vocal critique of rights theory in the nineteenth century underpinned his philosophy of Utilitarianism, which promoted the principle of the greatest good for the greatest number. Utilitarianism was promoted in many ways as an alternative to natural rights theory. In his work, *Anarchical Fallacies* (1843), Bentham contended that the idea of rights "is simple nonsense: natural and imprescriptible rights, rhetorical nonsense—nonsense upon stilts."[10] In a formulation which could not be more opposite from the natural rights view, Bentham rhetorically asks, "Whence is it, but from government, that contracts derive their binding force?" He concludes, "Contracts came from government, not government from contracts. It is from the habit of enforcing contracts, and seeing them enforced that governments are chiefly indebted for whatever disposition they have to observe them."[11]

The Utilitarian arguments of the English Bentham were a precursor to the legal positivist arguments of American jurists, including Oliver Wendell Holmes. Holmes rejected notions of natural right as a Supreme Court Justice in the early twentieth century and championed a legal positivism which largely believed in legislative deference and majoritarian rule. His philosophy often lacked moral reasoning and could, at times, appear rather nihilistic:

> I used to say, when I was young, that truth was the majority vote of that nation that could lick all others. Certainly we may expect that the received opinion about the … [First World] war will depend a good deal upon which side wins (I hope with all my soul it will be mine), and I think that the statement was correct in so far as it implied that our test of truth is a reference to either a present or an imagined future majority in favor of our view.[12]

Bradley C.S. Watson observes that Holmes's vision was of "an inexorable law of historical unfolding—[and] paints it as nothing more than a dominant opinion."[13] Holmes rejected the universal principles of natural rights when he wrote in the *Harvard Law Review* in 1918 that advocates of natural law possess "a naïve state of mind that accepts what has been familiar and accepted by them and their neighbors as something that must be accepted by all men everywhere."[14] Universality of rights was rejected by Holmes, as was the protection of minority opinion. Indeed this is the problem with both of the critiques by Bentham and Holmes. Neither provide an answer to majoritarian tyranny. Bentham assumed the greatest good for the greatest number would not conflict with essential liberties of individuals or minorities, and Holmes assumed the legitimate authority of majority opinion to be self-evident and beyond question.

There is an odd and irrational *might makes right* thesis to the arguments of Marx, Bentham, Holmes, and other critics of natural rights theory. The most essential aspect of the principle of natural rights is the autonomy and liberty of the individual against arbitrary oppression, and this is the very aspect that the critics of it cannot seem to convincingly counter or address. The American framers, for all of their moral faults and hypocrisies, embraced the theory of natural rights because of its recognition and protection of individual liberty and its logic in the proper exercise of constitutional governance and rule of law. Arguments by natural rights detractors, whether it is against the concept of private ownership by Marx, the desire to create a system which provides the greatest good for the greatest number by Bentham, or the legal positivism of Holmes which gives institutions a blank check to write legislation if its popularity can be substantiated; none of these alternatives solve the primary issue that rights theory tackles: the protection of the individual from the tyranny of others.

Natural Rights and Civil Rights

Rights theory generally subscribes to the primacy of both negative and positive rights, which is to say natural rights and civil rights. Simply defined, natural rights (or negative rights) are rights which require nothing from others for their expression. The right of free thought and free speech, for example, exist whether one lives within a society or not. The right of self-preservation is similarly a right which, by definition, is self-expressed. Civil rights (or positive rights) are those rights which should be afforded to someone in order to peacefully and orderly co-exist in a civilization. Essentially, natural rights are *rights from* and civil rights are *rights to*.

In a letter to Thomas Jefferson in the spring of 1788, Thomas Paine sought to define and distinguish natural and civil rights:

> I sat down to explain to myself ... my Ideas of natural and civil rights and the distinction between them.... Suppose 20 persons, strangers to each other, to meet in a Country not before inhabited. Each would be a sovereign in his own natural right. His will would be his Law, but his power, in many cases, inadequate to his right, and the consequence would be that each might be exposed, not only to each other, but to the other nineteen. It would then occur to them that their condition would be much improved, if a way could be devised to exchange that quantity of danger into so much protection, so that each individual should possess the strength of the whole number. As all their rights, in the first case, are natural rights, and the exercise of those rights supported only by their own natural individual power, they would begin by distinguishing between these rights they could individually exercise fully and perfectly and those they could not.... Having drawn this line they agree to retain individually the first Class of Rights or those of personal Competency; and to detach from their personal possession the second Class, or those of defective power and to accept in lieu thereof a right to the whole power produced by a condensation of all the parts. These I conceive to be civil rights or rights of Compact, and are distinguishable from Natural rights, because in the one we act wholly in our own person, in the other we agree not to do so, but act under the guarantee of society.[15]

Just as debates have raged over the very existence of natural rights, the degree of which civil rights should be afforded to citizens has also been a continuous discussion. Generally, however, in contradistinction to natural rights, few debate whether civil rights do exist, or should exist, at all. The debate over civil rights is less about their legitimacy and more a dispute over degrees. Civil rights, which include due process, legal representation, and right to a trial by jury, are rights which most people in the United States agree should be afforded to every citizen. Others, however, over the past century have called for rights to food, housing, and healthcare. Debates over whether these are, or should be, legitimate civil rights is a more complicated issue. The matter grows more complicated as some deny the existence of natural rights while others argue that all rights—including rights to housing and healthcare—are natural rights.

Rights theory historically, however, including in the expanding of rights recognition through judicial review in the United States over the past century, has generally recognized that civil rights emanate from natural rights. The legitimacy of civil rights is thus found in their inherent protection of natural rights. For example, the natural right of freedom of movement is protected and bolstered by the civil right of habeas corpus, a positive right that pre-dates the United States by several centuries. Because the freedom of movement is a fundamental, natural right, the civil right of requiring a judge—as an arbiter of state power—to defend imprisonment through a writ of habeas corpus, legally justifies the taking of one's natural right of free mobility. The civil right of habeas corpus thus informs and seeks to protect the natural right to move freely.

The broader principle of legal due process similarly is a matter of civil right, afforded those living in a modern state in order to mitigate whether one's natural rights should be taken away (through imprisonment or some other form of punishment, including milder forms of rights-taking such as monitorization, etc.). The civil right to have one's rights read, the right to an attorney, to trial by jury, etc., again protect against the taking of one's natural rights illegitimately. These are not civil rights which were always recognized and provided in the American system, but expanded over time largely through judicial review.

Thus civil rights are important and crucial to American rights history via judicial review. They do not contradict natural rights theory but support it. Civil rights, i.e., positive rights created by government and afforded to citizens to create a more just and free society, are themselves byproducts of natural rights theory. Civil Rights are state-created rights that facilitate the protection of natural rights. Civil rights, then, or as some call it positive law, is not an alternative to natural rights theory when exercised in its proper scope. It is informed by it and the progress of civil liberties expansion in American history owes whatever successes it has achieved to its understanding and devotion to natural rights theory. More will be discussed regarding the role of rights theory to specific cases of judicial review in Chapter Eight.

Classical Republicanism

To appreciate the history of rights theory in eighteenth-century America, a proper understanding of its cultural context is essential. Colonial America, prior to the imperial crisis of the 1760s, which altered its political and intellectual course, was a hierarchical society that largely based its social bonds on principles of deference. A level of patronage and reputation undergirded colonial life. Children were subservient to their parents, wives to their husbands, slaves to their masters, and the poor to the wealthy. Indeed, economics expressed and buttressed this cultural reality. Socially prominent members of society increased their wealth and reputations less through rents and the sale of lands than through the giving of personal loans to those in their community. In Colonial America—which was land rich and cash poor—some would increase their wealth and cultivate their status through this method. During a time when banks were essentially absent in the region, socially prominent men would themselves act as banks, charging very low interest for sometimes long durations. This helped members of the community, contributed to the local economy, and built reputations for men to be seen as leaders of their towns, counties, and colonies. This culture of paternalism and patronage reinforced a social and economic aristocracy that echoed the influence of the English nobility.[16] The master and apprentice system of skilled trade also expressed and reinforced the economic and social hierarchy. Apprentices, often indentured to their masters for a number of years for funding their migration to North America and teaching them a valuable vocation, became master tradesman themselves, usually within a decade, and the cycle would then repeat. Peter H. Wood observes, "For centuries apprenticeship had given a master craftsman reliable, cheap skilled labor, had provided a youth with the skills that would enable him to work as an adult, and had created a structure of authority within which the master and his apprentice conducted themselves."[17] Social deference thus informed nearly every aspect of everyday life in Colonial America, whether one found themselves at the giving or receiving end of such patronage.

Within Colonial America's culture of deference and patronage in the eighteenth century was a fondness for classical art and philosophy, including the works of Greek philosophers like Aristotle and the history of the Roman Republic. England's Civil Wars in the previous century and its Glorious Revolution in 1688–89, which brought William and Mary to the throne and established parliamentary authority, likely contributed to feelings of political equality, despite England's hierarchical culture and the colonies' inheritance of the brutal practice of slavery. Gordon S. Wood notes that for Americans in the middle of the eighteenth century, it "was truly a neo-classical age—the high point of their classical period. At one time or another almost every Whig patriot took or was given the name of an ancient republican hero, and classical references and allusions run through much of the colonists' writings, both public and private."[18]

Classical republicanism and its creed of civic virtue suited the psychological matrix of Colonial America's deferential society. Its notions of collective rights and self-sacrifice for the greater good reinforced social bonds and contributed to a culture of everyone having a place, and knowing their place. People were not equal within the social, economic, or political hierarchy, but all were equal in that each and every person carried an obligation to the greater community. In its Protestant tradition too, all were equal in the eyes of God. Such hierarchies were later thrown out of balance due to the sociopolitical ramifications of the American Revolution, but prior to the imperial crisis and the effects of the revolution, classical republicanism fit comfortably within Colonial America's cultural framework.

The influence of classical republicanism upon the American founding can be seen in that many of the founding generation were the first in their respective families to receive a college education, which in the eighteenth century centered largely upon the works of classical antiquity. This detail helps explain why a classical education was important to many founders. More importantly, however, it also acted as a bonding agent for the disparate group of men from differing economic backgrounds, religious affiliations, and geographic regions once the imperial crisis transpired. Their mutual notions of republicanism helped the nascent resistance, and ultimate revolution, remain united upon ideological grounds.

Principles of republicanism indeed go back to the ancient world, but a crucial reiteration of it occurred during the Italian Renaissance of the fifteenth and sixteenth centuries. Important republican figures like Bruni, Machiavelli, and Giannotti, just to name a few, formulated novel perspectives which laid the groundwork for ideas that followed in England and America in succeeding centuries. J.G.A. Pocock observes that the name of the Italian Renaissance itself, understood as a rebirth in art, science, and political thought, implies a nod to the best the classical world had to offer. "The idea of 'renaissance' after an age of barbarism would seem to owe something to a patriotic insistence on confronting the Florentine with the Roman republic and dismissing the intervening centuries of Roman and Germanic empire as an interlude of tyranny and barbarism."[19] Pocock identifies a shift in the intellectual history of Florence during the Renaissance, away from the Athenian philosophers and toward republican ideas about the structuring of society. Fifteenth-century Florence began to move away from the priority of lofty philosophical contemplation—practiced by the Greeks (Plato, Aristotle) as well as Christian scholars, and began to favor ideas dealing with the civic concerns of people living together.

Important matters of republican thought given voice during the Italian Renaissance connect explicitly to affairs of society and governance taken up during the American Revolution and the early republican period. These include the importance of people to exercise vocations that fulfill their potential and simultaneously contributes to the community, the need for members of a society to have integrity and be ever-vigilant in the promotion and cultivation of virtue, and the importance of a citizen militia. By looking at such examples of republican thought in fifteenth- and sixteenth-century Florence, the influence of the ideology upon England and ultimately upon the American founding becomes easier to apprehend.

Leonardo Bruni, author of *Historiarum Florentini populi libri XII* (*Twelve Books of Histories of the Florentine People*) from the Renaissance period and who translated works by Aristotle, Plato, and Plutarch, asserted the importance of historical knowledge, freedom of association, and the requirement that individuals strive for excellence. He insisted that first among all forms of study, "I place History: a subject which must not on any account be neglected by one who aspires to true cultivation," because "the careful study of the past enlarges our foresight in contemporary affairs.... From History, also, we draw our store of examples of moral precepts."[20] Bruni argued firmly for the role of human excellence and free association in the formulation of a healthy and virtuous polity. The cultivation of one's potential, and the ability to hone one's talents, contributed to the stability and advancement of the community. Pocock observes that "the case for the open society, as Bruni saw it, was that the excellence of one could only flourish when developed in collaboration with the excellences of others; not only was it better for any citizen there should be many rather than few others, but such civic if not directly political excellences as the arts and letters could flourish only under conditions of liberty."[21]

For political philosopher and statesman Niccolò Machiavelli, one of the most essential prerequisites of an enduring republic was the existence of a citizen army. In his work *The Art of War* (1520), Machiavelli states that the aim of the work was to "honor and reward virtue, not to have contempt for poverty, to esteem the modes and orders of military discipline, to constrain citizens to love one another, to live without factions, to esteem less the private than the public good."[22] In a single introductory statement, Machiavelli illustrated the republican connections he observed between liberty, civic virtue, and military organization. As Pocock explains, for Machiavelli, these appeared to exist in close relation to each other and that the *arte* of being a soldier "must be a public monopoly; only citizens may practice it, only magistrates may lead it, and only under public authority and at the public command may it be exercised at all."[23] The republican connection between citizenship and duty is thus emphasized. Only a citizen who possesses a personal stake in the preservation of a republic is qualified to raise arms in the republic's defense. Pocock elucidates Machiavelli's position further, observing that a "citizen called to arms, with a home and an occupation (arte) of his own, will wish to end the war and go home, where a mercenary, glad rather than sorry if the war drags on indefinitely, will make no attempt to win it."[24] Thus the republican concept of a citizen militia carries two purposes. First, it strengthens the health of the state because it depends upon those who have the most to lose in the outcome of the state's wars. The preservation of a citizen's home and freedom manifests investment in the outcome of a military conflict. Second, it binds the citizenry together through experiences of self-sacrifice, patriotism, and sharing of mutual values against the threats of a common enemy.

Political writer and playwright Donato Giannotti was described by seventeenth-century English political philosopher James Harrington as the intellectual heir of Machiavelli and the last significant writer of the Florentine republican legacy.[25] Giannotti put forward a convincing thesis establishing what he saw as the essentials of government under a republican system. He observed there are "four things which constitute the directive force of every republic: the creation of magistrates, the determination of peace and war, the making of laws, and the hearing of appeals."[26] Giannotti further implied the need for a separation of powers between a small body of consultants (*consultazione*) and a large body of deliberators (*deliberazione*). Pocock highlights that such a scheme did not necessarily have any democratic impulse in mind, noting that "we are looking at the origins of the doctrine of the separation of powers, and it should be observed both how far these origins lay in the fear of corruption, and how little a role was played by any clear theory of a democratic mode of understanding."[27] Giannotti echoed Machiavelli's argument for a citizen army, though disagreed with Machiavelli's assertion that a state's stability rested upon constant expansion. For Giannotti, it is natural to bear arms as it is natural to be a citizen, and for this reason their reciprocal and reinforcing relationship is expressed. Pocock observes, Giannotti communicated the conception that "the militia is a powerful, indeed an indispensable, socializing, and political agency."[28]

Classical republicanism grew in popularity in England in the seventeenth century as a result of the country's civil wars. They found themselves engaging in republicanism essentially by accident, in the absence of a monarchy which they had overthrown and even as Lord Protector Cromwell himself became more of a monarch in practice if not in name. James Harrington's *Oceania* (1656) was informed by the influence of republican thinkers of the Italian Renaissance and the events of the English Civil Wars. Harrington celebrated republican notions of property and an armed citizenry. The language of republicanism persisted in England, despite the ultimate restoration of the monarchy. When the Glorious Revolution transpired in the late 1680s, the role of political representation and parliamentary supremacy became the kingdom's defining feature.

Republicanism soon enough asserted itself less in the England of Europe and more so in its North American colonies. By the eighteenth century the British colonies of North America expressed a unique culture of deference informed by the hierarchical culture of the mother country, and republican values which England had temporarily entertained and then (to some degree) abandoned. Armed militias and the acquisition of land were promoted in the colonies by England less because of their republican values and more for their practical results. Militias allowed for law and order where local police forces were otherwise absent. The enticement of land ownership to those willing to migrate to the colonies from Britain facilitated population growth. This contributed to the ability to take lands from Native Americans and challenge regional land claims by other European powers. For the English monarch and for English politicians, the exercise of republican policies in the colonies was a pragmatic move. For British Americans it became a birthright and informed a belief that private property and an armed citizenry were essential to one's liberty. Without anyone aware of it at the time, the philosophical divide between England and its North American colonies had already begun.

The decline of classical republicanism in Colonial America began, arguably, with the imperial crisis of the 1760s, when the colonies began to express a different view of political liberty than that of the British. The English concept of parliamentary supremacy was challenged by the colonists who argued that their own local assemblies were essentially the legislative power of the individual colonies. When England continued to assert the Parliament's sovereignty through what the colonists saw as arbitrary rule, their republican sensibilities were both exercised and strained. They resisted England's authority through republican arguments even as their version of republicanism was transforming slowly into something different and new.

In their battle to retain their rights and liberties, colonists denounced the English government as having been corrupted. Gordon Wood suggests that when "the American Whigs described the English nation and government as eaten away by 'corruption,' they were in fact using a technical term of political science, rooted in the writings of classical antiquity, made famous by Machiavelli, developed by classical republicans of seventeenth century England, and carried into the eighteenth century by nearly everyone who laid claim to knowing anything about politics."[29] Americans came to see themselves as the rightful heirs of political liberty and the ultimate champions of republican values. The corruption they saw in their English rulers was a loss of virtue, through a thirst for power and as a result of political favors and perverted patronage. As a consequence, colonists not only did not recognize the authority of Parliament to intervene in colonial matters such as taxation, but also believed King George III had been corrupted. It thus became a matter of defending their rights, informed by a historical knowledge of classical republican principles, against the corrupted powers of England's Parliament and King. Clinton Rossiter observes in *Seedtime of the Republic* (1953) that by 1768, three years into the imperial crisis, American colonists had possibly become the most rights-conscious people in history.[30]

What began in the chaos of the imperial crisis was the beginning of a transformation of American republicanism which would, over a period of decades, morph into a more individualistic and liberalized form of social, economic, and political liberty as an outcome of the American Revolution and the founding of the constitutional republic. In the 1760s, however, it was nascent and as yet ill-defined. It would grow stronger and express itself more clearly as time went on. During the imperial crisis and the early years of the revolution, however, a new culture that rejected aristocratic paternalism, yet embraced the need for social bonds, manifested itself into a new form of republicanism. Though the culture would grow more self-interested and liberalized in the ensuing decades, certain elements of republican virtue either remained in subtler forms or found new avenues of expression later, in the nineteenth century, as social reform movements.

Gordon S. Woods's *Creation of the American Republic* (1969) was instrumental in forwarding what has become known as the republican thesis in American history. J.G.A. Pocock's *The Machiavellian Moment* (1975) utilized what Wood had done and supplied a rigorous European history which offers further intellectual context, focusing primarily on the intellectual history of the republican thinkers of Renaissance-era Florence. The importance of these works in understanding the influence of classical republicanism upon the American founding has been asserted for decades. Some scholars have questioned, however, if the republican thesis has been overstated. Michael P. Zuckert, for example, has argued that according to the republican thesis, "human beings are intensely political (Pocock) and/or communal (Wood); [however] according to the Declaration [of Independence], human beings are not originally or naturally political—the origin is a state of nature understood as an apolitical condition. Although polity is essential, it is not natural.... Politics, according to the Declaration is for the sake of natural rights, and natural rights are emphatically pre-political."[31] Zuckert thus contends that the republican thesis does not consider the weight of natural rights liberalism's influence upon the revolution. He further asserts that the "understanding of property likewise differs almost entirely between the two political theories [natural rights liberalism and classical republicanism]. For Pocock's republicans, property is for the sake of gentlemanly or citizenly independence, a precondition for the citizen's participation and public spiritedness. Property is, above all, a political, not an economic, phenomenon."[32] Zuckert contrasts this with the natural rights thesis that "property is a natural right and, therefore, not particularly tied to its political function."[33] Zuckert makes an important point that in order for the republican thesis to loom as large as it does in the work of Pocock and Wood, natural rights liberalism is necessarily de-emphasized. After all, John Locke's liberal influence (discussed in the following section of this chapter) is barely noted by the authors at all. This is more understandable for Pocock, considering the focus of *The Machiavellian Moment* to be the growth and influence of republicanism in (primarily) Florence. Wood, however, is an historian of revolutionary America and it does appear that his republican thesis suffers from an inability to incorporate or acknowledge its limits. Locke is barely mentioned in the six hundred and fifteen pages of *Creation of the American Republic*.

It may be the case that Locke had to be unfairly diminished for the republican thesis to work. Nevertheless, Zuckert may be missing some subtle points, including Wood's admission that—although important to American intellectual history prior to the revolution—classical republicanism was indeed replaced by natural rights liberalism. Zuckert and Wood may simply disagree as to when this occurred. Zuckert also seems to miss a point made earlier in this chapter: fundamental notions of rights theory in the American tradition such as private property and citizen militias appear to have begun as byproducts of republican principles and evolved over time to be embraced as principles of natural right. Republican policies of property and militias strengthened the growth and impact of England's power from across the Atlantic. This is true. As Americans came to see their way of life as a result of their natural right to liberty, the arguments for property rights and the right to bear arms became less republican and more liberal. This can also be true.

The Scots, Montesquieu, John Locke, and Natural Rights Liberalism

It is beyond the scope of this work to catalogue and assess the influence of every political philosopher who made an impact on American thought. That said, a number of writers should at least be given mention. Among these are the thinkers of the Scottish Enlightenment, most notably Adam Smith for his influence upon American economics and David Hume for his argument that human reason is, in actuality, a slave to passions.[34] Hume particularly gave voice to something quite similar to that of Alexander Hamilton and James Madison in their *Federalist* writings in which they warned against the fleeting passions of political thought. One of the basic principles of modern moral psychology asserts the Hume-influenced thesis: intuitions come first, strategic reasoning second. Psychologist Jonathan Haidt observes that "social and political judgments are particularly intuitive."[35] He has labelled this phenomenon *the elephant and the rider*. The *elephant* is one's intuitive passions and beliefs, and reason is the *rider*, struggling to maintain control.[36] Ultimately, following Hume's assertion in his *Treatise on Human Nature*, Haidt observes that it is "the rider's job to serve the elephant."[37] Human beings use reason to rationalize their passions. Hume's influence thus continues to shape American thought to this day. He observed a difficult truth which Hamilton and Madison echoed in the 1780s: passions are at the center of human existence and no good can come from ignoring that essential truth. Understanding the power of human passions, and recognizing the limits of human reason to keep such passions in check, is useful for designing governments and a rule of law that treats human beings as they actually are rather than what we wish them to be.

As noted in the introductory section of this work, the Frenchman Montesquieu played a crucial role in influencing the American design of government, particularly regarding the establishment of an independent judiciary and the principle of separation of powers. Montesquieu was also important in recognizing that a government could only survive if it included some kind of mechanism that facilitated self-correction. "In a word, a free government, that is, one always in a state of agitation, cannot survive if it cannot correct its faults by its own laws."[38] He asserted that such laws were required to establish forms of legal equality and that this was the primary purpose of government. He contended that "in a state of nature, men are equal … they lose this equality when they enter society— which can only be regained by laws."[39] Montesquieu argued that republics were the best form of government but doubted one could prosper over a large region. Amazingly, he openly wondered if a federation of republics might be the answer to such a problem. "This form of government [a federative republic] is an agreement by which a number of political units … consent to become citizens of that larger state they wish to form. This is a society of societies, which constitutes a new one capable of increasing even further by addition of any others that may care to join this union."[40] The influence this passage had upon James Madison's (and Alexander Hamilton's) vision of design for the United States federal government in the 1780s is compelling and clear. Jack Rakove submits that the "way in which Hamilton and Madison both invoke 'the celebrated Montesquieu' to introduce their respective discussions of the extended republic and the separation of powers in the Federalist essays (essays 9 and 47) demonstrates the authoritative status that the French baron's treatise *De l'spirit des lois* commanded."[41]

Though there were a number of Englishman whose thinking was critical to the evolution of American rights theory, one name looms far larger than any other.[42] John Locke's *Two Treatises of Government* (1689), particularly its second treatise, was referenced time and again by American political philosophers from the imperial crisis of the 1760s, through the revolution, and throughout the early republican period. Unlike the earlier Thomas Hobbes, who argued in his work *Leviathan* that man surrenders most of his rights in trade for protection from the state, Locke contended that human beings surrender almost none of their natural rights when leaving a state of nature and entering society. Crucially, for Locke, the powers given to government to manage the regulation of society must be based on consent. This acts as the basis of legitimate government, which must operate in a form that does not violate the rights which have not been surrendered and must be done through specific and enumerated laws:

> Absolute arbitrary power, or governing without settled standing laws, can neither of them consist with the ends of society and government, which men would not quit the freedom of the state of Nature for, and tie themselves up under, were it not to preserve their lives, liberties, and fortunes, and by stated rules of right and property to secure their peace and quiet ... whatever form the commonwealth is under, the ruling power ought to govern by declared and received laws, and not by extemporary dictates and undetermined resolutions.[43]

Implicit in Locke's vision of legitimate government founded upon the consent of the governed is something far more significant than merely representative government, vital as that is. Locke's thesis also requires governmental fidelity to the rule of law. This aspect of Lockean governance connects explicitly to the value of judicial review to hold the legislative (and executive) power to its express functions, granted by the consent of the governed, to safeguard the rights of the citizenry. Regarding legislation, Locke asserts that the legislative power is a sacred trust and cannot be delegated or transferred to another body. He states that "the legislative cannot transfer the power of making laws to any other hands, for it being but a delegated power from the people, they who have it cannot pass it over to others ... nobody else can say other men shall make laws for them; nor can they be bound by any laws but such as are enacted by those whom they have chosen and authorized to make laws for them."[44]

Locke's natural rights model of government based on the consent of the governed resonated with American colonists, especially as the imperial crisis transpired and political divisions between the colonies and England deepened. James Otis's essays, "Rights of the British Colonies Asserted and Proved" (1764–1765), echoed Locke, affirming that "if life, liberty, and property could be enjoyed in as great perfection in solitude, as in society, there would be no need of government."[45] Otis cites Locke liberally throughout the essays and reiterates Locke's argument that the "legislature cannot transfer the power of making laws to any other hands."[46] A pamphlet the following year, in 1766, by Richard Bland posits Locke's natural rights thesis explicitly, suggesting "though they [the people] must submit to the Laws, so long as they remain members of the Society, yet they retain so much of their natural Freedom as to have a Right to retire from the Society."[47] Bland's point is critical, as it recognizes the implied right of revolution in Locke's thesis, which Thomas Jefferson appropriated a decade later in the Declaration of Independence.

When events transformed from passive resistance (1764–1774) to armed resistance (1775–June 1776) to a declaration of independence (July 1776), the spirit of Locke's natural rights thesis of self-government and the right of revolution was made manifest. The American colonists-turned-American revolutionaries thus did not merely parrot the arguments of Locke's *Second Treatise*, they made it a political reality. Natural rights became the language and philosophy of the American Revolution, and the American republic that followed.

Conventions and the Sovereignty of the People

When the American colonies began to face the reality of declaring their independence in 1776, the Second Continental Congress adopted a resolution written by John Adams on May 10, which recommended "to the respective Assemblies and Conventions of the United Colonies, where no Government sufficient to the Exigencies of their Affairs, hath been hitherto established, to adopt such Government as shall in the Opinion of the Representatives of the People best conduce to the Happiness and Safety of their Constituents in particular, and America in general."[48] John Adams was instrumental not merely with the drafting of the May 10 resolution but also in providing for the specific architecture of government, based on his knowledge of classical republics and the writings of Locke and Montesquieu. His brief essay, *Thoughts on Government* (1776) argued for representative government based on the consent of the governed under a model establishing separation of powers. Regarding the stunning opportunity of history he and his colleagues were undertaking, Adams recognized that they had

> been sent into life at a time when the greatest lawgivers of antiquity would have wished to live. How few of the human race have ever enjoyed an opportunity of making an election of government, more than of air, soil, or climate, for themselves or their children! When, before the present epoch, had three millions of people full power and a fair opportunity to form and establish the wisest and happiest government that human wisdom can contrive?[49]

Adams's vision of republican government included a bicameral legislature and an independent judiciary. For Adams, himself a lawyer who had bravely defended the Boston Massacre soldiers in court in 1770 and had seen the arbitrariness of English rule with the writs of assistance[50] in the 1760s, he was driven to establish a government based on the rule of law:

The dignity and stability of government in all its branches, the morals of the people, and every blessing of society depend so much upon an upright and skillful administration of justice, that the judicial power ought to be distinct from both the legislative and executive, and independent upon both, that so it may be a check upon both, as both should be checks upon that. The judges, therefore, should be always men of learning and experience in the laws, of exemplary morals, great patience, calmness, coolness, and attention. Their minds should not be distracted with jarring interests; they should not be dependent upon any man, or body of men. To these ends, they should hold estates for life in their offices; or, in other words, their commissions should be during good behavior, and their salaries ascertained and established by law.[51]

As early as June 1775, Adams recommended that special conventions were the proper course to facilitate the creation of constitutions:

We must realize the Theories of the Wisest Writers and invite the People, to erect the whole Building with their own hands upon the broadest foundation. That this could be done only by Conventions of Representatives chosen by the People in the several Colonies, in the most exact proportions. That it was my Opinion, that Congress ought now to recommend to the People of every Colony to call such Conventions immediately and set up Governments of their own, under their own Authority: for the People were the Source of all Authority and Original of all Power.[52]

John Adams, **by Nicholas Eustache Maurin, copied after a work by Gilbert Stuart, 1828. Lithograph on paper (National Portrait Gallery).**

When Massachusetts sought to draft a new constitution in 1777, it ignored Adams's recommendation to do so through a convention and drafted the new constitution through its regular legislative process. The new Massachusetts Constitution was submitted to the people and was summarily rejected in 1778. Theosophilus Parsons, in a pamphlet known as the *Essex Result*, suggested that Massachusetts's evasion of the convention process was among the reasons for the constitution's rejection. According to the Commonwealth of Massachusetts's official website outlining the state's constitutional history, Parsons (who later became Chief Justice of the Massachusetts Supreme Court) "led the opposition [against ratification] ... in words demonstrating the influence of John Adams, [he] criticized the proposed constitution for not having been drafted by a body separate from the legislature, for lacking a declaration of rights (and for explicitly condoning slavery), and for failing to provide for the separation of powers among the executive, a bicameral legislature, and the judiciary."[53]

In August 1779, the Massachusetts legislature circulated a call to the towns for every male inhabitant to elect representatives to form a convention. With this act Massachusetts became the first government in history to set the precedent of establishing the convention process for the creation and ratification of its constitution. As the official Massachusetts constitutional history site observes, "Massachusetts thus created and clarified the distinction between ordinary legislation and the fundamental law contained in a constitution, which may be created and changed only by 'the people.'"[54]

The Massachusetts Constitution written and ratified through a convention in 1780 was largely drafted by John Adams, who had only recently returned from France. The charter addressed that which had been lacking in the version rejected in 1778. Made up of three sections (a preamble, a declaration of rights, and a design of government employing separation of powers), Adams achieved the making of a republic he had envisioned, and the establishment of a convention process which gave the government legitimacy. The convention process was eventually adopted by each of the states and became the same mode of constitutional ratification for the United States Federal Constitution in the late 1780s.

Gordon S. Wood has called the convention process of constitution making "an extraordinary invention" and "the most distinctive institutional contribution ... the American Revolutionaries made to Western politics. It not only enabled the constitution to rest on an authority different from the legislature's, but it actually seemed to have legitimized revolution."[55] Wood, of course, was speaking to how constitutional conventions act as a political method for transformation, giving space for a revolution through organization, rhetoric, and moral suasion as an alternative to revolution through arms and intimidation. Just as constitutional conventions legitimize revolution, however, the same can be said for the power of judicial review. As Louis H. Pollak observes, "the Constitution's most vital contribution to political theory and political practice was the development of a device which, in approximate fashion, has provided a constitutional alternative to revolution—the device of judicial review of actions undertaken by other branches of government."[56] Thus, judicial review too can be seen as an alternative to revolution and as a novel expression of revolutionary spirit. It acts as a restatement of the essential fundamental rights values of a self-governing people, and reasserts the established limits of the people's government.

The formation of constitutional conventions, which act as a body separate from and with authority over that of the regular legislative power, underscores the uniquely American political ethos that the people and the people's representatives are not one and the same. Thomas Tudor Tucker, a surgeon during the American Revolution and Representative for South Carolina during the first Congress, expressed this view of limited legislative power in 1784 when he declared, "It is a vain and weak argument that, the legislative being the representatives of the people, the act of the former is therefore always to be considered as the act of the latter. They are the representatives of the people for certain purposes only, not to all and purposes whatever."[57] This stood in stark contrast to the British, who saw no essential difference between the people and their representatives. In the 1770s and 1780s, a new interpretation regarding law and rights developed in America, which included the belief that constitutions are to be changed by the people themselves and not by their congressional representatives. This reinforces Locke's vision of a legislative power that is subservient to the people who created it. It also underscores the arguments of American founder and legal scholar James Wilson who challenged the notion of rights as nothing more than constructed privileges granted by government. Wilson refuted this legal positivist tenet thusly:

> [if] this view be a just view of things, then the consequence, undeniable and unavoidable is, that, under civil government, the rights of individuals to their private property, to their personal liberty, to their health, to their reputation, and to their life, flow from a human establishment, and can be traced to no higher source. The connection between man and his natural rights is intercepted by the institution of civil society ... then, under civil society, man is not only made *for*, but made *by* government: he is nothing but what the society frames: he can claim nothing but what the society provides.[58]

The American Revolutionaries and the United States' constitutional founders ultimately rejected arbitrary power because they instead embraced natural rights theory and devoted themselves to republican governance. Legislatures exceeding the authority afforded them by the people are illegitimate, as are legislative acts which change the constitution duly ratified by the people. Only the sovereign people can change their founding charters through a convention process which is separate from, and has authority over, such legislative power. Judicial review serves the same purpose. It acts as a counterrevolutionary force against illegitimate use of legislative and executive power.

A history informed by republican thought facilitated concepts of citizenship, virtue, and civic duty. An inherited language of natural rights contributed to notions of separation of powers, an independent judiciary, the limits of representative and legislative authority, and the principle of the sovereignty of the people. Once these intellectual components found their footing in the American scheme of law and governance, a uniquely American legal instrument emerged: judicial review, which acts as a consistent voice of the sovereign people through persistent reiteration of the founding charters of government. Judicial review's articulation and reassertion of constitutional principles counters fleeting passions among the electorate and defends the sovereign people's fundamental rights against legislative and executive overreach.

CHAPTER EIGHT

Rights Assertions via the Court in the Twentieth and Twenty-First Centuries

As discussed at the end of Chapter Six, the Supreme Court retreated from using the Privileges or Immunities Clause of the Fourteenth Amendment to apply the Bill of Rights against the states in totality during the last decades of the nineteenth century. The *Slaughter-House Cases* (1873) was highlighted as an example of this retreat by the Court to utilize the Fourteenth Amendment in a way its framers had intended. Similar cases in the same era include *Bradwell* v. *Illinois* (1873), which denied the Privileges or Immunities to women when aspiring attorney Maria Bradwell was kept from admittance to the bar and thus kept from practicing law. Bradwell's argument that the Privileges or Immunities Clause recognized the right of all American citizens, and not only men, was rejected by the Court. The 1876 ruling of *United States* v. *Cruikshank* further closed the door on the intended use of the Privileges or Immunities Clause. The Court sided with the defendants in that case, who had not only violated the rights of assembly and other political rights of their fellow countrymen, but had murdered approximately a hundred African Americans in the course of a political dispute in Louisiana in an event known as the Colfax Murders. The defendants had been charged with conspiracy to deny the political rights of African Americans, which not only violated fundamental principles of the Fourteenth Amendment, but also the 1870 Enforcement Act. That act had been passed to protect African Americans from groups like the Ku Klux Klan. Though the defendants had clearly violated the First and Second Amendment rights of the victims, the Court ruled that such amendments applied only to the federal government and not to the individual states or private citizens (again betraying the intent of the framers of the Privileges or Immunities Clause). This combination of cases in a handful of years, not long after ratification of the Fourteenth Amendment, made the Privileges or Immunities Clause a dead letter. The Court abandoned the principle of both the Bill of Rights and other unenumerated rights affirmed in the natural rights theory of the American founding and enshrined in the Ninth Amendment. As legal scholars Randy Barnett and Josh Blackman observe, "*Slaughter-House* and *Bradwell* involved what could be called *unenumerated rights*. That is, privileges or immunities that are not expressly stated in the Constitution.... *United States* v. *Cruikshank* ... held that the Privileges or Immunities Clause also did not bar a state from violating so-called *enumerated rights*: in this case, rights listed in the First and Second Amendments."[1] Barnett and Blackman imply an important aspect of the Privileges or Immunities Clause: it was meant to recognize the existence of natural rights not listed in the Constitution *and*, as outlined in Chapter Six, the enumerated rights which make up the Bill of Rights. Thus the Court failed to recognize and protect both listed and unlisted rights of citizens of the United States. It would not assert unenumerated rights for many years to come.

The Court failed to honor the intent of the authors of the Privileges or Immunities Clause of the Fourteenth Amendment almost immediately. However, over a period of decades the Court began to assert rights values related to personal autonomy, political expression, self-protection, and other matters of liberty instead through the appropriation of the Equal Protection and Due Process Clauses. The political and cultural history of the United States in the twentieth and twenty-first centuries, as a result, have become tied intrinsically with the evolution of the Court in its widening recognition and protection of rights.

Though the thrust of this chapter is to highlight specific moments of rights assertions over the past century, it is not to be construed in any way as a comprehensive legal history. Equally important, it is also not to be construed as a form of Whig-influenced history.[2] The belief that the arc of history bends toward justice is a pleasant but ultimately imprudent vision. It is a high-minded ideal to live by, but an unacceptable means for tracing the map of history. Similarly, the idea of the Court seamlessly evolving from an institution concerning itself with structural matters like the separation of powers to one that advocates for individual rights is simply too crude and reductionist of a formulation to be precisely accurate. The American judiciary has, much like Congress, regularly taken two steps forward and one step back with affording respect to the rights of the people. Though a macro evolution can and should be appreciated overall, as will be presented in the following pages, it has not been without serious missteps and outright constitutional violations. Ken Kersch articulates this point well in *Constructing Civil Liberties: Discontinuities in the Development of American Constitutional Law* (2004) when he asserts that over "the course of the last century, the Court both limited and extended constitutional criminal process rights.... Whiggish narratives positing an initial lack of concern and then a cresting solicitude for personal rights and privacy fail to capture these distinctive developmental dynamics."[3]

The Court, even in its best moments, regularly leveraged interests of the state against that of the citizen, the government versus the individual. It remains an institution made up of human beings and is thus prone to human failings, including siding with powerful forces over the rights of the weak and the unpopular. This is not to diminish the strides the Court has made in the recognition of rights values, but to evaluate it fairly and in its proper historical context. Indeed, leaving the egregious Dred Scott decision and the retreat from the Privileges or Immunities Clause behind and simply looking at the Supreme Court in the twentieth and twenty-first centuries, there are cases which challenge the wisdom in leaving the last word of the law to the judiciary. In the early twentieth century, for example, the Supreme Court was not finished in violating fundamental rights of the people, and any appreciation of what the Court has done—and would later do—must be measured with such matters in mind.

Rather than defend judicial review by ignoring the most egregious instances of the judiciary, it is instead better to address these matters— much as was done in Chapter Five—directly. The growth in the recognition of rights values by the Court, in fact, is all the more astounding once some of its worst cases are addressed. An advocacy for judicial review in no way means that the Supreme Court is sacrosanct. As will be seen, the early twentieth century, mid-twentieth century, and early twenty-first century presents decisions many regard as misguided and simply wrong. These cases are important to note not merely to appreciate that the American judiciary is imperfect, but also to further emphasize that defense of the Court's power of judicial review does not necessitate a Whiggish view of history, nor a naïve devotion to an institution capable of making serious errors. Rather than seeing such progress by the Court as inevitable and a byproduct of the natural progress of an enlightened history, it should be appreciated—and indeed preserved—precisely because of how unlikely it was to happen and how easy it can be lost.

The aim of this chapter, most of all, is to underscore that the Court came to become central to the American project and became a symbol of the best of what constitutionalism has to offer when it rested its decisions on the recognition of rights values. Conversely, its worst decisions have transpired when such rights values were abandoned or momentarily forgotten. Judicial review is legitimate because it empowers the Court to remind the state and federal governments, and indeed the American people, of the nation's fundamental mission to recognize individual rights. It thus must abide by these values to ensure its own legacy and continually foster a reiteration of separation of powers and the protection of individual liberty to reify the fundamental principles of the American republic.

Buck *v.* Bell, Korematsu, *and* Kelo

Before an exploration of the widening recognition of rights values via the Supreme Court in the twentieth and twenty-first centuries, then, some attention given to a handful of the Court's more troubling decisions in the same era is warranted. In 1927, for example, in *Buck* v. *Bell*, the Supreme Court upheld state sterilization laws for the mentally disabled. Sterilization laws, and the *Buck* v. *Bell* decision that upheld them, represented a dark period in American history when the pseudoscience of eugenics was at its zenith. Eugenics sought to weaponize biology by establishing a supposedly scientifically-based hierarchy of human races, with physically and mentally fit whites at the top. The field was promoted by academics, celebrated in the press, and found much support by the people's representatives in both state and federal government. The Supreme Court's decision in *Buck* v. *Bell* thus followed popular sentiment among the academic and governmental elite. Sterilization was used against racial minorities, the poor, as well as those sick or disabled with mental illness. The Buck family (Carrie Buck, her baby, and her mother) were registered as *feeble-minded* (the baby was designated an *imbecile*) by the Colony for Epileptics and Feeble Minded in Virginia. Carrie Buck was chosen to be sterilized because of the *weak stock* of her family line and to ensure she would not have any more children. History has shown that the competency designations were not correct, but this fact obscures the greater point, which is that the state of Virginia legalized forced sterilization and the Supreme Court upheld the law. Justice Oliver Wendell Holmes notoriously stated in the decision, "Three generations of imbeciles are enough."[4] *Buck* v. *Bell* should never be forgotten, because the Court eagerly supported the deprivation of the fundamental right of procreation. It should also never be forgotten, however, because it reveals how democratic majorities and their elected representatives may support legislation that blatantly violate essential rights. The Court should be derided for their decision in the case, but it should also be remembered that it was a law that received popular support by the press, academia, and the voting public. Judicial review was complicit in allowing a terrible, rights-violating, law to continue. The inception of that law, however, required support by a majority of the people's representatives, and such policies were popular all around the United States. Indiana was the first state to pass a forced-sterilization law in 1907 and before the end of the eugenics era, thirty states passed similar sterilization laws. This legislation proved to be popular and influential with the National Socialist Party of Germany in the 1920s and 1930s. After World War II, American eugenics-related policies lost support for obvious reasons, and its wide popularity in the United States during the Progressive Era is not often discussed today.

In late 1941, in response to Japan's attack upon Pearl Harbor, the United States entered World War II. As part of the war effort, the Roosevelt Administration ordered the internment of Japanese Americans in early 1942. The political loyalty of Japanese Americans was openly questioned by the United States government and these citizens were denied their natural and civil rights based solely upon their ethnicity. Fred Korematsu resisted internment and was thus arrested. Prior to arrest, Korematsu underwent plastic surgery and changed his name to avoid capture but was soon apprehended. Technically, it was Korematsu's arrest and detainment that was considered by the Court rather than the policy of broad internment itself, but the decision's implications nevertheless gave weight to the constitutionality of the order and its enforcement. The constitutionality of the internment was upheld by the Supreme Court in *Korematsu* v. *United States* (1944). Justice Black recognized the controversial nature of the policy because of its race-based rationale, but reasoned that it was nevertheless constitutional:

> It should be noted, to begin with, that all legal restrictions which curtail the civil rights of a single racial group are immediately suspect. That is not to say that all such restrictions are unconstitutional. It is to say that courts must subject them to the most rigid scrutiny. Pressing public necessity may sometimes justify the existence of such restrictions: racial antagonism never can.[5]

There were three dissents in *Korematsu*. Justice Murphy's dissent specifically targeted the naked racism involved with the policy of Japanese internment and with upholding its constitutionality:

> I dissent, therefore, from this legalization of racism. Racial discrimination in any form and in any degree has no justifiable part whatever in our democratic way of life. It is unattractive in any setting, but it is utterly revolting among a free people who have embraced the principles set forth in the Constitution of the United States. All residents of this nation are kin in some way by blood or culture to a foreign land. Yet they are primarily and necessarily a part of the new and distinct civilization of the United States. They must, accordingly, be treated at all times as the heirs of the American experiment, and as entitled to all the rights and freedoms guaranteed by the Constitution.[6]

Korematsu was one of the most egregious Supreme Court decisions of the twentieth century. It was evidence that the era of the Court depriving an entire group of people of their rights because of their race had not ended with *Dred Scott*. The United States federal government and the Supreme Court, in a post–Civil War and post–Fourteenth Amendment era, abided by justifications of racist policies instead of the rights values enshrined in the Declaration of Independence, the Constitution, and the Bill of Rights. Japanese American internment during World War II is a stain on the Franklin Roosevelt presidency and was a blatant miscarriage of justice.

Let it not be construed, however, that the Court's ability to ignore fundamental rights passed away with the last century, for inherent rights of property were compromised as well in the twenty-first. In *Kelo* v. *City of New London* (2005), the matter of *eminent domain* (the taking of private property by government for public use, the relevant clause of which is found in the Fifth Amendment) was stretched beyond its recognizable limits. The case centered on the town of New London, Connecticut, which sought to improve one of its neighborhoods by transferring property to the pharmaceutical company, Pfizer. In turn, Pfizer planned to open a new facility on the property which would bring job opportunities and increased tax revenue to the area. A group of home owners, including Susette Kelo, refused to sell their homes for the project. New London commenced a plan to condemn the homes and force the removal of the home owners through its power of eminent domain. Kelo argued in state court that New London's eminent domain efforts were illegal because they were not for public use. Historically, eminent domain had been recognized as valid only when a clear public-use justification could be made and the project would result in something beneficial for a public purpose, such as the construction of a bridge. Kelo asserted that the takings of private property by government simply to put into the hands of another private entity (in this case, Pfizer) was unconstitutional.

The Court ruled in favor of New London and against the home owners. The majority decided that economic benefit fulfilled the requirement, and was thus legally synonymous with, public use. The case enraged supporters across the political spectrum, from free market conservatives to political progressives critical of corporate favoritism. Justice Antonin Scalia criticized the idea that economic benefit was equal to public purpose during oral arguments, mockingly asserting, "You can take A to give to B if B pays more taxes."[7] Justice Sandra Day O'Connor expressed concern in her dissent:

> Under the banner of economic development, all private property is now vulnerable to being taken and transferred to another private owner, so long as it might be upgraded—i.e., given to an owner who will use it in a way that the legislature deems more beneficial to the public—in the process…. [The Court's decision] washes out any distinction between private and public use of property—and thereby effectively … deletes the words "for public use" from the Takings Clause of the Fifth Amendment.[8]

It is critical to remember decisions over the past century such as *Buck* v. *Bell*, *Korematsu* v. *United States*, and *Kelo* v. *City of New London* before examining instances of the Court asserting rights values in the same era. This is because ignoring recent and relevant errors does harm to an honest and sober analysis of judicial review. Far from a Whiggish narrative, this work argues that the Supreme Court's power to nullify state and federal legislation is legitimate and appropriate *despite* its failures to always fulfill its moral obligations. It is an interesting practice for some to question the legitimacy of judicial review due to the Court's many failings when debating the legitimacy of democracy is practically verboten, despite the many egregious laws passed with popular support. In this way, democracy gets a pass and jurisprudence does not. Of course, any institution that possesses the power to say *what the law is* has a sacred obligation to adhere to its constitutional purpose. The Court must fix its attention always on its objective to abide by the precepts of the nation's founding charters and philosophical principles. All the more reason to recognize instances of its failing to do so, even as its successes are brought into focus. With this in mind, we now examine (roughly) a century of rights assertions via the Supreme Court.

Economic Liberty: Lochner *and Its Backlash*

In 1905, the Court addressed constitutional matters related to economic liberty and labor regulations in *Lochner* v. *New York*. In 1895, the state of New York passed the Bakeshop Act, a law limiting the working hours of bakery employees to ten hours a day and sixty hours a week. The regulation was supported by New York's larger bakeries and the workers in their employ. Smaller bakeries, however, many of which were owned and operated by German immigrants, saw the regulation as a deprivation of their liberty. Joseph Lochner, a German immigrant who owned a bakery in Utica, New York, was charged with violating the law. Lochner's lifelong friend and employee, Arman Schmitter, worked more hours than the sixty-per-week limit. When Lochner refused to pay the fine imposed by the violation, he was arrested. Lochner argued in his appeal to the Supreme Court that the law was a violation of the Due Process Clause.

Among the provisions of the Bakeshop Act were health and safety regulations which the Court did not dispute as being among the legitimate police powers of the state of New York. These included sanitation standards. A majority of Justices departed, however, when it came to maximum hours legislation. Justice Peckham wrote the majority opinion, which stated in part:

There is no reasonable ground for interfering with the liberty of person or the right of free contract by determining the hours of labor in the occupation of a baker. There is no contention that bakers as a class are not equal in intelligence and capacity to men in other trades or manual occupations, or that they are able to assert their rights and care for themselves without the protecting arm of the State, interfering with their independence of judgment and of action. They are in no sense wards of the State. Viewed in the light of a purely labor law, with no reference whatever to the question of health, we think that a law like the one before us involves neither the safety, the morals, nor the welfare of the public, and that the interest of the public is not in the slightest degree affected by such an act. The law must be upheld, if at all, as a law pertaining to the health of the individual engaged in the occupation of a baker. It does not affect any other portion of the public than those who are engaged in that occupation. Clean and wholesome bread does not depend upon whether the baker works but ten hours per day or only sixty hours a week. The limitation of the hours of labor does not come within the police power on that ground.[9]

Justice Harlan's dissent, however, would prove influential over time. Harlan agreed with the majority that American citizens possessed a liberty of contract. However, he argued in his dissent that "when the validity of a statute is questioned, the burden of proof, so to speak, is upon those who assert it to be unconstitutional."[10] Harlan's dissent thus invoked the Thayerian view of constitutionalism. This inverted approach to individual rights—assuming a presumption of constitutionality rather than a presumption of liberty—would grow in the following decades, especially in regard to matters of economic liberty.

The New Deal era of the 1930s and early 1940s rolled back the principles of economic liberty asserted in *Lochner*. The majority of academics in the modern age are critical of *Lochner*'s liberty of contract assertion and generally applaud the regulations imposed later in the century. A combination of cases in the New Deal era, including *West Coast Hotel* v. *Parrish* (1937), *National Labor Relations Board* v. *Jones & Laughlin* (1937), *United States* v. *Darby Lumber* (1941), and *Wickard* v. *Filburn* (1942), expanded the federal government's Commerce Clause powers and significantly restricted economic liberty.

Criticism of the economic liberty recognized in *Lochner* began on the progressive left but over time tended to find bipartisan agreement. Randy Barnett observes that *Lochner* "came to be reviled, first by political progressives and populists, and most recently by judicial conservatives. Condemnation of *Lochner* has become de rigueur among law professors of nearly all stripes."[11] Though true, the reasonings often differ. Political progressives have often defended maximum-hours legislation as a means of protecting labor from the exploitation of their employers while conservatives have generally expressed critiques of *Lochner* due to its flouting of deference to legislative power. Economic liberty was one of the first assertions of rights values by the Court in the early twentieth century and although the principle was eroded significantly over time, it would reappear in the early twenty-first century in conjunction with speech rights in a case arguably as controversial in this century as *Lochner* was in the last. That case, *Citizens United* v. *FEC* (2010), will be discussed later in this chapter.

Footnote Four

During the same era that the economic liberty of *Lochner* was being tempered, a case known as *United States* v. *Carolene Products Company* (1938) was adjudicated. *Carolene Products* became important to the history of American jurisprudence not for the ruling of the case but for one of its footnotes. The case itself involved Milnut, a product known as *filled milk*, which was ostensibly a milk substitute that did not need to be refrigerated. The filled milk was manufactured through a process of removing the fat from dairy milk and replacing it with coconut oil. The dairy industry used its considerable influence to get legislation passed to ban this competition. Congress passed such a law in 1923, banning the transport of filled milk across state lines. Carolene Products challenged the law's constitutionality. They lost their appeal in the United States Supreme Court. The fourth footnote in the decision has come to be more significant to the trajectory of the Court than the case itself. Now known as Footnote Four, it outlines an approach for strict scrutiny regarding the constitutionality of laws, and by implication their otherwise rational basis.

Footnote Four forwards the rational basis presumption of constitutionality championed by Justice Harlan and others, while also articulating when a more rigorous scrutiny should be applied. It does this by asserting that the Court should utilize a "more searching judicial inquiry" when cases involve any of three specific factors.[12] First, when a law appears to violate an enumerated right, including those in the Bill of Rights. Second, when a law changes a political process of fundamental importance, such as organizing or elections. Third, when a law may bring harm to "discrete and insular minorities."[13] It is important to note Footnote Four because it made the rational basis approach to jurisprudence a matter of formal judicial practice. This is not an insignificant detail. As will be seen later in this chapter, there are complications with Footnote Four codifying rational basis as the Court's default position. Furthermore, its inability to address some of the most significant rights values in the twentieth century will be demonstrated, revealing that it ultimately failed in its purpose to articulate when and how the Court ought to scrutinize the constitutionality of legislation.

Free Speech Rights

Free speech rights were not considered by the United States Supreme Court until almost two decades into the twentieth century. The first such case presented to the Court (and several thereafter) was not a victory for free expression. It nevertheless deserves attention both for the reasoning of the ruling, which is often quoted by Americans who lack knowledge of the details of the case, and for understanding the ultimate recognition of speech rights over time. The first free speech case, *Schenck* v. *United States* (1919), involved Charles Schenck and Elizabeth Baer, members of the Socialist Party who were arrested for violating the Espionage Act of 1917 for handing out leaflets which argued that the military draft was unconstitutional. Among other prohibitions, the Espionage law made acts of so-called disloyalty against the United States illegal. Supposedly, the distribution of content critical of the military draft qualified as promotion of mutiny and obstructed the work of the armed forces. Along with arguments against conscription, the leaflet quoted the United States Constitution's Thirteenth Amendment, which forbids involuntary servitude.

In an oft-quoted but rarely contextualized statement, Justice Oliver Wendell Holmes—speaking on behalf of a unanimous Court that upheld the speech restrictions against Schenck and Baer—stated that the "most stringent protection of free speech would not protect a man falsely shouting fire in a theatre and causing a panic…. The question in every case is whether the words used are used in such circumstances and are of such a nature as to create a clear and present danger that they will bring about the substantive evils that Congress has a right to prevent."[14] This ruling established the *clear and present danger* standard, which was then replaced in the ensuing years with first the *bad tendency test*, followed by the *preferred freedoms test*, and then the *clear and probable danger* standard in the 1950s. The criterion was again reformed in the late 1960s with the *imminent lawless action* standard, which will be discussed presently. Holmes's line about falsely shouting fire in a theater was never intended to be used as a standard of law, and—more to the point—it is a terrible analogy. Justice Holmes compared the distribution of leaflets condemning military conscription, which celebrated the Thirteenth Amendment, with putting people in danger for disingenuously causing immediate public panic. Though the comparison is awkward at best and was never meant to be interpreted as a literal standard of speech law, it is nevertheless quoted by apologists for speech restrictions to this day.

Other speech cases heard by the Court the same year were upheld, including *Debs* v. *United States* (1919), in which the Socialist presidential candidate Eugene Debs was also charged for violating the Espionage Act. In that case, Debs had criticized U.S. involvement in World War I. The Wilson Administration ensured that Debs was prosecuted to the fullest extent of the law. In 1921, President Harding commuted Debs' sentence and the socialist politician was granted his freedom. In another Supreme Court case in 1919, *Abrams* v. *United States*, the Supreme Court upheld the prosecution of factory workers who organized a strike. They too were charged with violating the Espionage Act because they were employed at a munitions factory and the strike was interpreted as an obstruction to the legitimate exercise of military power. The workers had distributed leaflets among themselves for the purpose of organizing, and the content of the leaflets was construed by the government as disloyal.

In 1925, an important decision was made by the Court although the restriction on speech in question was once again upheld. In *Gitlow* v. *New York*, the Court upheld the conviction of Benjamin Gitlow and his colleague Alan Larkin, who had been arrested on the charge of criminal anarchy for the publication of communist content that promoted the overthrow of the United States. Though the convictions were upheld, the Court's majority nevertheless ruled that First Amendment protections against state governments existed due to incorporation by the Fourteenth Amendment. This recognition, along with dissents by Justices Holmes and Brandeis who noted that there was no present danger inherently in the publication of such content, began a slow evolution in how the Court examined speech restrictions going forward.

When *Stromberg* v. *California* was decided in 1931, for the first time in the history of the United States a conviction related to speech and the relevant state law connected to it were ruled unconstitutional. The defendant, Yetta Stromberg, was arrested for flying a red banner in support of Soviet Russia, thus violating California's Red Flag Law. The legislation had made it illegal to wave a red flag in symbolic opposition to the United States government. The historic decision by the Supreme Court which nullified the California statute and Stromberg's conviction began the actual practice of holding state governments to free speech standards outlined in the First Amendment. The Court first overruled a federal law violating the First Amendment in 1965, in *Lamont* v. *Postmaster General*.

Free speech standards were further articulated by the Court in 1969, in *Brandenburg* v. *Ohio*. Clarence Brandenburg was a member of the Ku Klux Klan who was arrested for one of his public speeches, which had been recorded by local media. The speech included disparaging remarks against the Jewish community and African Americans. Brandenburg's language also explicitly included messages articulating and promoting reprisal by the white population against racial minorities and the government. He was charged for violating an Ohio law that criminalized speech which advocated lawless acts. The Supreme Court ultimately ruled the Ohio law and Brandenburg's conviction unconstitutional and refined free speech standards to their most liberal degree. The Court effectively overruled previous standards and replaced it with the standard of *imminent lawless action*. Doing so, the Court liberalized the free exercise of speech to a line just before action itself. Advocacy of crime and violence were ruled constitutionally protected, so long as they were not declarations which promoted imminent harm. Advocacy in the abstract was constitutionally protected. *Brandenburg's imminent lawless action* remains the standard for speech cases where political speech that advocates violence and other crimes by individuals is considered.

Twenty years after *Brandenburg, Texas,* v. *Johnson* (1989) underscored the liberalization of free speech values the Court had undergone through the twentieth century. The case was in a number of ways reminiscent of those previously mentioned. Only the manner of speech was different. In 1984, outside of the Republican National Convention in Dallas, Texas, Gregory Lee Johnson publicly burned an American flag to protest the policies of President Ronald Reagan and the Republican Party. Johnson was soon arrested and charged for violating a Texas law which criminalized the desecration of the American flag. He was tried and convicted in a Texas state court. Johnson appealed to the United States Supreme Court, asserting that his burning of the flag was protected under the First Amendment as symbolic political speech. The majority of the Court agreed with Johnson that the desecration of the American flag, by burning or otherwise, was a form of speech protected under the First Amendment. The Court criticized the Texas law not merely for restricting speech, but for its clear intention to restrict a particular viewpoint. As Justice Scalia asked (somewhat rhetorically) during oral arguments, "Will you give me an example where … somebody desecrates the flag in order to show that he agrees with the policies of the United States?… It will always be to criticize the country."[15] The law itself was thus a form of viewpoint discrimination.

Texas v. *Johnson* symbolized a moment when the Court proved to be more liberal in their political philosophy than much of the public or the elected class. After the ruling, both Democrat and Republican officials condemned the decision. President George H.W. Bush called for a constitutional amendment to make flag burning illegal and the Democratic leadership in Congress called for immediate anti-flag burning legislation. A law was indeed passed in late 1989, and the Court naturally nullified the new law. Much of these events appear to have been political posturing because

Democrats must have known that the new anti-flag burning law would be ruled unconstitutional, but it granted them an opportunity to score points with their constituents who were disturbed by the *Texas* v. *Johnson* decision. Keith Whittington observes in *Political Foundations of Judicial Supremacy* (2007), "Flag burning was a nonissue before the Court placed it on the agenda with its 1989 ruling…. Opinion surveys instantly showed roughly 70 percent of the public disapproving of the decision and supporting a constitutional amendment to ban flag burning."[16] Thus the Democrats took the opportunity to pass a law they must have known would be overturned so as to not have their patriotism questioned by Republicans. In turn, Republicans could use flag burning as a political wedge issue for the next many years, knowing that if no amendment was achieved they would be none the worse for it. The posturing by members of both major political parties was surely influenced by the broad distaste for the *Texas* v. *Johnson* decision among the voting public. This is not a positive feature of the elected class, and it underscores how popular opinion can compel political representatives to retreat from constitutional principles. All the more reason not to leave the final word about constitutionality to a body obsessed with political maneuvering, as it is so easily shaken by fleeting public passions.

Texas v. *Johnson* is an important case, not merely for exemplifying the liberalization of the Court's rights values regarding free speech, but also for recognizing how it cast everyone else in 1989, from Republicans to Democrats to the American people generally, as placing little value in the protection of free speech rights. If left to a popular vote, certain controversial political speech would not have survived constitutional protection as recently as the end of the last century. The same is likely true of today.

Liberty and Equal Protection: Vocation, Education, and Marriage

Political speech was not the only liberty the federal government and states were restricting during the First World War and the Progressive Era. Nebraska criminalized the teaching of so-called *alien* languages to children, including German, Italian, French, and Spanish, in 1919. Ancient languages such as Hebrew, Greek, and Latin were exempt from this law. Robert Meyer, a teacher at Zion Parochial School, was charged with violating the law in 1920 when it became known he had been teaching a child German. When *Meyer* v. *Nebraska* reached the Supreme Court in 1923, the majority ruled the nativist-motivated law unconstitutional. The Court expressed an understanding that for some the law had made sense in order to prioritize the importance of children learning English, but nevertheless found the law extreme and arbitrary. Important to the constitutional reasoning expressed in the decision, however, was the recognition of economic liberty for teachers and tutors to practice their trade and make a living. Justice James C. McReynolds remarked on the liberty recognized in the Fourteenth Amendment:

> While this court has not attempted to define with exactness the liberty thus guaranteed, the term has received much consideration and some of the included things have been definitely stated. Without doubt, it denotes not merely freedom from bodily restraint but also the right of the individual to contract, to engage in any of the common occupations of life, to acquire useful knowledge, to marry, establish a home and bring up children, to worship God according to the dictates of his own conscience, and generally to enjoy those privileges long recognized at common law as essential to the orderly pursuit of happiness by free men.[17]

Nebraska's law forbidding the teaching of modern foreign languages to children was not thus merely arbitrary and extreme, but also violated the principle of liberty for educators to practice their trade. The economic liberty required for citizens to cultivate their skills, which simultaneously benefits the greater community (in this case, the education of children), is a value that can be easily overlooked. The Court, however, recognized that the arbitrariness of the Nebraska law was unfortunate, but the deprivation of liberty it cast upon educators was central to ruling the law unconstitutional.

Justice McReynolds wrote the majority opinion for the Court again in an education-related case two years later in *Pierce* v. *Society of Sisters* (1925). The state of Oregon had passed the Oregon Compulsory Education Act in 1922. In the early twentieth century, state governments passed laws making the schooling of children mandatory. Oregon's compulsory education law was different, however, as it required all children to attend public schools exclusively. Parents with children in private schools were guilty of a misdemeanor according to the law. Two private schools in Oregon, Hill Military Academy and the Society of Sisters, challenged the constitutionality of the law. According to Leo Pfeffer, legal scholar and author of *Church, State, and Freedom* (1953), the law was enacted by popular referendum, when "the people of Oregon were largely under the influence of Ku Klux Klan elements."[18] The Klan element represented a larger, more widespread anti–Catholic sentiment. The law was thus an attempt to subvert Catholic-rooted education and cultural influence found in certain private schools.

The Court ruled Oregon's compulsory education law unconstitutional. Justice McReynolds emphasized the liberty of parents to decide for themselves the manner of learning for their children:

> The fundamental theory of liberty upon which all governments in this Union repose excludes any general power of the State to standardize its children by

forcing them to accept instruction from public teachers only. The child is not the mere creature of the State; those who nurture him and direct his destiny have the right, coupled with the high duty, to recognize and prepare him for additional obligations.[19]

The fact that the Oregon Compulsory Education Act had been passed through popular referendum should also not be ignored. The nullification of the state law by the United States Supreme Court was a direct rebuke of a local act of direct democracy that exceeded its legitimate powers, insisting that the liberty of individuals eclipsed the popular wishes of the citizenry when the two were in conflict. The *Pierce* v. *Society of Sisters* decision underscored the liberty interests of parents in the realm of educating their children. Nearly three decades following *Pierce*, constitutional questions about public education turned to matters regarding equal protection. Questions arose as to whether a national policy of separate but equal could continue to be tolerated in an era where rights values became more central to the public discourse.

Brown v. *Board of Education* (1954) was a consolidation of four relevant cases in different states (South Carolina, Virginia, Kansas, and Delaware) relating to segregation policies based upon race in public schools. Though *Brown* was the result of a combination of lower court rulings, its namesake and the details of that particular case are noteworthy. Oliver Brown of Topeka, Kansas, attempted to register his daughter in the school located closest to their residence. They were denied, requiring Brown's daughter, Linda Carol Brown, to walk several blocks to a bus stop and then be bussed much farther away to a segregated school for African American children. Brown and several other families challenged the constitutionality of the segregation policy in Kansas. The state Supreme Court in Delaware had ruled in a separate case that African American students in that state should be admitted to the white schools that had denied them access. The U.S. District Court for the District of Kansas, however, ruled against Brown and the other families in his case. There was thus a conflict of constitutionality between various lower courts.

The U.S. District Court of Kansas had ruled against Brown by citing the precedent established in *Plessy* v. *Ferguson* (1896), which had upheld the legal doctrine of *separate but equal* regarding differing treatment for African Americans concerning public spaces and accommodations. *Plessy* belongs on the long list of egregious decision by the Court. Its lone dissent, however, authored by Justice Harlan, proved influential on the later decision in *Brown*. Harlan's dissent in *Plessy* asserted:

> I deny that any legislative body or judicial tribunal may have regard to the race of citizens which the civil rights of those citizens are involved. Indeed, such legislation as that here in question is inconsistent not only with that equality of

rights which pertains to citizenship, national and state but with the personal liberty enjoyed by everyone within the United States....

The arbitrary separation of citizens, on the basis of race ... is a badge of servitude wholly inconsistent with the civil freedom and the equality before the law established by the Constitution. It cannot be justified upon any legal grounds.[20]

The consolidation of segregation cases in *Brown* were challenged at the United States Supreme Court by NAACP attorney and future Supreme Court Justice, Thurgood Marshall. During oral argument in December 1953, Marshall powerfully illustrated the incongruity between the principles enshrined in the Constitution and the treatment of African Americans under segregation:

Nobody will stand in the Court and urge that, and in order to arrive at the decision that they want us to arrive at, there would have to be some recognition of a reason why of all of the multitudinous groups of people in this country you have to single out Negroes and give them this separate treatment.

It can't be because of slavery in the past, because there are very few groups in this country that haven't had slavery some place back in history of their groups. It can't be color because there are Negroes as white as the drifted snow, with blue eyes, and they are just as segregated as the colored man.

The only thing can be is an inherent determination that the people who were formerly in slavery, regardless of anything else, shall be kept as near that stage as is possible, and now is the time, we submit, that this Court should make it clear that that is not what our Constitution stands for.[21]

Marshall successfully persuaded the Court that school segregation violated the Equal Protection Clause of the Fourteenth Amendment. The *Plessy* standard of separate but equal was overturned. Less cited in popular culture today but similarly noteworthy was the case of *Bolling* v. *Sharpe*, decided the same day

Thurgood Marshall, attorney for the NAACP, by Thomas J. O'Halloran, 1957. Photographic portrait (Library of Congress).

(May 17) as *Brown* in 1954. Though *Brown* addressed the issue of segregated public schools in the separate states, schools in the federal District of Columbia were also racially segregated. The Court ruled in *Bolling* v. *Sharpe* that racial segregation by public schools in the District of Columbia violated the Due Process Clause of the Fifth Amendment. The *Bolling* decision asserts the role of the Fifth Amendment's Due Process Clause rather than the Due Process or Equal Protection Clauses of the Fourteenth Amendment because the Fourteenth Amendment applies specifically to the states. The Court ruled that such segregation in the federal district was "a burden that constitutes an arbitrary deprivation of [African American students'] liberty."[22]

A year later, in a continuation of the case known as *Brown II*, the Court laid out a legal process for fulfilling the requirement established in *Brown* v. *Board of Education*. *Brown II*, however, concerned only those states that were party to the original *Brown* case. This left open the question for some as to whether states not involved in *Brown* were subject to its jurisdiction. This matter was addressed following events in Arkansas.

After a number of legal challenges, Arkansas Governor Orval Faubus used the state's National Guard to block nine African American students from entering Central High School in Little Rock. In an address on September 24, 1957, in response to the actions of Arkansas's government, President Eisenhower asserted that "under the leadership of demagogic extremists, disorderly mobs have deliberately prevented the carrying out of proper orders from a Federal Court."[23] In response, President Eisenhower sent the 101st Airborne to Arkansas:

> Whenever normal agencies prove inadequate to the task and it becomes necessary for the Executive Branch of the Federal Government to use its powers and authority to uphold Federal Courts, the President's responsibility is inescapable. In accordance with that responsibility, I have today issued an Executive Order directing the use of troops under Federal authority to aid in the execution of Federal law at Little Rock, Arkansas.[24]

The show of force convinced Arkansas's governor to stand down. The African American children were allowed to enter and were given the protection of federal guards while at school for the remainder of the academic year. Arkansas's governor and legislature argued that the *Brown* decision was not legally binding upon them, as they were not a party to the case. President Eisenhower clearly disagreed. This question was addressed by the Supreme Court in 1958, in *Cooper* v. *Aaron*:

> As this case reaches us, it raises questions of the highest importance to the maintenance of our federal system of government. It necessarily involves a claim by the Governor and Legislature of a State that there is no duty on state officials to obey federal court orders resting on this Court's considered

interpretation of the United States Constitution. Specifically, it involves actions by the Governor and Legislature of Arkansas upon the premise that they are not bound by our holding in *Brown* v. *Board of Education*, 347 U.S. 483. That holding was that the Fourteenth Amendment forbids States to use their governmental powers to bar children on racial grounds from attending schools where there is state participation through any arrangement, management, funds or property.[25]

Cooper v. *Aaron* saw the Court explicitly express its power of judicial review, echoing John Marshall's assertion in *Marbury* v. *Madison* (1803) and affirming that the Court's decisions were binding upon the separate states. The Court declared that "Article VI of the Constitution makes the Constitution the 'supreme Law of the Land.'"[26] Additionally, "No state legislator or executive or judicial officer can war against the Constitution without violating his undertaking to support it."[27]

Despite its defense in ending school segregation, critics of judicial review have expressed little love for *Cooper* v. *Aaron*. Larry D. Kramer, for example, in *The People Themselves* (2004), called the ruling "just bluster and puff."[28] When the Court paraphrased John Marshall in saying that *Marbury* declared that the federal judiciary is supreme in regard to interpreting the Constitution, Kramer argues that "Marbury says no such thing."[29] Marshall was in fact even clearer than *Cooper* implies, as he asserted that it was "emphatically the province and duty of the Judicial Department to say what the law is."[30] Perhaps Kramer's point was that John Marshall did not assert the Court's role in enforcing the Bill of Rights against the states in 1803 (which is already known to us via *Barron* v. *Baltimore*). This is a distraction, however, as the Fourteenth Amendment, long after Marshall's tenure, made manifest this protocol. For those who prefer legislative supremacy, *Cooper*'s reiteration of the legitimacy of judicial review is a bitter pill.

The Fourteenth Amendment's guarantee of equal protection and liberty turned to matters related to interracial marriage in the 1960s. Virginia had passed a miscegenation law in 1924 called the Racial Integrity Act that barred interracial marriage and also prohibited interracial couples from living together as though they were married.[31] Mildred Jeter, an African American woman, and Richard Loving, a Euro-American man, were residents of Virginia. Wanting to be married and being aware of the state's prohibition, they travelled to Washington, D.C., and got married in 1958. Upon their return they were arrested. Their door was broken in by police and the two were dragged off to jail in the middle of the night. Though Richard Loving was able to post bail, Mildred Loving—who was pregnant—was forced to stay in the local jail through the weekend. Though the two were convicted to one year in jail, their sentence was suspended on the condition they leave Virginia. It was included in their plea deal that they would not return for twenty-five years. They challenged the conviction in 1963 but it was upheld by the state court of Virginia. The Lovings challenged the constitutionality of the law, appealing to the United States Supreme Court.

On June 12, 1967, the Supreme Court unanimously ruled that the Virginia law had deprived the Lovings of their liberty, thus violating the Due Process Clause of the Fourteenth Amendment. Chief Justice Earl Warren, in expressing the ruling by the Court, declared that the "freedom to marry has long been recognized as one of the vital personal rights essential to the orderly pursuit of happiness by free men.… Under our Constitution, the freedom to marry, or not marry, a person of another race resides with the individual and cannot be infringed by the State."[32] Miscegenation laws were at last nationally nullified in 1967, more than a century after the end of the Civil War.

Procedural Due Process

The rather bizarre practice of utilizing the Due Process Clause to assert fundamental rights in place of the Privileges or Immunities Clause created two separate forms of due process-oriented rights. Rights of life, liberty, and property asserted by the Court through the Fourteenth Amendment's Due Process Clause came to be known as *substantive due process* rights. Formal rights regarding protections when under suspicion, arrest, or trial are known as rights related to *procedural due process*. The ridiculousness of this term is evident in that *procedural* and *process* are practically synonyms. Nevertheless, a different terminology was required to define more traditional and practical aspects of due process rights, in contrast to the so-called substantive due process rights established after the Court had retreated from privileges or immunities. This collection of procedural due process protections evolved over the twentieth century along with substantive due process rights. Most notably, two cases in the 1960s raised the bar for rights of the accused: *Gideon* v. *Wainwright* (1963) and *Miranda* v. *Arizona* (1966).

Clarence Gideon was charged in Florida for a felony due to breaking and entering with intent to commit a misdemeanor. Gideon requested that the court provide him with an attorney. Though the Bill of Rights provides that an attorney will be appointed if a defendant cannot afford one in federal cases, states had differing laws concerning legal representation for poor defendants. Florida's relevant statute only provided free legal representation to a poor defendant in capital cases. Due to this, Gideon represented himself at trial. He was found guilty and convicted to five years in prison. In response, he filed a habeas corpus petition in the Florida Supreme Court, claiming his right to counsel had been violated. His writ was denied.

Gideon appealed to the United States Supreme Court. The Court considered whether the Fourteenth Amendment incorporated the Sixth Amendment's right to counsel in criminal cases, thus extending the privilege to felony defendants in state courts. In a unanimous decision, the Court ruled that it did. Legal scholar Erwin Chemerinsky observes the importance of *Gideon*, noting that an "adversarial system of justice requires some semblance of equality between the two sides.... It holds that all facing the power of the state to take away their liberty, however poor, are entitled to representation."[33] Chemerinsky also observes that *Gideon* is unique in the Court's demand that governments (federal and state) provide a positive right, which is unusual and infrequent in a system generally defined by the negative rights of citizens and the limited express powers of the state. "*Gideon* holds that there is something the government must pay for and provide: an attorney to those who cannot afford one and who face the loss of liberty by imprisonment."[34]

Whereas the rights of the accused on trial was the focus of *Gideon*, it was the rights of the accused while under arrest that was deliberated in *Miranda* v. *Arizona* (1966). The case, like *Brown*, was a consolidation of cases, each of which included a defendant who confessed their guilt following interrogation by police. In each case, the Fifth Amendment rights of the accused had not been disclosed to them by the authorities. The Court thus had to consider whether the Fifth Amendment's protection against self-incrimination applied to those in police custody while under arrest. Chief Justice Earl Warren delivered the majority opinion that the Fifth Amendment's protection against self-incrimination applied in all settings. Suspects must be made aware of their right to remain silent, right to an attorney, to have an attorney provided if necessary, that they may waive these rights at any time, and that once they request counsel no more questioning will be done until an attorney is present.

Erwin Chemerinsky similarly notes the importance of *Miranda*, its early controversy, and subsequent wide-ranging acceptance. "Initially, *Miranda* was very controversial, with critics seeing it as unduly limiting police questioning and fearing that it would let criminals off on a technicality."[35] However, over time, *Miranda* came to be generally celebrated. "In 2000, the Court had the chance to overrule Miranda and declined to do so. Even police organizations filed a brief urging the Court to keep Miranda. They explained to the Court that the Miranda warning provides clear guidance to the police about what to do in questioning a suspect."[36]

The expansion of rights recognition for those in police detainment and those facing a criminal trial in the mid-twentieth century can be easily overlooked or taken for granted. There is some level of human instinct to possess contempt for those accused of an awful act. It can thus be easy for some to fail to appreciate how rights protections for the accused can be a benefit to all, particularly the innocent. In times when accusations are equated with automatic implications of guilt, privileges extended to the accused become all the more precious.

Liberty and Privacy

Matters of privacy and personal autonomy were also contended with by the Court in the 1960s. *Griswold* v. *Connecticut* (1965) marked a new age for the Court in this regard, as the ruling's ramifications were to be felt for decades to come. The case centered on whether a Connecticut law dating back to 1879 that prohibited the distribution of contraceptives was unconstitutional. Furthermore, it raised questions as to whether the law violated the privacy rights of married couples to hold autonomy over such interests. The Court ruled the Connecticut law to be unnecessarily broad. Though the Constitution does not specifically describe a right to privacy, the Court asserted that privacy rights certainly exist when the combination of the First, Third, Fourth, Fifth, and Ninth Amendments are taken into consideration. The First Amendment recognizes the liberty of private speech and the free exercise of religion (a matter of personal conscience). The Third Amendment protects against the quartering of soldiers in one's home. The Fourth Amendment asserts protections from unreasonable search and seizure of one's person and property, and the Fifth Amendment recognizes a privacy right to withhold self-incriminating information from the authorities. In conjunction, the Court recognized that there are *penumbras* of rights that exist though they are not enumerated in the Constitution. Critical to this point is the Ninth Amendment, which was also mentioned in Justice Goldberg's concurring opinion in *Griswold*. The Ninth Amendment simply states, "The enumeration in the Constitution, of certain rights, shall not be construed to deny or disparage others retained by the people."[37] The existence of unenumerated rights is informed by the natural rights philosophy of the framers; a philosophy that insists that rights precede the existence and formation of government. Justice Goldberg explained the role of the Ninth Amendment in *Griswold* and in jurisprudence broadly:

> The Ninth Amendment simply shows the intent of the Constitution's authors that other fundamental personal rights should not be denied such protection

or disparaged in any other way simply because they are not specifically listed in the first eight constitutional amendments....

In sum, the Ninth Amendment simply lends strong support to the view that the "liberty" protected by the Fifth and Fourteenth Amendments from infringement by the Federal Government or the States is not restricted to rights specifically mentioned in the first eight amendments.[38]

Griswold influenced a series of cases over the following decades. Most immediately and dramatically was *Roe* v. *Wade* (1973), which recognized a woman's right to an abortion. Abortion was not an issue that fell across easily decipherable ideological or partisan lines as it does today. The evidence of this is that the Court's majority, at the time of the *Roe* decision, were appointed by Republican administrations. Four of the Justices were recent appointees of President Richard Nixon, and one of the most vocal dissenters in *Roe* was President Kennedy-appointed Justice Byron White. Though *Roe* recognized a woman's right to an abortion, the Court also ruled that there did exist a state interest as a pregnancy advanced. The categorization of different levels of state interest during different trimesters of pregnancy received more criticism over time. Anti-abortion activists argued that the trimester model was devoid of scientific justification, and abortion advocates who defended the result of *Roe* nevertheless recognized flaws in its reasoning. Regardless of the various views surrounding the abortion debate, however, the relevant case law for thirty years was not *Roe* v. *Wade* but *Planned Parenthood* v. *Casey* (1992).

Planned Parenthood v. *Casey* upheld abortion rights but formulated their limits and the area of state interest involved. *Casey* was also emblematic of similar interests engaged in both *Roe* and *Griswold* (abortion and marriage), as the law in dispute was a 1989 Pennsylvania statute requiring married women to notify their husbands prior to having an abortion. The Supreme Court struck down the provision but also articulated a refined standard of abortion law, informed by the same liberty interests first raised in *Griswold*. The Court rejected the trimester model formulated in *Roe* and asserted that the state has legitimate interests throughout the nine-month period of pregnancy. Nevertheless, the Court did not apply the standard of strict scrutiny but instead ruled that no law should provide an *undue burden* upon a woman's right to an abortion. The Court affirmed that women were not to be seen as legally subordinate to their husbands, declaring that a "husband has no enforceable right to require a wife to advise him before she exercises her personal choices ... [and a man does not have] the kind of dominion over his wife that parents exercise over their children."[39] Furthermore, the balance of legitimate state interests and the extent to which abortion rights were to be recognized were not defined by the Court as matters of privacy, but rather liberty. In a rare joint opinion authored by

Justices O'Connor, Kennedy, and Souter, the Court relied on the Fourteenth Amendment. They also invoked the Ninth Amendment's assertions of unenumerated rights, just as Justice Goldberg had done in *Griswold*. "Neither the Bill of Rights nor the specific practices of States at the time of the adoption of the Fourteenth Amendment marks the outer limits of the substantive sphere of liberty which the Fourteenth Amendment protects. See U.S. Const., Amdt. 9."

In June 2022, with *Dobbs* v. *Jackson Women's Health Organization*, the Court upheld a Mississippi law that banned abortions after fifteen weeks. Five of the six-member majority, more significantly, ruled that *Roe* and *Casey's* recognition of constitutionally protected abortion rights were deeply flawed, legally dubious, and not rooted either in the U.S. Constitution nor in the nation's history. The Court decreed that abortion was not, in fact, a constitutionally-protected right. Chief Justice Roberts, though in agreement to uphold Mississippi's post-fifteen week abortion ban, did not agree with overturning *Roe* and *Casey* entirely.

The Court's majority opinion was written by Justice Alito, whose draft opinion was originally leaked to the press in May 2022. The decision was deeply critical of *Roe's* viability and trimester formulations, and similarly dismissive of *Casey's* undue burden standard, asserting them to be arbitrary and possessing no constitutional merit. Though the decision proved immediately divisive, it is noteworthy that even progressive legal scholars who support abortion rights have criticized the legal reasoning for abortion in the realm of American jurisprudence for decades, particularly *Roe*. Justice Ruth Bader Ginsburg, for example, was a critic of the *Roe* decision for having gone farther than necessary to protect some minimum level of abortion rights, rather than creating a complete standard of abortion policy throughout pregnancy (which is what *Roe* v. *Wade* indeed set out to do).

The *Dobbs* decision, however, did not ultimately question the role of substantive due process rooted in *Roe* and *Casey*, and furthermore, explicitly states that the *Dobbs* ruling should not be construed as though other rights protected under substantive due process (including contraception and same-sex marriage) are at similar risk of being overturned. It asserts that the decision speaks only to the lack of constitutional recognition of the right to abortion. Justice Thomas, in his concurrence, was the only member of the Court to criticize the role of substantive due process. He argued that the Court should instead analyze the constitutionality of such controversies via the Privileges or Immunities Clause of the Fourteenth Amendment.

Though critics of the *Dobbs* decision viewed it as a move by an arch-conservative majority, the fact is that not one Justice among the majority sought to create a national ban on abortion. Not one member of the majority expressed a claim that there was *no right* to an abortion (merely that there was no constitutionally-recognized right), or that no state could allow it to be practiced. Instead, the opinion held that abortion is a political matter that the judiciary had been unable to satisfactorily settle over a period of nearly fifty years and that, as a political matter, it should be attended to instead by the people's elected representatives. Some among the Pro-Life legal camp indeed leaned toward advocating for a complete national abortion ban, asserting that the procedure is a violation of the rights of unborn human beings who are legal persons under the Equal Protection Clause of the Fourteenth Amendment. Prominent constitutional scholars, including Princeton professor Robert George, filed an amicus brief on behalf of the anti-abortion contingent in the case utilizing this very legal reasoning for ending constitutionally-protected abortion throughout the United States. Though in the conclusion of his amicus brief, George simply maintains that the Mississippi law should stand, the Equal Protection implications would potentially drive future arguments for a nationwide ban. It should be noted that the *Equal Protection for the unborn* argument is its own kind of rights-assertion position, but one that essentially went nowhere in *Dobbs*. The Court's majority ultimately rejected this line of argument.

The response to *Dobbs* was significant and explosive. The Pro-Life movement celebrated the judicial reversal of constitutionally-recognized abortion rights and Pro-Choice advocates criticized the Court's overturning of precedent. Political polarization in the United States deepened, with not only protests as a result, but also acts of vandalism and violence. This included an assassination attempt on Justice Kavanaugh following the leaked draft opinion and prior to the opinion's official announcement. *Dobbs* stalled, or reversed, the trend of rights assertions via the Court over the course of the previous century, for good or for ill. The political and cultural ramifications for the Court and the nation post-*Dobbs* will be discussed further in the conclusion of this book.

The Ninth Amendment

The invocation of the Ninth Amendment in Goldberg's concurrence in *Griswold* implies an incorporation of the amendment against the individual states. Because of the unique nature of the Ninth Amendment, however, as an amendment that asserts the existence of unenumerated rights, it can be better understood that the Ninth Amendment's implications existed as a standard against any form of government, federal or state, since the American founding. Indeed the assertion of inherent rights of self-protection recognized by Georgia's Supreme Court in the 1840s gives weight to this view (see Chapter Six). Though the Ninth Amendment was not referenced by the United States Supreme Court until the 1960s in *Griswold*—lying quiet in the realm of American jurisprudence for the better part of two centuries—it underscores the rights values of the founding and reiterates the existence of rights regardless of whether they have been written down and recognized by state agents. Sotirios A. Barber remarked on the importance of the Ninth Amendment in a 1988 article, "The Ninth Amendment: Inkblot or Another Hard Nut to Crack?" Barber observed that "legal instruments for insuring justice can never be fully codified. The ninth amendment is thus express authorization for a power that Federalist No. 78 assumes already in the possession of our courts: the power to mitigate governmental injustices that occur within the scope of unjust but not expressly proscribed means to authorized governmental ends."[40] This understanding of the purpose and power of the Ninth Amendment thus emphasizes and reinforces the Court's role in practicing judicial review. *Griswold* represents a moment when the Court explicitly affirmed the importance of recognizing unenumerated rights and invoked the Ninth Amendment to underscore the historical and philosophical underpinnings of American rights values.

Liberty interests were similarly cited in the early twenty-first-century case, *Lawrence* v. *Texas* (2003). The case involved John Lawrence, who was arrested for violating a Texas anti-sodomy law when Houston police entered his home and discovered him engaging in a consensual sex act with another man, Tyron Garner. The Texas State Court of Appeals upheld the conviction, ruling the anti-sodomy law constitutional. Lawrence appealed to the United States Supreme Court. The case sought to resolve not only the relevant liberty interests, but also precedent, as the Court had ruled a Georgia anti-sodomy law constitutional in 1986 (*Bowers* v. *Hardwick*).

The Court ruled the Texas law unconstitutional. Such laws were a deprivation of liberty by criminalizing the private behavior of consenting adults. Any similar laws in the several states were thus unconstitutional. The earlier decision of *Bowers* v. *Hardwick* was overturned. Justice Kennedy's opinion, writing for the Court's majority, declared that the Texas law furthered "no legitimate state interest which can justify its intrusion into the personal and private life of the individual."[41]

An organization which filed amicus briefs on behalf of Lawrence and was referenced twice in the Court's decision was the libertarian Cato Institute. Cato (and libertarians generally) is often cast into the category of the political right or the conservative camp due to a shared devotion to free market capitalism. Cato's involvement in the *Lawrence* case, however, reveals the notable differences between libertarians and conservatives regarding their views on private behavior and cultural matters. Underscoring the disparity between Cato's libertarians and political conservatives regarding jurisprudence, the organization published a critique of prevailing conservative thought in 1986. The work was authored by Stephen Macedo and was titled *The New Right v. The Constitution.* Macedo deftly illustrated the ideological difference between libertarians and conservatives during the era, at a time when conservatives had grown vocal in their opposition to individual rights assertions via judicial review. Macedo observed, "When conservatives like [Court of Appeals Judge Robert] Bork treat rights as islands surrounded by a sea of government powers, they precisely reverse the view of the Founders as enshrined in the Constitution, wherein government powers are limited and specified and rendered as islands surrounded by a sea of individual rights."[42]

The New Right v. The Constitution was published one year prior to Robert Bork's nomination by President Reagan to the Supreme Court in 1987. Bork's confirmation hearings were a disaster. The Democratic majority on the Judiciary Committee challenged Bork's form of constitutionalism. Some conservatives have interpreted the Bork hearings and his failure to become a Supreme Court Justice as the beginning of the politicization of the Court and the erosion of the nomination process (this book's conclusion will discuss politicization). This version of the events, however, ignores the complicity of Bork himself. When asked about the role and value of the Ninth Amendment in jurisprudence, for example, Bork did not cite *Griswold*, privacy, liberty, or unenumerated rights. Instead, Bork declared that he knew nothing of the meaning of the Ninth Amendment and compared it to an ink blot.

Griswold, Roe, Casey, and *Lawrence,* when taken together, make up a collection of cases related to liberty interests that illustrate an enormous transformation in the recognition of rights values by the Court over a period of less than fifty years. Taken collectively, they also underscore the limits, even the failings, of Footnote Four. The justification for utilizing rational basis save for the exceptions that Footnote Four outlines played no role in the liberty interest cases just discussed. Instead, an unenumerated right to privacy was asserted in *Griswold* and *Roe,* and the language of privacy was changed (and arguably improved) to interests of liberty in *Casey* and *Lawrence.* Footnote Four's prescription for applying strict scrutiny in matters related to suspect classes, the changing of political procedures, or the possible violation of an enumerated right had no relevance in the *Griswold* case, for example. The Court, seeming to be aware of this, did not attempt to reconstruct Footnote Four into a new form. They instead ignored it. Despite the reversal of constitutional protections on abortion rights via *Dobbs*, the legal and intellectual history surrounding the cases discussed above are significant and noteworthy

Where Footnote Four was of no use, the Court instead employed a jurisprudence that was far more deeply connected to the Constitution, the Bill of Rights, and the rights values that informed them. By acknowledging the role of unenumerated rights identified in the Ninth Amendment and asserting them in *Griswold*, the Court pivoted away from New Deal era procedural guidelines that were unfit to address matters of liberty. This is not to necessarily argue that Footnote Four has no legitimate role, but its inherent presumption of constitutionality does seem at odds with the presumption of liberty that the Declaration of Independence, the Constitution, the Bill of Rights, the Ninth Amendment, and the Fourteenth Amendment appear to embody.

Second Amendment

The early twenty-first century saw the Court address Second Amendment rights. Two cases, one in 2008 and another in 2010, affirmed the right of individual gun ownership. The first, *District of Columbia* v. *Heller*, concerned a law in the federal district that made it illegal to carry an unregistered firearm. The law also banned the registration of handguns but included an exception which allowed the chief of police to issue one-year licenses on a per-case basis. Additional provisions in the law included the requirement for firearms to be kept unloaded and disassembled in one's home. Alternatively, if they were to be loaded and assembled they were required to be bound by a trigger lock or a similar device.

Dick Heller was a police officer for the District of Columbia and was thus certified to carry a gun for his job. He applied for a one-year license for a handgun. His application was denied. Noting the contradiction in his ability to carry a gun as part of his occupation but denied the right to keep a gun in his own home for personal use, Heller sued the District of Columbia for violating his Second Amendment right to keep and bear arms. Heller's complaint was dismissed by the District of Columbia, however the U.S. Court of Appeals for the District of Columbia reversed that decision and held that Heller's rights had been infringed.

The United States Supreme Court deliberated the case and ruled in 2008 that the federal district's law was unconstitutional due to its violation of the Second Amendment. Not only was the registration procedure unconstitutional but also was the requirement to keep firearms unloaded or otherwise non-functional in one's private residence. The Court's majority observed that the term *militia* in the Second Amendment did not intend to make such a right exclusive to government agents. Quite the contrary. Justice Scalia observed, "The militia consisted of all male citizens capable of military service. That was thought to be a protection against, not only attack from abroad, but tyranny at home.... The lesson learned, if the people cannot have arms, there will be no people's militia."[43] Scalia and the majority rejected that the two relevant clauses of the Second Amendment, the *well-regulated militia* clause and the *shall not be infringed* clause, were in conflict. The amendment declares, "A well regulated Militia, being necessary to the security of a free State, the right of the people to keep and bear Arms shall not be infringed."[44] Instead, Scalia asserted, the two clauses were in harmony. "The two clauses go together beautifully: Since we need a militia, the right of the people to keep and bear arms shall not be infringed."[45]

Two years later, the Court heard a similar case. Because *Heller* involved a law in the federal district, constitutional questions remained concerning comparable matters relating to gun laws in the separate states. The Court ruled in favor of individual gun ownership again in *McDonald* v. *City of Chicago* (2010). *McDonald* proved arguably more historic than *Heller*. By 2010, the Court had incorporated most of the Bill of Rights against the states via the Due Process Clause of the Fourteenth Amendment. This, as has been seen, after abandoning incorporation in totality via the Privileges or Immunities Clause in the late nineteenth century. Nevertheless, by 2010, most (though not all) of the Bill of Rights had been incorporated incrementally via the Due Process Clause over the preceding century. The Second Amendment was one of the few that had not.

The *McDonald* case involved a 1982 Chicago law that banned the registration of handguns and required registration for any other firearm. Residents of Chicago, including Otis McDonald, filed suit against the city for violating their Second Amendment rights. Lower courts ruled against the Chicago residents but when the case was brought before the United States Supreme Court the lower court decisions were overruled.

Prior to a discussion of the majority opinion and its concurrences, some attention to the dissents in *McDonald* is warranted. The four dissenters in *McDonald*: Justices Sotomayor, Ginsburg, Breyer, and Stevens, all denied that the Fourteenth Amendment incorporated the Second Amendment against the states. This interpretation was thus a denial of the intention of the Privileges or Immunities Clause that Congressman John Bingham and others had affirmed in the 1860s. As discussed in Chapter Six, not only did Bingham and other Republicans intend to apply all of the Bill of Rights (including the Second Amendment) against the states, but other legislation passed in the same era asserted similar aims. Most notably, the Freedmen's Bureau legislation passed to recognize the right of former slaves to keep and bear arms. The dissenters in *McDonald* thus argued against incorporation and that the Second Amendment was not a fundamental right.

Justice Alito's remarks regarding the relevant history of support for gun rights during Reconstruction by the very people who wrote the Fourteenth Amendment and related legislation is particularly enlightening:

> Armed parties often consisting of ex-Confederate soldiers serving in the state militias forcibly took arms from newly freed slaves and other blacks. The Reconstruction era Congress was alarmed by these practices. Union Army Commanders tried to stop these abuses by issuing orders, securing the right of all people to keep and bear arms, but Congress decided that more was needed. It first turned to ordinary legislation. It enacted the Freedman's Bureau Act of 1866 which explicitly guaranteed the right of all citizens "to have the full and equal benefit of the constitutional right to bear arms." The Civil Rights Act of 1866 had a similar aim, but Congress feared that these Civil Rights Laws would be held to exceed Congress' power and Congress then proposed the Fourteenth Amendment which was ratified.[46]

The Court's majority, Justices Alito, Scalia, Roberts, Thomas, and Kennedy, though together in their opinion to incorporate the Second Amendment, differed as to their legal reasoning, with Justice Thomas to one side and the rest of the majority to the other. Scalia, Roberts, Alito, and Kennedy accepted and affirmed incorporation but did so through the now traditional route of the Due Process Clause. Indeed, when McDonald's attorney, Alan Gura, asserted the Privileges or Immunities Clause during oral arguments, he was challenged by some of the conservative Justices. Justice Roberts countered Gura's Privileges or Immunities assertion and remarked that such an "argument is contrary to the *Slaughter-House Cases*, which have been law for 140 years."[47] Justice Scalia argued the same, and asked, "Why are you asking us to overrule ... 140 years of prior law, when you can reach your result under substantive due process?"[48] Such remarks are an important reminder that originalism is at times no match for judicial precedent, including for legal conservatives.

It was only Justice Thomas who asserted incorporation of the Second Amendment as a result of the Privileges or Immunities Clause, thus separating himself from the rest of the majority's devotion to the precedence of Due Process incorporation. Justice Thomas's assertion of the Privileges or Immunities Clause and his criticism of incremental and selective Due Process incorporation by the Court over the previous century-and-a-half underscores one of the major themes of this work. Substantive due process achieved through incorporation by way of the Due Process Clause has benefited citizens of the United States in comparison to the theoretical alternative of non-incorporation. Nevertheless, its foundation is fundamentally ahistorical and philosophically flawed when contrasted with the totality of incorporation which *should* have transpired via the Privileges or Immunities Clause following ratification of the Fourteenth Amendment. Thomas underscores this point when he observes that the Privileges or Immunities Clause is "far more likely to yield discernible answers than the substantive due process questions the Court has for years created on its own, with neither textual nor historical support."[49] By 2010, the Court's devotion to substantive due process relied more on judicial precedent than on the language and intent of the Fourteenth Amendment. This was true not merely of the progressive wing but for much of the supposedly originalist, conservative wing as well.

Heller and *McDonald* are critical moments in the history of the Supreme Court for their assertion of Second Amendment rights values. Though arguably cited less often than *Heller*, *McDonald* is the more historic decision between the two, because it raised the question of Second Amendment incorporation where *Heller* had not. Furthermore, *McDonald* is a historic decision because of the powerful assertions of the Privileges or Immunities Clause by Justice Thomas. Additionally, Justice Thomas's critique of the Court's long application of so-called substantive due process is noteworthy. The progressive wing of the Court denied the intent of the Fourteenth Amendment's framers to incorporate the Second Amendment against the states. Moreover, Justice Thomas illustrated that the conservative members of the Court appeared more devoted to consistency of jurisprudence and judicial precedence than fidelity to the vision of the framers of the Fourteenth Amendment.

Same-Sex Marriage

The Defense of Marriage Act was passed in 1996 by a Republican Congress and signed into law by Democratic President Bill Clinton. The federal law defined marriage as a union between one man and one woman. In the following years, individual states began to legalize same-sex marriage. This brought legal challenges to the Defense of Marriage Act and lower federal courts began ruling the law constitutional. The Supreme Court considered the issue in *United States* v. *Windsor* in 2013. Edith Windsor was the widow and sole executor of the estate of her late spouse, Thea Clara Spyer. The two had been married in Toronto, Canada and their legal union was recognized by the state of New York. Because the federal government did not recognize the legality of their marriage, when Spyer died the government imposed $363,000 in taxes on the Spyer estate.

The Supreme Court's majority held that the separate states have the authority to define marital relationships. As a result, the Defense of Marriage Act was unconstitutional and had denied the legal privilege marriage provides to same sex-couples in states that recognized such unions. The Court ruled that the law imposed the disadvantage of a separate and inferior status to same-sex couples, which violated the Fifth Amendment's guarantee of equal protection. The *Windsor* decision did not settle the matter regarding same-sex marriage so much as raise further questions once it was regarded as legally legitimate in the states that recognized it. As Keith Whittington observes, "In the aftermath of *Windsor*, the remaining states rapidly moved toward recognizing same-sex marriage (primarily by court decision)."[50] Suddenly the question over the constitutionality of same-sex marriage was inverted. Prior to *Windsor*, the question was whether the federal government could deny the recognition of same sex unions in states that had legalized the practice. In the post–*Windsor* scenario, the question soon became whether states that had not recognized same sex marriage could continue to do so.

In 2015, the Court's *Obergefell* v. *Hodges* decision established a federal recognition of same-sex marriage nationwide, thus nullifying all state-level prohibitions. Justice Kennedy, writing for the majority of the Court, asserted that the "fundamental liberties protected by the Fourteenth Amendment's Due Process Clause extend to certain personal choices central to individual dignity and autonomy, including intimate choices defining personal identity and beliefs."[51] He added, "same-sex couples seek in marriage the same legal treatment as opposite-sex couples, and it would disparage their choices and diminish their personhood to deny them this right."[52] Justice Kennedy further remarked that restrictions against same-sex marriage in the states where such restrictions persisted (at the time of the *Obergefell* decision, that number was thirteen) burdened "the *liberty* of same-sex couples, and they abridge central precepts of *equality*."[53] By making these assertions, the constitutionality and full legality of same-sex marriage was recognized through both the Due Process and Equal Protection Clauses of the Fourteenth Amendment.

The conservative dissenters argued that there was no such liberty or equal protection guarantee which provided for the legal recognition of same sex marriage. Chief Justice John Roberts articulated strong disagreement over the Court rejecting the historical roots of biologically-defined marriage and for not continuing to leave the matter to the individual states. In his *Obergefell* dissent, Roberts lamented, "Allowing unelected federal judges to select which unenumerated rights rank as 'fundamental'—and to strike down state laws on the basis of that determination—raises obvious concerns about the judicial role."[54] Though his argument concerning the importance of federalism should not be dismissed, his criticism of the judicial power's role in recognizing the existence of fundamental rights—especially those which are unenumerated—is disconcerting. It poses the question as to whether Chief Justice Roberts denies the Court should ever assert an unenumerated right as fundamental. If rights are to be retained by the people, including unenumerated rights—which the Ninth Amendment asserts exist—and if the role of the Court is to nullify laws which infringe on the rights of the people, then such determinations are precisely within the purview of the Court.

Intertwined Liberties

Free speech issues that simultaneously involved facets of economic liberty posed constitutional questions for the Court in the second decade of the twenty-first century. In 2010, the Court ruled on *Citizens United* v. *Federal Election Commission.* The case concerned a federal election law called the Bipartisan Campaign Reform Act (BCRA), passed in 2002. The law was often referred to in the press as McCain-Feingold, referring to the bipartisan sponsors of the legislation, Arizona Republican Senator John McCain and Wisconsin Democratic Senator Russ Feingold. Among the provisions of the legislation, which amended aspects of the Federal Election Campaign Act of 1971, were disclosure requirements for campaign donors and restrictions upon what the law deemed *electioneering communications.*

A conservative nonprofit corporation called Citizens United sought to broadcast a film called *Hillary: The Movie,* in 2008 with a message that explicitly opposed the candidacy of New York Senator Hillary Rodham Clinton for President of the United States. At the time of the making of the film, Clinton was the predicted nominee for the Democratic Party for the 2008 Presidential Election. In reality, she would lose late in the primary season to Illinois Senator Barack Obama. Citizens United had wanted to broadcast the film to video-on-demand formats and advertise the film prior to the beginning of the 2008 Democratic Primary. The corporation anticipated financial and criminal penalties for broadcasting the film due to the proscriptions outlined in the campaign law. The relevant provision of the BCRA prohibited the broadcast of media, funded by corporate or union general treasury funds, that unambiguously referred to a specific candidate (either in support or opposition) for federal office sixty days prior to a general election and thirty days prior to a primary election. Citizens United ultimately challenged several provisions of the BCRA as unconstitutional.

When the United States Supreme Court handed down its opinion in 2010, after having ordered reargument the following term on the broader questions raised by the case, it upheld the disclosure requirements outlined in the Bipartisan Campaign Reform Act, as well as the law's prohibition against direct contributions from corporations and unions. The controversy arising from the decision, however, came from the Court's ruling that restrictions on political speech funded by corporations (or unions) was a violation of the First Amendment. Justice Kennedy observed, speaking for the Court's majority, "If the First Amendment has any force, it prohibits Congress from fining or jailing citizens, or associations of citizens, for simply engaging in political speech."[55] He further asserted that political speech is no less indispensable and no less true merely "because the speech comes from a corporation rather than an individual."[56]

The criticism of the decision in regard to the protection of speech rights for corporations was considerable. Justice Stevens's dissent illustrated what many who disagreed with the *Citizens United* decision felt. Justice Stevens argued that the American founders "held a cautious view of corporate power and a narrow view of corporate rights."[57] He further asserted that the creators of the First Amendment did not subscribe to "a principle that could be used to insulate corporations from even modest restrictions on electioneering expenditures."[58] Stevens ardently contended in his dissent that money "is property, it is not speech…. These property rights are not entitled to the same protection as the right to say what one pleases."[59]

There were many Americans who saw the decision in the manner Justice Stevens had framed it in his dissent: that if the utilization of funds by a corporation is a protected form of political speech, then those with money have more speech than those who do not. Stevens, and critics of *Citizens United* who shared his view, believed the decision granted free speech rights onto money itself. Justice Scalia, in his concurrence with the majority, disputed Stevens's view of the decision and of the First Amendment. Scalia maintained that Stevens was in "splendid isolation from the text of the First Amendment…. The Amendment is written in terms of 'speech,' not speakers … [and] offers no foothold for excluding any category of speaker, from single individuals to … incorporated associations of individuals."[60]

The significance of the free speech element of the *Citizens United* case is often ignored, though it motivated the reasoning behind the decision. Enticing as it may be for some to interpret the ruling as a carte blanche giveaway to corporate power and the enormous wealth associated with it, an examination of the oral arguments reveal a more nuanced truth. When Justice Alito asked Deputy Solicitor General Malcolm Stewart during oral argument if the provisions of the BCRA could restrict political speech in the form of a book much as it could in the form of a film or video, Stewart affirmed that it could. Some of the Justices recognized the significance of this. Alito responded, "That's pretty incredible. You think that if a book was published, a campaign biography that was the functional equivalent of express advocacy, that could be banned?"[61] The Deputy Solicitor General answered yes.

When the case was re-argued several months later, the new Solicitor General (now Justice), Elena Kagan, was asked this question again—this time by Justice Ruth Bader Ginsburg. Solicitor General Kagan declared that the federal government's position had changed and that it was no longer making this legal argument. Justice Alito was apparently not satisfied with the government's position, however much it had ostensibly shifted. He remarked, "In light of your retraction, I have no idea where the government would draw the line with respect to the medium that could be prohibited."[62] This is arguably the crux of the argument on the free speech side of this debate. The government had originally argued its case that the BCRA could legitimately restrict film and video funded by corporations and unions during election season, and could do the same with print media including books. When re-arguments transpired half a year later the government changed its tune, but the Court then became more fixated upon First Amendment concerns as a result.

Critics of *Citizens United* would need to demarcate where the speech limits for corporations and unions should be placed if there are to be such constraints. This would not be an easy thing to do, as the federal government made evident. Furthermore, it is a mistake to see the decision as merely a benefit to corporations when the decision recognized the same speech rights for labor unions as well. Additionally, many nonprofits that are politically oriented would have endured dramatically diminished speech rights if the decision had gone the other way. As Keith Whittington observes, such bans "would impose criminal sanctions on the Sierra Club, the National Rifle Association, or the American Civil Liberties Union if any of them ran ads near Election Day urging Americans to vote in a particular way."[63] How this is not a violation of First Amendment protections of speech, organizing, and association is a burden to be proven by those who seek to restrict such rights. The federal government failed to offer that proof.

Those in academic scholarship must similarly address the free speech questions at the heart of *Citizens United* if they are to offer a convincing alternative. Critiques about the role of money in elections underscores a notable and understandable concern. Nevertheless, if the principle of free speech is avoided in such discussions, then no alternative will be sufficient for many civil libertarians. Erwin Chemerinsky, as one example, in *The Case Against the Supreme Court* (2014), references or discusses *Citizens United* in fourteen pages of his book. Nowhere, however, does he ever address matters of free speech within the context of that case. The influence of money in American elections and campaigns is not a problem to be dismissed, but ignoring core matters of free speech in this regard will not lead to a remedy.

In 2017, the Court handed down a decision which shared some features with *Citizens United*, most notably in regard to its connection between matters of economic liberty and freedom of speech. *Matal* v. *Tam* involved the Portland, Oregon, dance rock group The Slants. The band's application for a trademark was denied in 2010 by the U.S. Patent and Trademark Office on the grounds that the group's name violated the Disparagement Clause of the Lanham Act (1946). The relevant clause prohibited the trademarking of names deemed to disparage particular groups of people, institutions, or national symbols. The Slants were a group of Asian American musicians specifically seeking to co-opt the term to own it for themselves as a means of disempowering the dated slur and to wear it as a form of ethnic pride. When the Trademark Office denied their application, seemingly with the rationalization that such a trademark would be disparaging to the band themselves, the group's leader Simon Tam appealed. The Patent Trial and Appeals Board upheld the rejection of trademarking The Slants due to its connotation as an Asian slur, citing (again) the Disparagement Clause of the Lanham Act. Tam then appealed to the U.S. Court of Appeals for the Federal Circuit. The Court of Appeals initially ruled against The Slants, but in a radical move reversed themselves several days later and opened the case *en banc* (a rare instance when the U.S. Circuit Court of Appeals deems a case to be of enough significance so as to be heard by the entire twelve-judge panel). The Court of Appeals ultimately ruled in favor of The Slants. The U.S. Patent and Trademark Office appealed the decision to the United States Supreme Court.

In a unanimous decision, the Court ruled the Disparagement Clause of the Lanham Act unconstitutional. Justice Alito wrote the majority opinion, with Justices Kennedy and Thomas writing concurrences. Alito observed the importance of protecting all forms of speech, including that which many would find disparaging. "Speech that demeans on the basis of race, ethnicity, gender, religion, age, disability, or any other similar ground is hateful; but the proudest boast of our free speech jurisprudence is that we protect the freedom to express 'the thought that we hate.'"[64] He added that the Lanham Act's Disparagement Clause sought to police both the content and tone of speech through administrative law. He asserted that the Disparagement Clause "is not an anti-discrimination clause; it is a happy-talk clause. In this way, it goes much further than is necessary to serve the interest asserted."[65]

Mutually, *Citizens United* and *Matal* v. *Tam* recognize the precarious balance and deep-rooted connection between free speech and economic liberty. In *Citizens United*, this balance concerned the political speech rights of unions, nonprofits, and corporations during campaigns. *Matal* v. *Tam* involved the speech rights of artists and entrepreneurs bringing creative content into the commercial sphere and being free to utilize labels and names not everyone may like or understand. In both cases, rights of speech were inextricably linked with facets of economic liberty in ways that are not easy—and may not be entirely possible—to sever.

More Than a Century of Rights Assertions

Ramos v. *Louisiana* (2020), referenced in the introduction of this work, is merely a recent example of the United States Supreme Court nullifying a law due to its violation of rights values enshrined in the Constitution. Some Court decisions have nullified state statutes, such as *Ramos*. Others have overruled federal laws, whether those enacted by Congress such as the Defense of Marriage Act or administrative rules written by agencies like the U.S. Patent and Trademark Office. Assertions of rights values have at times recognized explicit language in the Constitution or the Bill of Rights that protect enumerated rights. In other moments, the Court has observed the existence of unenumerated rights—a concept informed by the natural rights assertions of the American founders and alluded to in the Ninth Amendment.

The Court slowed the progress of rights recognition when it retreated from employing the Privileges or Immunities Clause in its fully-intended capacity. Over time, however, through a novel theory of substantive due process, many of the amendments in the Bill of Rights were nevertheless incorporated as a standard against the separate states. This process of incremental and selective incorporation was nowhere near as immediate or radical as the full application of the Bill of Rights would have been through the Privileges or Immunities Clause. That said, the success in the expansion of rights recognition through the twentieth and twenty-first centuries in the United States via judicial review is noteworthy. A utilization of the principles of substantive due process and equal protection slowly revolutionized the nation. This is not because the Supreme Court has fulfilled a Whiggish view of inevitable historical human progress. On the contrary, the Court's many failures of judgment regarding constitutional fidelity make its successes all the more significant.

The administrative approach of Footnote Four created in the late 1930s informed a desire to articulate a protocol for when strict scrutiny ought to be applied in cases brought to the Court. For all its attempts to convey a way forward, however, Footnote Four's default position to treat legislation with a presumption of constitutionality—i.e., rational basis— drove American jurisprudence still further away from its core principles of inherent individual rights and limited state powers. Furthermore, it was a procedure that offered no help when unenumerated rights of privacy and liberty came to the fore beginning in the 1960s.

The cases discussed in this chapter highlight the essential role of rights values regarding the power of judicial review. The ultimate purpose in discussing such cases is to underscore that the Court tends to forsake its constitutional mandates at the moment it abandons the rights values that inform them. One need not agree with every decision discussed above. Indeed, a belief that the Court has always been correct betrays the nuanced argument within this work. It is critical, however, to recognize the relationship between a devotion to the role of individual rights, both enumerated and unenumerated, which inform the natural and civil rights philosophy of the Constitution, and the Court's power to nullify laws which violate those very rights. Any legitimate argument for judicial review necessitates constitutional commitment and respect to the rights values that are foundational to the American project.

Conclusion

Judicial Review and the Court Today

The Supreme Court's power of judicial review is unique to the American project and fundamental to its operation. It has been routinely attacked by politicians and scholars across the ideological spectrum for nearly as long as the republic has been in existence. Thomas Jefferson rejected the Court's power to determine a law's constitutionality and nullify legislation it deemed repugnant in the early nineteenth century. The power was utilized for the most egregious purposes in the mid-nineteenth century with the *Dred Scott* decision and its application in that case deserved condemnation in the 1850s and after. Progressives in the late nineteenth and early twentieth centuries saw the judicial power as a threat to the legislature. Conservatives critical of the expansion of rights recognition during the Civil Rights era in the middle of the twentieth century similarly accused the Court of legislating from the bench, and the next generation of conservative politicians and legal scholars in the 1980s and 1990s also condemned judicial review for not expressing deferential treatment to Congress. Attacks against the judicial power in the first two decades of the twenty-first century became more bipartisan overall, but political progressives have been more vocal in expressing a desire to make the Court more representative and democratic.

The threat of so-called *packing* the Court with likeminded legal minds, once thought to be a relic of a failed strategy of the Franklin Roosevelt administration, was re-introduced in the Democratic Primary in 2019. A commission was established to investigate the possibility of packing the Court (as well as other potential reforms, including judicial term limits) in April 2021, and several members of Congress expressed advocacy for such changes. The commission ultimately rejected the idea in its report in December 2021, but such proposals may well persist into the future. It is an idea that threatens the very purpose of the Court. The judiciary is not meant to be another representative body. To act as though the interpreters of law, and defenders of the supreme law, which is the Constitution of the United States, are no different than the House of Representatives or the U.S. Senate is a terribly misguided premise. Furthermore, preserving the Court's present size and procedural makeup advocates neither a conservative nor a progressive position. Though conservatives and libertarians may at the moment express the most apprehension regarding packing the Court, progressives like Justice Ruth Bader Ginsburg—not long before her death—expressed her desire for the Court (as we know it) to endure. Justice Stephen Breyer expressed a similar sentiment in April 2021, warning that packing the Court could erode the public trust.

The Court has changed in size over the centuries, from as few as five to as many as ten. The fact that the size of the Court has changed over time provides (for some) a rationalization to do so again. The size of the Court changed for various reasons. Some of those reasons were due to westward expansion and an increase in Circuit Courts, while others were, like present-day, political. It is difficult to comprehend doing so in the modern era, however, as it would be to achieve such overtly self-serving aims. It would arm one party with amplified power over another, and in turn, would encourage the opposition party to do the same whenever they regain majority status. Congress, however, regardless of party, has a knack for exploiting short-term political advantage that ultimately yields long-term damage to its credibility and the health of the nation. Thus, court-packing may yet come to pass.

Unlike most previous eras, it appears that instead of disputing the legitimacy of the judicial power itself, however, proponents of legislative supremacy seek to dilute the Court by transforming it into something closer to a third house of Congress. What would the Court look like if it became a third representative body of the federal government? What would be the ramifications if a political party with majority power—regardless of whether it was the Democratic Party, the Republican Party, or any other—increased the size of the Court in order to make it more friendly to its particular platform? The purpose of the Court would no longer be to interpret the law and defend the individual rights of the people. Rather, it would be to abide by the political platform of those in power, regardless of whether or not such a platform aligns with constitutional principles. There would be a potential erosion of the separation of powers to a degree never before seen in the history of the United States.

There is a sort of inherent hubris to American politics. This hubris involves a majority party assuming its majority position will endure. Political parties in power understandably seek avenues and policies that will increase their chances of continued dominance. Playing with the makeup of the Court is one possible means of doing so. That said, what is to become of a Court—transformed by one political party in power—if the opposition party then prevails at a later time? The implicit legitimacy of precedent would thus allow the next party in power to further increase the size of the Court to represent *its* interests. A practice could soon develop in which a regular part of the American political process would be an increase in the Court's number of Justices in response to a new political regime taking power, thus representing the party that was victorious in the most recent election. The result of a Court that increases in number for the express purpose of mirroring the prevailing political party of a given era will subvert the purpose of an independent judiciary and make the role of Justice no less political than that of a member of Congress. The people would lose the one body that was intended to be most removed from the political process; most removed precisely because they are to interpret the constitutionality of laws based on a fidelity to the country's founding charters and the rights values that informed them. The judiciary was designed to be a branch not representative of the passions of a voting public or the posturing of elected officials. A Court transformed so routinely by political trends, platforms, and election cycles is a mark of an unstable regime, not an enduring nation of laws. A durable constitutional republic founded upon individual rights and separation of powers requires an independent judiciary, not a Court that acts as a secondary Senate.

None of this is to say that there has not been a growing politicization regarding the judiciary over the years. Nearly every nomination process becomes fodder for grandstanding and predictions of falling skies by members of one party or another. It is significant to note, however, that the growing politicization of the judiciary, including the nomination process, is employed by those in elected positions. Thus, it is elected politicians who are most guilty of politicizing the judiciary and the judicial nomination process. Considering this fact, it is a bizarre assumption to think that making judges and Justices less independent would be a solution to this problem. Interpreting this politicization as somehow the fault of judges and those in the legal field rather than those who make politics their living also misses a larger point: the inevitability of increased politicization when rights are at stake.

Using the Judiciary for Seeking Justice

The 1963 Supreme Court decision of *NAACP* v. *Button* affirmed the constitutional legitimacy of litigation as a form of political expression. For much of American legal history prior to this, the utilization of so-called *test cases* (in which persons intentionally have themselves arrested in order to challenge a law's constitutionality) was seen as an abuse of the judicial process. The Court in *Button*, however, held that the courts are sometimes the last and only means for persons—particularly minorities (racial, political, or otherwise)—to find a remedy regarding the deprivation of their rights. The Court thus affirmed that the American judicial system was available to those who may not possess significant political representation. This is significant, as it underscored the judiciary's role in the recognition and protection of fundamental rights, particularly because the rights of certain groups or individuals might be dismissed if left exclusively to elected politicians and majority rule. With this in mind, it becomes far less remarkable that the Court has been viewed in more political terms since the early-to-mid twentieth century, as it became more central to recognizing individual rights, at the cost of reining in members of both major political parties in the other branches of government. It is thus not surprising that politicians who make their success from the popular will of their constituencies would condemn the Court for not being more deferential or representative. This is all the more relevant when considering that advocacy through the Court has been necessary at times to protect the rights of those with far less political power. When one's bread and butter is reliant upon popular majorities, denouncing an institution that exists to protect political minorities and restrain democratic overreach becomes a convenient and effective strategy. It is a tactic employed by members of both major political parties, and it is these tactics—in combination with the Court's exceeding role in the recognition of rights values—that contributes to politicization.

The Court's role in recognizing rights, however, and its authority to assert an unconstitutional law void through its power of judicial review, is its most salient feature. It is up to the elected politicians, then, to stop criticizing the Court for doing precisely what it was designed to do and respect its power to say what the law is. If politicization of the judiciary, and particularly the judicial nomination process, is going to be tempered, it will have to be done by those representing the people. Elected officials simply cannot constitutionally flout the rulings of the Court. It is in their power, however, and is arguably their duty, to restrain the worst tendencies of demagoguery and instead use their platform to appeal to the better angels of their constituencies. Urging the American people to not respect or appreciate the role of the Court to act as an undemocratic check against the otherwise democratic design of government is to undermine the constitutional system itself.

Ideologies and Misconceptions

There are some deep misconceptions regarding the ideology of the Court, contributed to in no small manner by an ill-informed population and an exceedingly politicized press. Though there are certainly differences of opinion regarding jurisprudence and constitutionality on the Supreme Court, reducing the variety of legal opinion to a conservative wing versus a progressive wing obscures a more nuanced truth. For example, the *Ramos* v. *Louisiana* (2020) decision, discussed in the introduction of this book, contended with the incorporation of the Sixth Amendment's right to a jury trial and a state's use of nonunanimous jury convictions. A simplistic and dichotomous view of the Court as *progressives versus conservatives* might lead one to assume that incorporation in the *Ramos* case would have been denied by conservatives and embraced by progressives. This is because it is too often accepted that conservatives resist change and progressives welcome it. Such crude assumptions do not reflect reality. The supposedly conservative Justice Neil Gorsuch, writing for the majority of the Court, embraced incorporation of the Sixth Amendment against the states via the Fourteenth Amendment. Among the legal reasoning employed by Justice Gorsuch was the blatantly racist motivations in the history of nonunanimous jury convictions and the importance of upholding rights for the accused. Those who voted against incorporation of the Sixth Amendment's right to a trial by jury included the supposedly progressive Justice Elena Kagan. Furthermore, in the final Supreme Court decision discussed in Chapter Eight, *Matal* v. *Tam* (2017), the Court ruled unanimously for the dance rock group, The Slants, to be able to trademark their name regardless of its known history as a disparaging term for Asian Americans. Every member of the Court who deliberated the *Matal* v. *Tam* case understood the intertwining liberties of artistic expression, political expression, and entrepreneurship involved. Attempting to frame every legal decision through a progressive/conservative, left/right lens is a fool's game and intellectually limiting. The premise of the Court as a body with warring ideological wings is far too simplistic of a supposition to be particularly accurate. It evades the nuances of various legal interpretations and how they may overlap, and misses the apolitical mission of the Supreme Court as one with specific constitutional interests as its focus. Certainly, different members of the Court provide different interpretations. Written majority decisions, concurrences, and dissents are provided for the very reason of articulating differing perspectives. Reducing the differences of legal opinion to naked partisanship, however, does not withstand honest and objective scrutiny. Doing so also emphasizes a view that the Court is a political body like any other, which is a premise this work roundly rejects, precisely because of its role as a counter-majoritarian check against the more overtly political aspects of the United States government.

The Precarious Position of the Court

There is, however, a precarious position the American judiciary and the United States Supreme Court in particular finds itself. Though its most important function is to enforce an (at times) undemocratic safeguard against undue legislative or executive power to preserve the rights of We the People, its legitimacy is dependent upon the confidence of the American populace. The irony is, then, that the undemocratic Court must measure its power to provide unpopular decisions against the ability of the population to honor and respect such rulings. The people will endure unpopular decisions, and indeed have. Some rulings by the Court were initially quite unpopular but eventually became widely accepted and even celebrated, including the *Miranda* case discussed in Chapter Eight. In this way, the American people have accepted the role of judicial review, including some of its most controversial iterations. The Court must nevertheless remain cognizant, however, that the patience and confidence of the people is not an unlimited reservoir. Even an institution designed to exercise an undemocratic impulse against the representative branches must recognize the limits of its own power and its own legitimacy to do so. Just as elected politicians endanger the credibility of the Court when they unnecessarily politicize the nomination process, members of the judiciary may potentially endanger their own reputation when they overstep their bounds and must never forget that the will of the people is a factor in every decision, even (and especially) when a ruling goes against popular opinion. Just as judicial review acts as a check against unrestrained democracy, the will of the people restrain the Court from becoming a tyranny itself because its credibility requires the implicit acceptance of the people for its own survival.

It is to be remembered that this question of legitimacy was similarly brought to the fore as a result of the *Bush* v. *Gore* decision in 2000. The Court's decision to stop Florida's recount was seen by many among the American people as a violation of the electoral process and an egregious move that put George W. Bush into power. Though there remain many who criticize the Court for that ruling, and the domestic and foreign policy blunders that followed in its wake (including after Bush's re-election in 2004), the Court was able to more or less rehabilitate itself in the eyes of the American people. That said, decades after *Bush* v. *Gore*, the American people are far more politically polarized. Perhaps, in due time, the legitimacy of the Court and its power of judicial review will survive and even thrive, much as it lost legitimacy after *Dred Scott* v. *Sandford* in 1857, yet nevertheless became an essential advocate of rights values over the many decades that followed. Perhaps recent accusations of the Court's illegitimacy will ultimately prove to be overstated. Time will tell.

Reviewing Judicial Review: History and Practice

Following the introduction, this book began by providing a wealth of primary source evidence for judicial review's legitimacy and practice going back to the American Revolution and the creation of the new constitutional republic. The work of scholars such as William E. Nelson reveal the practice to have been alive and well going farther back still to the colonial era. The work of historians such as Gordon Wood and Pauline Maier have also demonstrated how the dissolution of independent courts during the imperial crisis has been an oft-overlooked motivator for the American Revolution. In the 1780s, prior to establishing a new national Constitution, state courts employed aspects of judicial review in noteworthy and substantial ways. In some cases they challenged the legitimacy of legislation, such as *Rutgers* v. *Waddington* in New York in 1784, and other cases rebuked egregious practices dating back to the earliest decades of Colonial America, including when the Massachusetts Court declared slavery unconstitutional and repugnant to its charter's Declaration of Rights in 1783.

The newly established federal judiciary exercised judicial review in the 1790s with a Supreme Court that included figures who had recognized and championed the judicial power during the state ratification debates. Various members of the Philadelphia Convention had asserted that the judiciary would be empowered to nullify unconstitutional legislation. Antifederalists who urged opposition to ratification also alluded to judicial review, with figures like Brutus issuing it as a warning of the judiciary's supremacy over the legislature and Patrick Henry claiming that the new federal judiciary would not possess the fortitude necessary to exercise its legitimate power to counter unconstitutional laws. The primary sources provided in Chapter One were presented to arm the reader with such evidence prior to an analysis of judicial review scholarship. This evidence was also offered to underscore that the practice by the judiciary to review and check the legislative power was discussed and practiced long before Chief Justice John Marshall's assertion of the judicial power in *Marbury* v. *Madison* in 1803.

The scholarship relating to judicial review in Chapter Two included a combination of political science, legal research, and historical works. Because of this, the chapter discussed scholarship that was rooted in legal history while other works were more prescriptive. Judicial review is an inherently interdisciplinary enterprise, and contending with studies of not merely differing interpretations but also different goals is to some degree inevitable. This is true especially of a topic like judicial review because it includes champions and detractors, as well as those who recognize its history but not necessarily its legitimacy. Still others have denied its historical role. Thus, the chapter sought to wrestle with many schools of thought and aims at once.

Most of all, with the additional help of the first chapter, Chapter Two sought to refute the claim that the judicial power was not rooted in the American founding and was unimaginable to the framers. Its objective then was to address the common criticisms among scholars advocating for legislative supremacy as an alternative. The faith in legislative power via elected officials from James Bradley Thayer in the late nineteenth century to Jeremy Waldren in the early twenty-first century do not sufficiently address the threat of majoritarian tyranny that constitutionalism and judicial review offer. Criticism of the use of judicial review in particular circumstances is warranted and this work has offered condemnation of its misuse throughout. However, Chapter Two's examination of the scholarship asserts that a critique of the Court and advocacy of unrestrained democracy need not be conflated. The chapter additionally intended to demonstrate that deep analysis of the history of judicial review in recent decades has not been accomplished generally by historians (William E. Nelson and Mary Sarah Bilder excepted) as by political scientists like Keith Whittington. Whittington's statistical analysis of judicial review in his 2019 work, *Repugnant Laws*, will be helpful to scholars of judicial review from numerous fields for years to come.

Some works, however, have provided critiques without offering many answers. Erwin Chemerinsky's 2014 work, *The Case Against the Supreme Court*, for example, offers hundreds of pages of denunciation regarding the Court, but despite this (and despite the book's title), Chemerinsky refuses to abandon judicial review in the end. Some of the literature, then, condemns the judicial power but presents no significant alternative. Other works by scholars previously mentioned advocate absolute eradication of judicial review for legislative supremacy and implicitly assume elected representatives will not exclude or exploit political minorities. Neither of these approaches are satisfactory.

It is hoped that by offering a historiography of judicial review scholarship from various fields and with various objectives, that the uniqueness of this work can be appreciated. Analysis of judicial review among historians—particularly beyond the scope of the early nineteenth century—has been lacking in recent decades. Legal scholars such as Akhil Reed Amar and Randy Barnett have provided valuable understanding into matters of legal theory but not always the most thorough analysis of the pertinent intellectual history. Political scientists have offered useful statistics to draw from in some cases but in other instances have championed a form of legislative supremacy that borders on utopianism. This work has instead sought to utilize the best data from the realm of political science, cogent insights offered by leading legal theorists, and the most relevant evidence provided by legal and intellectual historians to offer something new.

Thomas Jefferson and James Madison asserted the principle of state nullification to resist the enforcement of unconstitutional federal laws in the late 1790s. This has rarely been appreciated by historians as a possible alternative for judicial review and has too often been conflated with later instances of nullification and ties with southern slavery. Jefferson and Madison's nullification arguments did not offer the stability and final word of constitutionality that judicial review would prove to accomplish, but it was nevertheless an understandable theory of state power employed to challenge the legitimacy of the Alien and Sedition Acts of the Adams Administration. The speech restrictions and other provisions of the Alien and Sedition Acts acted as a lynchpin to events that transpired from 1798 to 1803. The controversy motivated Jefferson and Madison to interpose with their theory of nullification, John Marshall ran for Congress against the policy, and the unpopularity of the legislation ultimately contributed to the downfall of President John Adams and his Federalist Party. The Republicans swept Congress and Jefferson ultimately won the White House. As a result, to shore up and secure vestiges of political power for his party, Adams appointed Federalists to judgeships in the final days of his tenure, including the appointment of John Marshall to Chief Justice. This series of events led to the *Marbury* v. *Madison* case in 1803, in which Chief Justice Marshall explicitly asserted judicial review to be a key component of American jurisprudence. Though the practice had previously been exercised by both state and federal courts, the *Marbury* decision marked a new era for the Court and the nation. The Marshall Court generally contributed to federal power in the succeeding decades, helping to facilitate the mission of national power and westward expansion. One important exception to this was the *Barron* v *Baltimore* decision in 1833 that affirmed that the Bill of Rights did not apply to the individual state governments. The nationalist policy of the Marshall Court, however, generally assisted in the growth of a federal government that enforced Indian Removal in the 1830s. The Taney Court that followed eroded federal restrictions upon slavery in the 1850s and contributed to the coming of the Civil War.

The Fourteenth Amendment was ratified both to reverse the egregious Dred Scott decision and to enforce the Bill of Rights against the separate states. The Supreme Court failed to interpret the Fourteenth Amendment in this way initially but over a period of many decades began to apply selective incorporation in place of immediate and full incorporation of the Bill of Rights. Though the progress was slow and failed to immediately abide by the intent of the framers of the Fourteenth Amendment, the expansion of rights recognition via the Court in the twentieth and twenty-first centuries underscored the centrality it began to occupy in the American project. Many rights recognized and respected today would never have come to pass if they had been left to a democratic majority, and it is only through judicial review and the enforcement of the Bill of Rights against the states via the Fourteenth Amendment that made it possible.

The Legitimacy and Limits of Emergency Powers

At the time of this writing, the United States and the world has endured about three years of complications resulting from a global pandemic. Beginning in March 2020, public spaces, schools, and businesses that operate with public accommodations were shut down for the sake of public health. Since then, states and countries have reopened and restrictions have lifted, though the threat of other strains make potential closures and restrictions in the future a possibility. The development and distribution of vaccines progressed at a pace never before seen. In many pockets of the nation and the world, something resembling life prior to the pandemic has returned.

The Supreme Court ruled in November 2020 (*Roman Catholic Diocese of Brooklyn, New York,* v. *Andrew Cuomo, Governor of New York*) and again in February 2021 (*South Bay United Pentecostal Church* v. *Gavin Newsom, Governor of California*) that broad and arbitrary restrictions implemented against the organizing of persons attending religious services were unconstitutional. More rulings regarding the deprivation of liberty among Americans due to policies implemented over recent years are likely to continue. Those critical of such decisions must contemplate whether restrictions against political protest, also a notable feature of 2020, could or should be restricted under the same rationale for restricting church attendance. Defending the First Amendment under the right of protest and defying First Amendment values regarding rights of fellowship and worship is to cherry pick rights which emanate from the same principle. Natural rights of speech, movement, and organization do not belong to one policy or platform. Rights know no party, and exist within friend and foe alike.

On January 13, 2022, the United States Supreme Court nullified President Joe Biden's Executive Order that sought to impose a vaccine mandate through the Occupational Safety and Health Administration (OSHA) upon private businesses with one hundred or more employees. Such impositions require, at the very least, laws made by the duly elected representatives of the people and cannot be directed by the executive branch from on high. It is doubtful that the U.S. Congress could find the necessary votes for such a mandate within their ranks, considering the controversial nature of such decisions. Furthermore, whether the Court would recognize the constitutionality of such a mandate, even if it were the result of a vote by legislators, is a separate question that may find its way to the Supreme Court one day. *Jacobson v. Massachusetts* (1905) saw the Court uphold a smallpox vaccine mandate. Seeing the case as potential precedent, however, may be misguided, as comparisons between Covid-19 and smallpox (and their respective vaccines) may strain credulity for some. Furthermore, the mandate that was upheld in 1905 derived from a state law that allowed for enforcement through a city ordinance and was not a federal directive. Thus far, the Court has not ruled explicitly on the constitutionality of a federal vaccine mandate put forward by the legislative branch.

It can be fairly acknowledged that the judiciary has otherwise exercised a reasonable level of patience, seeking to allow the other federal branches and the separate states (and their subsidiary counties and municipalities) to exercise their legitimate powers, especially in a time of emergency. Emergency powers, however, cannot be legitimately exercised indefinitely, and the day may soon come when the Court begins overruling more policies that have otherwise been allowed to persist. In times when matters concern something like a global pandemic, most reasonable people can understand the need for governments to exercise certain powers for the sake of protecting public health. This is true particularly when concerns regarding international relations, economic policy, public education, and medicine all hang in the balance. No defense of liberty necessitates an attack upon scientifically-based, public welfare-oriented measures intended to curtail a legitimate threat to public health.

Regardless, the history of the United States is littered with instances of emergency powers, from the Espionage Act to Japanese American internment to the Patriot Act, that sought to rationalize state power in the name of public safety. Warning against state overreach is arduous enough during times of peace and prosperity. Advocating for measured policies that address the matter at hand while not betraying fundamental principles of natural and civil rights becomes potentially dangerous in times of calamity, underscoring that a defense of liberty grows in difficulty as rationalizations for government power gain steam.

Protagonists of history are often pariahs in their own time. Those who protested against the military draft during World War I were vilified as traitors to their country and jailed for their dissent. A century later, a number of American politicians and media figures who previously supported both the Patriot Act and the Iraq War now regret those decisions.

They include members of both major political parties who possess vary-ing views and beliefs. It is only in retrospect that some are able to compre-hend that they had at some point in their past abandoned the rights values they otherwise embraced and championed. In such a scenario, democ-racy was of little help, because popular opinion was on their side. Only a system employing a process of checking and countering popular opinion can address such challenges. This process too can fail in its duty to uphold rights values, as the Court has at times done, but the United States would not benefit from possessing no such check at all, particularly in times of crisis.

As for the political and cultural ramifications of the *Dobbs* decision from June 2022, it could be that the abortion issue may prove to represent the limits of judicial review. If it is a matter that is ever—to any reasonable degree—settled, it is currently unknowable to us whether such a settle-ment will be achieved through federalism (state legislatures), congressio-nal statute, or some future judicial decree. The difficult truth may well be that no resolution is possible. If true, it is an open question as to how the republic that is the United States will endure.

Perhaps the era of judicial review, particularly rights assertions via the Court, is over. Perhaps the next phase of the unfolding of history of the United States is an overt return to Jefferson and Madison-style arguments for nullification, circa 1798. Perhaps calls by nullification advocates for a *national divorce* will be heeded by more Americans along the political spectrum. Perhaps the nineteenth, twentieth, and early twenty-first centu-ries will become known as the era of judicial review, or possibly the *rights assertion age* of the Court. Perhaps federal laws over abortion and other divisive issues will vacillate wildly back and forth, subject to the whims of the political party that happens to wield power at a given moment. For all of the upheaval over current controversies, it is difficult to believe that such unrest every election cycle would be a preferable alternative. These are the choices before the American people and their representatives, as there is no indication that a constitutional amendment to either protect or to criminalize abortion would ever possess the support necessary by a super-majority of the citizenry to achieve passage.

The American constitutional system is built upon a multi-layered dialectical process between states, between the states and the federal gov-ernment, and between the Court and the other branches. This mixture of horizontal separation of powers and vertical separation of powers is dynamic and complex by design. It is a form of rights-centered political architecture that checks and re-checks power. It is a beautifully sophisti-cated structure intended to serve a simple though critical purpose: nav-igating the limits of legitimate governance through the recognition of individual rights. It is an audacious enterprise, the most challenging in all political history. It is thus prone to stumble, as any endeavor taken up by human beings is bound to be. It is a system that nevertheless acknowledges human fallibility and the threat of concentrated power.

A rejection—or at least a vocal critique—of substantive due process could inform a positive evolution for the Court, but this has not transpired. Alito's opinion in *Dobbs*, and most of the concurrences, saw no mission to question substantive due process or its legitimacy. Justice Clarence Thomas's concurrence was the only one to do so. Nevertheless, if the Court were to turn away from substantive due process sometime in the future but do so without repositioning its focus on the Privileges or Immunities Clause, and the presumption of liberty enshrined in the principle of unenumerated rights in the Ninth Amendment, then it may take the judiciary yet farther from the rights values that have informed it for the past century.

Justice Thomas was right that substantive due process was an invention of the Court. It would be wrong, however, to assume that unenumerated rights ought not to be asserted and recognized by the Court, whether that be through the Privileges or Immunities Clause or the Ninth Amendment. The immunities referenced in the Fourteenth Amendment implies natural (or negative) rights (i.e., "rights from"). Considering that most natural rights are not enumerated, an argument can easily be made that the Fourteenth Amendment's Immunities include such unenumerated rights. If that argument does not suffice and it is settled that the Privileges or Immunities Clause was meant to recognize only the first Eight Amendments (which would itself finally establish full incorporation as the amendment's authors had intended), the power and the principle of the Ninth Amendment nevertheless endures and should be asserted more forcefully and directly in order to avoid a later generation of jurists (conservative, progressive, or otherwise) falling into the morass of positive law and arbitrary government power.

There is a notable difference between the Court using its power of judicial review to refer a difficult and politically divisive matter back to the people's representatives, as controversial as such a decision may be, and doing so because of a motivation to distance itself more fundamentally from its role in recognizing rights. However enflamed the warring sides of the abortion debate surely are, the longer-term and bigger question for the Court going forward will be whether it abandons its historical role as an institution that recognizes and protects unenumerated rights. Doing so could lead to the kind of legislative supremacy and positive law that betrays the essential rights values of the nation. It is ironic that the kind of legal philosophy progressives promoted in the late nineteenth and early twentieth centuries (by figures like Thayer and Holmes) might be achieved by a conservative Court in the early twenty-first century. To some degree, however, it should not be surprising. This book has clearly laid out that many all along the political spectrum in American history (and today) have favored legislative supremacy, despite its inherent majoritarian defects. It may be a direction taken in which deference to the states appeases conservatives and deference to the U.S. Congress appeases progressives; a synthesis of deference prioritization that retreats from the duty to recognize the constitutional limits of those very institutions.

Turning away from substantive due process (as unlikely as that is for the foreseeable future) would be advisable but not because of its assertion of fundamental or unenumerated rights. The problem with substantive due process is its lack of constitutional merit. It was an invention of the Court that grew stronger over time not because of constitutional veracity but because of precedent and the role of *stare decisis*. Instead, the Privileges or Immunities Clause of the Fourteenth Amendment should take its rightful place as the standard for adjudicating matters related to enumerated rights, as should the Ninth Amendment in regard to unenumerated rights. Doing so would not mean a full eradication of cultural and political controversies. That is not possible in a nation the size of the United States, with a variety of opinions regarding the most contentious of issues. It would, however, align the Court with the Bill of Rights, the intent of the framers of the Fourteenth Amendment, and the natural rights thesis of the Ninth Amendment. For all the good substantive due process did over the course of a century, it unnecessarily complicated American jurisprudence, and its flaws and limitations have become as evident as those of Footnote Four.

Rights Reign Supreme

If any chapter represents the heart of this work, it is Chapter Seven. It detours from the history of the Fourteenth Amendment's Privileges or Immunities Clause in Chapter Six and transitions through a history of American rights theory prior to exploring Supreme Court decisions over the past century in Chapter Eight. The reason for structuring the work in this way is to contextualize the role of rights values in the scheme of legal theory and constitutional thought in the American system. The United States judiciary is to some degree an accident of history. It is the culmination of an intellectual history based, uniquely, on the use of written charters that represent supreme law. Supreme law that, paradoxically, does not subscribe to the sort of legal positivism that written law implies, but to a philosophy of natural rights theory that seeks to locate the limits of legitimate state power and employs the kind of civil rights that make peaceful and prosperous societies possible.

Through the early use of colonial charters and the oversight of England's Privy Council in the seventeenth and eighteenth centuries, a political and legal culture was fostered that ignited an appreciation and devotion to constitutions and independent courts in Colonial America. Following the rise of England's Parliament in the late 1680s, the mother country became defined by its practice of legislative supremacy. Representative democracy ascended and the English courts (and the monarchy) yielded. Though local representation and principles of self-government were championed in Colonial America as well, a long and intimate history of judicial review in the colonies also contributed to a political culture separate from that of England. Though the American colonies were deprived judges who would serve during good behavior in the eighteenth century, as was practiced in England, their use of judicial review developed a deeper appreciation for the importance of an independent judiciary.

Following revolution and independence, American colonies-turned-states struggled with understanding the proper application of self-government. This struggle was in no small part related to the principle of natural rights that revolutionaries had championed throughout the war, which had been instilled in them throughout the eighteenth century in the form of treatises by Enlightenment figures like Montesquieu and Locke. The American founding generation was led by a number of figures who had been educated in history, science, and political philosophy. These framers were beneficiaries of a classical republican influence from the history of England's civil wars and Glorious Revolution, but inherited a liberal natural rights philosophy as well that focused on fundamental individual rights and the limits of state power. A history of utilizing written charters and judicial independence (including judicial review), and their precarious experiments with democracy in the 1770s and 1780s, contributed to the most unique invention in the history of political and legal theory. This novel legal theory included the following principles: (1) legislatures are not the people themselves, (2) laws do not supersede constitutions, and (3) it is the role of an independent judiciary to say what the law is and to rule unconstitutional legislation null and void. Thus We the People is not a principle of unrestrained democracy, legislative supremacy, and positive law. American self-governance is instead defined by fidelity to a constitutional order of separation of powers and the protection of fundamental rights.

The establishment of judicial review would have been a noteworthy contribution to political philosophy even in its pre–1860s form. The Court's *Barron* v. *Baltimore* decision in 1833, affirming that the Bill of

Rights did not apply to the separate states, was a legally correct but morally unsettling ruling that protected the institution of slavery. The institution was thus able to continue to grow and in some states free speech rights, including the right to protest the practice, were restricted. The creation of the Fourteenth Amendment, however, with its intent to apply the Bill of Rights against the states, later empowered the Court and repositioned it into a body that explicitly connected the power to nullify unconstitutional laws with the protection of fundamental rights. The Court stalled and stumbled over such efforts in the late nineteenth and early twentieth centuries because it failed to honor the original intent of the Privileges or Immunities Clause. Though immediate and total incorporation of the first eight amendments was not achieved, the Court's eventual application of substantive due process brought the nation closer to the aims of John Bingham and others who believed that the states were to be held to the same obligation of rights recognition as the federal government.

The early twentieth century saw the Court turn to a presumption of constitutionality in jurisprudence, advocated by scholars like James Bradley Thayer and supported by jurists like Justices Harlan and Holmes. Rational basis of constitutionality thus became the default position of the Court. Attempts to convey exceptions to rational basis, as to when strict scrutiny ought to be instead applied, were articulated and became codified, most notably in Footnote Four of the *Carolene Products* decision in 1938. Though the protection of rights of discrete and insular minorities—also known as suspect classes—were included as to when to apply strict scrutiny, the Footnote Four standard nevertheless failed to rule the internment of Japanese Americans unconstitutional in 1944.

When constitutional matters of privacy were brought to the Court in the 1960s and 1970s, and matters of liberty were presented in the 1990s and the early twenty-first century, rational basis and Footnote Four's prescription for when to apply strict scrutiny were ignored due to their uselessness in such matters. Instead, appeals to natural rights of liberty and the Ninth Amendment's assertion of unenumerated rights were employed. The recognition of rights values, both listed and unlisted, offered a remedy where the rational basis of Footnote Four and its exceptions for strict scrutiny failed. Thus, two centuries after the ratification of the Bill of Rights, the Court found the history of American rights values and the U.S. Constitution to be of help where presumptions of constitutionality and modes for navigating exceptions to the presumption had fallen short.

* * *

Americans generally charge the notion of democracy with a positive spark, and it is understandable why this is so. There exists a sincere and common belief in the enfranchisement of the entire constituency. This admirable impulse, combined with the cultural association Americans make between democracy and legal equality, nevertheless obscures the revolutionary aims of the American project and its purpose, which includes an independent court that possesses the power to nullify unconstitutional legislation. Rather than seeing judicial review as a threat to democracy, it would be an improvement to recognize that its purpose—articulated as far back as the founding—is to protect fundamental rights that may at times otherwise be insecure if left in the hands of political majorities. Fundamental rights are not a threat to a legitimate democratic process, but an unrestrained democracy certainly may be a threat to fundamental rights. It is thus incumbent upon the people to understand and appreciate the role and the purpose of judicial review in the American project. Fidelity to a constitution is not to be confused with subscribing to a philosophy of legal positivism, because legal positivism is antithetical to a belief in natural rights. Similarly, assertions that rights precede government and that certain rights are superior to majority rule is not an outright rejection of democracy. The purpose is, instead, to weigh the value of popular opinion against the virtue of fundamental individual rights. Thus, the tensions in American thought, outlined in the introduction of this work, endure. The mission, then, is to accommodate, wherever possible, the competing rights of opposing parties. This is the principle of *ordered liberty.*

It is not to be construed that recognizing and protecting rights is a straightforward affair. Indeed, the Supreme Court does not generally consider cases that are blatantly one-sided. Instead, they deliberate matters characterized by the fact that the rights of one party are in conflict and competition with the rights of another. It is not a simple matter, and the long and complicated history of American jurisprudence bears this out. This work does not make the claim that a proper ruling is always easy to apprehend or achieve. It is the purpose of this work, however, to assert that the role of judicial review is historically-rooted, constitutionally legitimate, and philosophically sound. Furthermore, this work affirms that the Court should utilize its power to nullify laws where appropriate and that such appropriateness can often be ascertained by evaluating the law in question against the United States Constitution and the rights values that inform it.

Above all, this work of intellectual history is intended to bring attention to the incredibly unique history of the judicial power in the United States. Too often couched in academic and popular history as an eccentric legal feature expressed in the early republic, such a framework ignores the intellectual history of rights theory that preceded and informed the concept of judicial review. This characterization also ignores the evolution of judicial review into an important instrument of rights theory as the United States progressed. Once the Court was armed with the power of enforcement of the Bill of Rights against the separate states through the Fourteenth Amendment, the past century particularly saw an expansion of rights recognition in the United States. It is the evolution in both the judicial power and the role of rights theory in the American project that detractors of judicial review must contend with. Simply put, advocates of legislative supremacy must overcome a difficult truth: many of the advancements in rights recognition over the past hundred and fifty years would not have been possible under a system based on mere majority rule.

Judicial review is a function of the American courts that enforces the principle of separation of powers when the executive or legislative branches overstep their constitutional bounds. It similarly legitimizes democracy by demarcating the limits of majoritarian rule. Most importantly, however, the judicial power asserts the essentiality of fundamental rights and their primacy in a political system based on the rule of the governed. This unique feature of American constitutional governance was influenced by a history of philosophical thought derived from both classical republican precepts and tenets of natural rights theory. These philosophical influences, combined with the experience of written charters in the colonial era and dalliances with democracy during the revolutionary era, created a system of governance never before seen in human history.

Utilizing representation but rejecting its supremacy, and championing home rule but leaning toward national and continental aims, the framers of the United States Constitution and advocates of judicial review forged a new way forward that was recognizably different from what had come before. The United States was to be a democratic system that rejected democracy as a sole arbiter of rights. This premise, articulated through the judicial power, was honed and evolved further over time, leading to a revolution of rights recognition over succeeding centuries. Rather than a design based on bandwagon rationales or arbitrary rule, judicial review—perhaps more than any other feature in the American system—acts as a reminder to the government and to the people themselves that rights reign supreme.

Chapter Notes

Introduction

1. *Ramos* v. *Louisiana*, 590 U.S. _ (2020).

2. *Ibid.*

3. *Ibid.*

4. *Ibid.*

5. *Ibid.*

6. *Ibid.*

7. Sir Edward Coke, *Bonham Case*, 1610. Co. Rep. 113b. 118a, 77 Eng. Rep. 646, 652 (C.P. 1610).

8. William Blackstone, 1 *Commentaries on the Laws of England*, 91 (1760).

9. John V. Orth, "Did Sir Edward Coke Mean What He Said?" *Constitutional Commentary* 16, no. 1 (Spring 1999), 34–35. Orth quotes Bailyn's *Ideological Origins of the American Revolution* (Cambridge: Belknap Press, 1967), 177.

10. *Ibid.*, 36.

11. *Ibid.*, 37.

12. Charles de Secondat Montesquieu, *The Spirit of the Laws*, 1748. Reprinted in *Montesquieu: Selected Political Writings*, ed. and trans. Melvin Richter (Indianapolis: Hackett, 1990), 182.

13. Alexis de Tocqueville, *The Ancien Régime and the French Revolution*, eds. Jon Elster and Arthur Goldhammer (Cambridge: Cambridge University Press, 2011), 55.

14. *Ibid.*, 144–145.

15. *Ibid.*, 203.

16. Keith Michael Baker, *Inventing the French Revolution: Essays on French Political Culture in the Eighteenth Century* (New York: Cambridge University Press, 1990), 93.

17. *Ibid.*

18. Germantown Mennonite Historic Trust, http://www.meetinghouse.info/1688-petition-against-slavery.html.

19. Germantown Petition Against Slavery, 1688, "A Minute Against Slavery, Addressed to Germantown Monthly Meeting, 1688," Germantown Mennonite Historic Trust, http://www.meetinghouse.info/uploads/1/9/4/1/19410913/a_minute_against_slavery.pdf.

20. Virginia Declaration of Rights, June 12, 1776, George Mason, National Archives, Founding Documents, https://www.archives.gov/founding-docs/virginia-declaration-of-rights.

21. Declaration of Independence (original draft), 1776, Thomas Jefferson. Reprinted in *For the Record: A Documentary History of America; Volume 1: From First Contact Through Reconstruction*, eds. David E. Shi and Holly A. Mayer (New York: W.W. Norton, 1999), 119.

22. *Ibid.*, 121.

23. New England Antislavery Society Constitution (Boston: Garrison and Knapp, 1832).

24. Frederick Douglass, Frederick Douglass Biography, *Battlefields*, https://www.battlefields.org/learn/biographies/frederick-douglass.

25. *First Convention Ever Called to Discuss the Civil and Political Rights of Women*, Seneca Falls, New York, July 19, 20, 1848. Online Text. https://www.loc.gov/item/rbcmiller001107/.

26. *Ibid.*

27. Martin Luther King, Jr., "Letter from Birmingham Jail," 1963, African Studies Center—University of Pennsylvania, https://www.africa.upenn.edu/Articles_Gen/Letter_Birmingham.html.

28. Martin Luther King, Jr., "I Have a

Dream," 1963, *Full Text March on Washington Speech*, NAACP, https://www.naacp.org/i-have-a-dream-speech-full-march-on-washington/.

29. "The Black Panther Party: Platform and Program," *The Black Panther*, July 5, 1969, in Judith Clavir Albert and Stewart Edward Albert, *The Sixties Papers: Documents of a Rebellious Decade* (New York: Praeger, 1984), 159–64.

Chapter One

1. Bernard Bailyn, *The Ideological Origins of the American Revolution* (Cambridge: Belknap Press of Harvard University Press, 1967), 105.

2. Gordon S. Wood, *Empire of Liberty: A History of the Early Republic, 1789–1815* (New York: Oxford University Press, 2009), 400.

3. Bernard Bailyn, *The Ideological Origins of the American Revolution*, 105.

4. *Ibid.*, 106.

5. William E. Nelson, *Marbury v. Madison: The Origin and Legacy of Judicial Review* (Lawrence: University Press of Kansas, 2018), 23.

6. Mary Sarah Bilder, "Idea or Practice: A Brief Historiography of Judicial Review." *Journal of Policy History* 20, no. 1 (Cambridge: Cambridge University Press, 2008), 7.

7. Keith E. Whittington, *Repugnant Laws: Judicial Review of Acts of Congress from the Founding to the Present* (Lawrence: University Press of Kansas, 2019), 43.

8. Sharon Hamby O'Connor and Mary Sarah Bilder, "Appeals to the Privy Council Before American Independence: An Annotated Digital Catalog," *Law Library Journal* 104, no. 1 (2012), 84.

9. Pauline Maier, *American Scripture: Making the Declaration of Independence* (New York: Alfred A. Knopf, 1997), 110.

10. William E. Nelson, *Marbury v. Madison: The Origin and Legacy of Judicial Review* (Lawrence: University Press of Kansas, 2018), 46.

11. *The Boston News-Letter*, September 1, 1774, reprinted in *Making the Revolution: 1763–1791*, Primary Source Collection, *America in Class*, National Humanities Center, http://americainclass.org/sources/makingrevolution/crisis/text7/coerciveactsresponse.pdf.

12. Edmund Randolph, *Notes of Debates in the Federal Convention of 1787 Reported by James Madison* (Athens: Ohio University Press, 1966), 31–32.

13. Elbridge Gerry, *Notes of Debates in the Federal Convention of 1787 Reported by James Madison*, 61.

14. Rufus King, *Notes of Debates in the Federal Convention of 1787 Reported by James Madison*, 61.

15. Elbridge Gerry, *Notes of Debates in the Federal Convention of 1787 Reported by James Madison*, 61.

16. James Wilson, *Notes of Debates in the Federal Convention*, 61.

17. *Ibid.*, 336–337.

18. James Madison, "Vices of the Political System of the United States," April 1787, *Founders Online*, National Archives, founders.archives.gov/documents/Madison/01-09-02-0187. Madison's concern regarding growing democratic sentiment in the individual states expressed his fear of majoritarian tyranny: "Place three individuals in a situation wherein the interest of each depends on the voice of the others, and give to two of them an interest opposed to the rights of the third. Will the latter be secure? The prudence of every man would shun the danger. The rules and forms of justice suppose and guard against it. Will two thousand in a like situation be less likely to encroach on the rights of one thousand?"

19. Elbridge Gerry, *Notes of Debates in the Federal Convention*, 338.

20. *Ibid.*, 342.

21. John Rutledge, *Notes of Debates in the Federal Convention*, 343. This same philosophy is regularly asserted by judicial nominees during the confirmation process when brought before the Senate Judiciary Committee.

22. James Madison, *Notes of Debates*, 462.

23. Charles Pinkney, *Notes of Debates*, 462.

24. John Mercer, *Notes of Debates*, 462.

25. John Dickinson, *Notes on Debates*, 463.

26. *Ibid.*

27. James Wilson, *Notes on Debates*, 464.

28. Madison's essays, specifically

"Federalist No. 10" and "No. 51," are among the most celebrated political writings in the history of the United States. They address how conflicting interests, or as Madison refers to them, "factions," may act as checks against each other and protect minority interests from majoritarian influence. These factions may be political interests, individuals, organizations, states, or the separate branches. Though Hamilton authored the majority of the Federalist essays, it is Madison's that are arguably more significant and compelling in their advocacy of the new republican model the Constitution was to establish.

29. "Federalist No. 22," Publius (Alexander Hamilton), 1787, reprinted in *Citizen Hamilton: The Wit and Wisdom of an American Founder* (Lanham, MD: Rowman & Littlefield, 2006), 83.

30. "Federalist No. 34," Publius (Alexander Hamilton), 1788, *The Federalist Papers*, ed. Clinton Rossiter (New York: Mentor/New American Library, 1961), 172–173.

31. "Federalist No. 78," Publius (Alexander Hamilton), 1788, *The Federalist Papers*, ed. Clinton Rossiter (New York: Mentor/New American Library, 1961), 435.

32. The moniker "Antifederalists," labelled against those opposed to ratification, was intended to cast them in contradistinction to the Constitution-supporting "Federalists." The term is ideologically confusing, however, as it was the Federalists who sought to concentrate power in a central authority. Thus, ironically, it was the so-called Antifederalists who supported a more substantial form of federalism (by preserving a weaker central authority) and it was in fact the Federalists who were antifederalist in their aims.

33. "Centinel XVI," Centinel (presumed to be Samuel Bryan), 1788, reprinted at *Teaching American History*, Documents Archive, https://teachingamericanhistory.org/library/document/centinel-xvi/.

34. The identity of Brutus is believed by modern scholars to have been either Melancton Smith or John Williams. See Zuckert and Webb, *The Anti-Federalist Writings of the Melancton Smith Circle* (2009) and Joel Johnson, "'Brutus' and 'Cato' Unmasked: General John Williams's Role

in the New York Ratification Debate," *American Antiquarian Society* (2008).

35. "Essay XII," Brutus, 1788, *The Anti-Federalist Papers and the Constitutional Convention Debates*, ed. Ralph Ketcham (New York: Signet Classics, 1986), 316.

36. *Ibid.*

37. "Essay XV," Brutus, 1788, *The Anti-Federalist Papers and the Constitutional Convention Debates*, ed. Ralph Ketcham (New York: Signet Classics, 1986), 325.

38. James Wilson, Pennsylvania Ratification Convention, "Response to [William] Findley," December 1, 1787, *The Debate on the Constitution: Federalist and Antifederalist Speeches, Articles, & Letters During the Struggle Over Ratification, September 1787 to August 1788*, ed. Bernard Bailyn (New York: The Library of America, 1993), 823.

39. Oliver Ellsworth, Connecticut Ratification Convention, January 3–9, 1788, *The Debate on the Constitution: Federalist and Antifederalist Speeches, Articles, & Letters During the Struggle Over Ratification, September 1787 to August 1788*, ed. Bernard Bailyn (New York: The Library of America, 1993), 883.

40. Patrick Henry, Virginia Ratification Convention, "Elaboration of His Main Objections," debate between Henry and James Madison, June 12, 1788, *The Debate on the Constitution: Federalist and Antifederalist Speeches, Articles, & Letters During the Struggle Over Ratification, September 1787 to August 1788*, ed. Bernard Bailyn (New York: The Library of America, 1993), 684–685.

41. Elbridge Gerry, *Notes of Debates in the Federal Convention of 1787 Reported by James Madison*, 61.

42. Peter Charles Hoffer, *Rutgers v. Waddington: Alexander Hamilton, the End of the War for Independence, and the Origins of Judicial Review* (Lawrence: University Press of Kansas, 2016), 30.

43. *Ibid.*, 46.

44. *Ibid.*, 44.

45. *Ibid.*, 70.

46. The law of nations was a principle concerning the obligation of sovereign states, particularly to each other, and establishing norms of international law. It developed first from Greek and Roman

thinkers in antiquity. Seventeenth- century philosophers and legal scholars, including the Dutch Hugo Grotius and the German Samuel von Pufendorf, popularized the concept when the idea of the nation-state was on the rise. The term arguably reached its apex in the eighteenth century with *Les Droit de gens [The Law of Nations]*, first published in 1758 and written by the Swiss Emer de Vattel. Vattel's work sought to resolve international law with principles of natural rights.

47. Peter Charles Hoffer, *Rutgers v. Waddington: Alexander Hamilton, the End of the War for Independence, and the Origins of Judicial Review* (Lawrence: University Press of Kansas, 2016), 82.

48. *Holmes* v. *Walton* (1780), "Holmes v. Walton: Case File Transcriptions and Other Materials," *New Jersey Digital Legal Library*, http://njlegallib.rutgers.edu/hw/.

49. "*Commonwealth* v. *Canton*, 8 Va. (4 Call) 5 (1782)," *George Wythe Encyclopedia*, a project of the Wolf Law Library at the College of William & Mary's Marshall-Wythe School of Law, https://lawlibrary.wm.edu/wythepedia/index.php/Commonwealth_v._Caton#Decision_of_the_Court_of_Appeals.

50. "Africans at the End of Slavery in Massachusetts," *Massachusetts Historical Society*, https://www.masshist.org/endofslavery/index.php?id=54.

51. Justice William Cushing, "Notes from the Quock Walker Case at the Supreme Judicial Court of Massachusetts," April 1783, *Massachusetts Historical Society*, MHS Collections Online, https://www.masshist.org/database/viewer.php?item_id=630&mode=transcript&img_step=13&br=1#page13.

52. *Ibid.*

53. Arthur Zilversmit, "Quok Walker, Mumbet, and the Abolition of Slavery in Massachusetts," *The William and Mary Quarterly* 25, no. 4 (1968), 623.

54. "Nathaniel Jennison to the House of Representatives," June 18, 1782 (11 Memorial of) H.R. doc. no. 956 (1782 session), Massachusetts Archives.

55. William Michael Treanor, "Judicial Review Before Marbury," *Stanford Law Review* 58, no. 455 (2005), 534.

56. *Ibid.*

57. *Hayburn's Case*, 2 U.S. (2 Dall.).

58. *Ibid.*

59. Treanor, "Judicial Review Before Marbury," 534.

60. *Chisolm* v. *Georgia* (1793), 2 U.S. 419.

61. *Ibid.*

62. Eleventh Amendment (1795), U.S. Constitution.

63. *Hylton* v. *United States*, 3 U.S. 3 Dall. 171 171 (1796).

64. *Ibid.*

65. Keith E. Whittington, *Repugnant Laws: Judicial Review of Acts of Congress from the Founding to the Present* (Lawrence: University Press of Kansas, 2019), 71.

Chapter Two

1. Joseph Story, *Commentaries on the Constitution of the United States: with a Preliminary Review of the Constitutional History of the Colonies and States Before the Adoption of the Constitution* (Boston: Little, Brown, 1873), 266.

2. *Ibid.*, 266–267.

3. *Ibid.*, 272.

4. James Bradley Thayer, "The Origin and Scope of the American Doctrine of Constitutional Law," *Harvard Law Review* VII, no. 3 (October 25, 1893), 130.

5. *Ibid.*

6. *Ibid.*, 149.

7. *Ibid.*, 156.

8. *Ibid.*

9. Louis B. Boudin, "Government by Judiciary," *Political Science Quarterly* XXVI, June 1, 1911, Internet Archive, 242.

10. *Ibid.*, 249.

11. Charles A. Beard, "The Supreme Court—Usurper or Grantee?" *Political Science Quarterly* 27, no. 1 (March 1912), 28.

12. *Ibid.*, 30.

13. *Ibid.*, 31.

14. William M. Meigs, *The Relation of the Judiciary to the Constitution* (New York: Neale, 1919), 9.

15. *Ibid.*, 10.

16. *Ibid.*, 11.

17. *Ibid.*, 17.

18. *Ibid.*, 103–104.

19. Cecelia M. Kenyon, "Men of Little Faith: The Anti-Federalists on the Nature of Representative Government," *William and Mary Quarterly* 12, no. 1 (Jan. 1955), 51.

20. *Ibid.*

21. Alexander M. Bickel, *The Least Dangerous Branch*, Second Edition (New Haven: Yale University Press, 1986), 16–17.

22. *Ibid.*, 18.

23. Charles S. Hyneman, *The Supreme Court on Trial: How the American Justice System Sacrifices Innocent Defendants* (New York: Atherton Press, 1963), 125.

24. Clinton Rossiter, *1787: The Grand Convention; The Year That Made A Nation* (New York: Macmillan, 1966), 315.

25. *Ibid.*, 50.

26. Gordon S. Wood, *Creation of the American Republic, 1776–1787* (Chapel Hill: University of North Carolina Press, 1969), 454–455.

27. Forrest McDonald, *Novus Ordo Seclorum: The Intellectual Origins of the Constitution* (Lawrence: University Press of Kansas, 1985), 276.

28. Jack N. Rakove, *Original Meanings: Politics and Ideas in the Making of the Constitution* (New York: Vantage/Random House, 1996), 186.

29. *Ibid.*, 175.

30. Mark Tushnet, *Taking the Constitution Away from the Courts* (Princeton: Princeton University Press, 1999), 194.

31. *Ibid.*, ix.

32. *Ibid.*

33. *Ibid.*, 12.

34. *Ibid.*, 126.

35. Larry Kramer, *The People Themselves: Popular Constitutionalism and Judicial Review* (New York: Oxford University Press, 2004), 249.

36. Akhil Reed Amar, *America's Constitution: A Biography* (New York: Random House, 2005), 307.

37. *Ibid.*, 217.

38. *Ibid.*, 213.

39. Jeremy Waldren, "The Core of the Case Against Judicial Review," *The Yale Law Journal* 115, no. 6 (April 2006), 1346.

40. *Ibid.*, 1353.

41. *Ibid.*, 1356.

42. *Ibid.*, 1357. Waldren discusses the role rights play in constitutional judicial decisions: "statutes are scrutinized for their conformity to individual rights."

43. *Ibid.*

44. *Ibid.*, 1406.

45. Randy Barnett, *Our Republican Constitution: Securing the Liberty and Sovereignty of We the People* (New York: HarperCollins, 2016), 126.

46. *Ibid.*, 128.

47. *Ibid.*, 271.

48. William E. Nelson, *Marbury v. Madison: The Origins and Legacy of Judicial Review*, Second Edition, Revised and Expanded (Lawrence: University Press of Kansas, 2018), 151.

49. Keith E. Whittington, *Repugnant Laws: Judicial Review of Acts of Congress from the Founding to the Present* (Lawrence: University Press of Kansas, 2019), 61.

50. *Ibid.*, 60.

51. *Ibid.*

52. *Ibid.*, 62.

53. *Ibid.*

54. *Ibid.*, 119.

Chapter Three

1. Alien and Sedition Acts (1798), Fifth Congress, Enrolled Acts and Resolutions; General Records of the United States Government; Record Group 11, *Our Documents*, National Archives, https://www.ourdocuments.gov/doc.php?flash=false&doc=16&page=transcript#.

2. Asa Earl Martin, *History of the United States: Volume I* (Boston: Ginn and Company, 1928), 329.

3. Woody Holton, *Abigail Adams: A Life* (New York: Free Press, 2009), 353.

4. *Ibid.*

5. Ron Chernow, *Washington: A Life* (New York: Penguin, 2010) 792–793.

6. *Ibid.*, 793.

7. Alexander Hamilton, Letter to Oliver Wolcott, Junior (June 29, 1798), *Founders Online*, National Archives. Original source: *The Papers of Alexander Hamilton*, vol. 21, April 1797–July 1798, ed. Harold C. Syrett (New York: Columbia University Press, 1974), 522–523, https://founders.archives.gov/documents/Hamilton/01-21-02-0296.

8. James Morton Smith, "Alexander Hamilton, the Alien Law, and Seditious Libels," *The Review of Politics* 16, no. 3 (July 1954), 305–333, Cambridge University Press for the University of Notre Dame on behalf of *Review of Politics*, http://www.jstor.com/stable/1405146, 308.

9. *Ibid.*

10. *Ibid.*

11. Edward Livingston, "Opposition

to the Alien and Sedition Acts," reprinted in *Logic of History. Five hundred political texts being concentrated extracts of Abolitionism; Also results of Slavery Agitation and Emancipation; Together with Sundry Chapters on Despotism, Usurpations and Frauds*, pub. and ed. S.D. Carpenter, 1864.

12. U.S. Constitution, Article I, Section 6.

13. Akhil Reed Amar, *America's Constitution: A Biography* (New York: Random House, 2005), 101–102.

14. *Ibid.*

15. Thomas Jefferson, letter to John Taylor, November 26, 1798, *Founders Online*, National Archives, https://founders.archives.gov/documents/Jefferson/01-30-02-0398. Original source: *The Papers of Thomas Jefferson*, vol. 30, 1 January 1798–31 January 1799, ed. Barbara B. Oberg (Princeton: Princeton University Press, 2003), pp. 588–590, https://founders.archives.gov/documents/Jefferson/01-30-02-0398.

16. Thomas E. Woods, *Nullification* (Washington, D.C.: Regnery, 2010), 56.

17. Jonathan Gienapp, "How to Maintain a Constitution: The Virginia and Kentucky Resolutions and James Madison's Struggle with the Problem of Constitutional Maintenance," *Nullification and Secession in Modern Constitutional Thought*, ed. Sanford Levinson (Lawrence: University Press of Kansas, 2016), 53.

18. Kentucky Resolution of 1798 (Thomas Jefferson), "Resolutions Adopted by the Kentucky General Assembly, in the House of Representatives, November 10th, 1798," *The Papers of Thomas Jefferson* 30, January 1, 1798 to January 31,1799 (Princeton: Princeton University Press, 2003), 550–56.

19. Virginia Resolution of 1798 (James Madison), "Virginia Resolutions, 21 December 1798," *Founders Online*, National Archives, https://founders.archives.gov/documents/Madison/01-17-02-0128. Original source: *The Papers of James Madison*, vol. 17, 31 March 1797–3 March 1801 and supplement 22 January 1778–9 August 1795, eds. David B. Mattern, J.C.A. Stagg, Jeanne K. Cross, and Susan Holbrook Perdue (Charlottesville: University Press of Virginia, 1991).

20. Edward Lazarus, "Why the Tenth Amendment 'Nullification' Arguments Against the Stimulus Bill Are Sheer Folly—and Why It's Disturbing that So Many Years After the Civil War, They Are Still Being Raised," March 12, 2009, *FindLaw*, https://supreme.findlaw.com/legal-commentary/why-the-tenth-amendment-nullification-arguments-against-the-stimulus-bill-are-sheer-folly-and-why-its-disturbing-that-so-many-years-after-the-civil-war-they-are-still-being-raised.html.

21. U.S. Constitution, Article I, Section 1.

22. Allen West, quoted in "Allen West Wrong on Nullification and Supremacy Clause," Joe Wolverton II, January 4, 2014, *The New American*, https://www.thenewamerican.com/usnews/constitution/item/17317-allen-west-wrong-on-nullification-and-supremacy-clause.

23. U.S. Constitution, Article VI, Clause 2.

24. Gordon S. Wood, *Revolutionary Characters: What Made the Founders Different* (New York: Penguin, 2006), 145.

25. Jack Rakove, *Original Meanings: Politics and Ideas in the Making of the Constitution* (New York: Vantage/Random House, 1996), 367.

26. James Madison, "Vices of the Political System of the United States," April 1787, *Founders Online*, National Archives, founders.archives.gov/documents/Madison/01-09-02-0187.

27. Gordon S. Wood, *Revolutionary Characters: What Made the Founders Different* (New York: Penguin, 2006), 155.

28. Jonathan Gienapp, "How to Maintain a Constitution: The Virginia and Kentucky Resolutions and James Madison's Struggle with the Problem of Constitutional Maintenance," *Nullification and Secession in Modern Constitutional Thought*, ed. Sanford Levinson (Lawrence: University Press of Kansas, 2016), 56.

29. Edward Lazarus, "Why the Tenth Amendment 'Nullification' Arguments Against the Stimulus Bill Are Sheer Folly—and Why It's Disturbing that So Many Years After the Civil War, They Are Still Being Raised," March 12, 2009, *FindLaw*, https://supreme.findlaw.com/legal-commentary/why-the-tenth-amendment-nullification-arguments-against-the-stimulus-bill-are-sheer-folly-and-why-its-disturbing-that-so-many-

years-after-the-civil-war-they-are-still-being-raised.html.

30. *Ibid.*

31. *Ibid.*

32. Thomas E. Woods, *Nullification* (Washington, D.C.: Regnery, 2010), 79.

33. *Ibid.*, 75.

34. Wisconsin Joint Resolution, March 19, 1859, *General Laws Passed by the Legislature of Wisconsin*, Wisconsin State Legislature official website, https://docs.legis.wisconsin.gov/1859/related/joint_resolutions/4.pdf.

35. Federalist No. 51, Publius (James Madison), *The Federalist Papers*, ed. Clinton Rossiter (New York: Mentor/New American Library, 1961), 288–293.

36. John Ferling, *Adams vs. Jefferson: The Tumultuous Election of 1800* (New York: Oxford University Press, 2004), 115.

37. Gordon S. Wood, *Empire of Liberty: A History of the Early Republic, 1789–1815* (New York: Oxford University Press, 2009), 270.

38. "Pennsylvania House Resolution Refuting Nullification," reprinted in *American Sovereigns: The People and America's Constitutional Tradition before the Civil War*, ed. Christian G. Fritz (Oxford: Cambridge University Press, 2008), https://hdl-handle-net.proxy.lib.pdx.edu/2027/heb.07867. EPUB.

Chapter Four

1. Ron Chernow, *Washington: A Life* (New York: Penguin, 2010), 787.

2. William E. Nelson, *Marbury v. Madison: The Origin and Legacy of Judicial Review* (Lawrence: University Press of Kansas, 2018), 79.

3. *Ibid.*

4. Francis N. Stites, *John Marshall: Defender of the Constitution* (Boston: Little, Brown, 1981), 67.

5. Nancy Isenberg, *Fallen Founder: The Life of Aaron Burr* (London: Penguin, 2007), 338.

6. John Ferling, *Adams vs. Jefferson: The Tumultuous Election of 1800* (New York: Oxford University Press, 2004), 204.

7. *Ibid.*, 199.

8. Thomas Jefferson, letter to Abigail Adams, June 13, 1804, reprinted in *The Adams-Jefferson Letters: The Complete Correspondence Between Thomas Jefferson & Abigail & John Adams*, ed. Lester J. Cappon (Charlotte: University of North Carolina Press, 1959), 270.

9. R.B. Bernstein, *Thomas Jefferson* (New York: Oxford University Press, 2003), 149.

10. Bruce Ackerman, *The Failure of the Founding Fathers: Jefferson, Marshall, and the Rise of Presidential Democracy* (Cambridge: Belknap Press of Harvard University Press, 2007), 113.

11. Francis N. Stites, *John Marshall: Defender of the Constitution* (Boston: Little, Brown, 1981), 91.

12. *Marbury* v. *Madison*, 5 U.S. (1 Cranch) 137 (1803), ruling by Chief Justice John Marshall, *U.S. Reports*, Library of Congress, https://www.loc.gov/item/usrep005137/.

13. *Ibid.*

14. *Ibid.*

15. Thomas Jefferson, letter to Abigail Adams, September 11, 1804, reprinted in *The Adams-Jefferson Letters: The Complete Correspondence Between Thomas Jefferson & Abigail & John Adams*, ed. Lester J. Cappon (Charlotte: University of North Carolina Press, 1959), 279.

16. *Ibid.*

17. Thomas Jefferson, *Notes on the State of Virginia* (1781–1782) (New York: Harper Torchbooks, 1964), 113–114.

18. Thomas Jefferson, letter to James Madison, March 15, 1789, *Founders Online*, National Archives, https://founders.archives.gov/documents/Jefferson/01-14-02-0410. Original source: *The Papers of Thomas Jefferson*, vol. 14, 8 October 1788–26 March 1789, ed. Julian P. Boyd (Princeton: Princeton University Press, 1958), 659–663.

19. *Ibid.*

20. Thomas Jefferson, letter to James Madison, March 15, 1789, *Founders Online*, National Archives, https://founders.archives.gov/documents/Jefferson/01-14-02-0410. Original source: *The Papers of Thomas Jefferson*, vol. 14, 8 October 1788–26 March 1789, ed. Julian P. Boyd (Princeton: Princeton University Press, 1958), pp. 659–663.

21. Randy Barnett, *Restoring the Lost Constitution: The Presumption of Liberty* (Princeton: Princeton University Press, 2004), 269.

22. Gordon S. Wood, "The Trials and Tribulations of Thomas Jefferson," *Jeffersonian Legacies* (Charlottesville: University Press of Virginia, 1993), 412.

23. Thomas Jefferson, letter to James Madison, September 6, 1789, *Founders Online*, National Archives, https://founders.archives.gov/documents/Madison/01-12-02-0248. Original source: *The Papers of James Madison*, vol. 12, 2 March 1789–20 January 1790, and supplement 24 October 1775–24 January 1789, ed. Charles F. Hobson and Robert A. Rutland (Charlottesville: University Press of Virginia, 1979), 382–388.

24. Circuit-riding was an obligation of Supreme Court Justices to preside over lower federal court proceedings, which required them to *ride circuit* and travel across vast geographic areas. The practice was abolished with the Judiciary Act of 1801 but reinstated, though in a less-arduous form, with the Judiciary Act of 1802. Separate circuit judgeships were established again in 1869 and circuit-riding was officially ended by an act of Congress in 1911. "Circuit Riding," *Federal Judicial Center*, https://www.fjc.gov/history/timeline/circuit-riding.

25. Bruce Ackerman, *The Failure of the Founding Fathers: Jefferson, Marshall, and the Rise of Presidential Democracy* (Cambridge: Belknap Press of Harvard University Press, 2007), 114.

26. *McCulloch* v. *Maryland*, March 6, 1819, "Minutes of the Supreme Court of the United States," Record Group 267, *National Archives*, https://www.ourdocuments.gov/doc.php?flash=false&doc=21&page=transcript.

27. Fifth Amendment, U.S. Constitution.

28. Akhil Reed Amar, *America's Constitution: A Biography* (New York: Random House, 2005), 387.

29. *Barron* v. *Mayor & City Council of Baltimore*, 32 U.S. 243 (1833).

Chapter Five

1. Jason Edward Black, *American Indians and the Rhetoric of Removal and Allotment* (Jackson: University Press of Mississippi, 2015), 28.

2. *Ibid.*, 23.

3. Roger G. Kennedy, *Mr. Jefferson's Lost Cause: Land, Farmers, Slavery, and the Louisiana Purchase* (New York: Oxford University Press, 2003), 194.

4. *Ibid.*, 188.

5. Thomas Jefferson, letter to John Breckinridge, August 12, 1803, *Founders Online*, National Archives, https://founders.archives.gov/documents/Jefferson/01-41-02-0139.

6. Jeffrey Ostler, *Surviving Genocide: Native Nations and the United States from the American Revolution to Bleeding Kansas* (New Haven: Yale University Press, 2019), 215.

7. Paul Finkelman and Tim Garrison, "U.S. Indian Policy: Congress and the Executive, 1803–1848," *Encyclopedia of United States Indian Policy and Law* (Washington, D.C.: CQ Press, 2009), 14.

8. *Ibid.*

9. President Andrew Jackson's Message to Congress, "On Indian Removal," December 6, 1830; *Records of the United States Senate, 1789–1990*; Record Group 46, National Archives.

10. *Ibid.*

11. Jeffrey Ostler, *Surviving Genocide: Native Nations and the United States from the American Revolution to Bleeding Kansas* (New Haven: Yale University Press, 2019), 248.

12. Tim Alan Garrison, *Legal Ideology of Removal: The Southern Judiciary and the Sovereignty of Native American Nations* (Athens: University of Georgia Press, 2002), 234.

13. Francis N. Stites, *John Marshall: Defender of the Constitution* (Boston: Little, Brown, 1981), 160.

14. Jason Edward Black, *American Indians and the Rhetoric of Removal and Allotment* (Jackson: University Press of Mississippi, 2015), 55.

15. Francis N. Stites, *John Marshall: Defender of the Constitution* (Boston: Little, Brown, 1981), 162–163.

16. *Worcester* v. *Georgia*. 31 U.S. (6 Pet.) 515 (1832).

17. Tim Alan Garrison, *Legal Ideology of Removal: The Southern Judiciary and the Sovereignty of Native American Nations* (Athens: University of Georgia Press, 2002), 178.

18. Jeffrey Ostler, *Surviving Genocide:*

Native Nations and the United States from the American Revolution to Bleeding Kansas (New Haven: Yale University Press, 2019), 267.

19. *Ibid.*, 271.

20. Tim Alan Garrison, *Legal Ideology of Removal: The Southern Judiciary and the Sovereignty of Native American Nations* (Athens: University of Georgia Press, 2002), 237.

21. Jason Edward Black, *American Indians and the Rhetoric of Removal and Allotment* (Jackson: University Press of Mississippi, 2015), 58.

22. Akhil Reed Amar, *America's Constitution: A Biography* (New York: Random House, 2005), 215.

23. Keith Whittington, *Repugnant Laws: Judicial Review of Acts of Congress from the Founding to the Present* (Lawrence: University Press of Kansas, 2019), 113.

24. *Ibid.*, 253.

25. *Ibid.*, 100.

26. Paul Finkelman, "James Buchanan, Dred Scott, and the Whisper of Conspiracy," *James Buchanan and the Coming of the Civil War*, eds. John W. Quist and Michael J. Birkner (Gainesville: University Press of Florida, 2013), 27.

27. Henry Clay, "On the Boundaries of Texas," Senate debate, June 8, 1850, *The Speeches of Henry Clay, Volume 2*, ed. Calvin Colton (New York: A.S. Barnes, 1857), 507.

28. *Dred Scott v. Sandford*. 60 U.S. (19 How.) 393 (1857).

29. *Ibid.*

30. Akhil Reed Amar, *America's Constitution: A Biography* (New York: Random House, 2005), 98.

31. Paul Finkelman, "James Buchanan, Dred Scott, and the Whisper of Conspiracy," *James Buchanan and the Coming of the Civil War*, eds. John W. Quist and Michael J. Birkner (Gainesville: University Press of Florida, 2013), 24.

32. James Wilson, Remarks at the Pennsylvania Ratification Convention, December 3, 1787, reprinted in *Collected Works of James Wilson Volume 1*, eds. Kermit L. Hall and Mark David Hall (Indianapolis: Liberty Fund, 2007), 210.

33. *Ibid.*, 241.

34. Mark A. Graber, *Dred Scott and the Problem of Constitutional Evil* (Cambridge: Cambridge University Press, 2006), 18.

35. *Ibid.*, 28.

Chapter Six

1. Damon Root, *Overruled: The Long War for Control of the U.S. Supreme Court* (New York: Palgrave Macmillan, 2014), 26.

2. Eric Foner, *The Second Founding: How the Civil War and Reconstruction Remade the Constitution* (New York: W.W. Norton, 2019), 63–65.

3. *Ibid.*, 67.

4. Randy Barnett, *Restoring the Lost Constitution: The Presumption of Liberty* (Princeton: Princeton University Press, 2004), 324.

5. Michael Kent Curtis, *No State Shall Abridge: The Fourteenth Amendment and the Bill of Rights* (Durham: Duke University Press, 1986), 30–31.

6. *Ibid.*, 31.

7. *Congressional Globe*, 35th Congress, 2nd Session, 982 (1859).

8. Michael Kent Curtis, *No State Shall Abridge: The Fourteenth Amendment and the Bill of Rights* (Durham: Duke University Press, 1986), 60.

9. Beyond Bingham's likeminded contemporaries, the idea of rights values being imposed against the individual states and the role of fundamental rights recognition as a limit to government power was asserted as far back as Justice Bushrod Washington's reference to Article IV's privileges and immunities clause in *Corfield v. Coryell* in 1823. Justice Washington's reference to privileges *and* immunities within Article IV of the Constitution inspired Bingham's reference to privileges *or* immunities in the Fourteenth Amendment.

10. *Congressional Globe*, 38th Congress, 1st Session, 1202 (1864).

11. Randy Barnett, *Restoring the Lost Constitution: The Presumption of Liberty* (Princeton: Princeton University Press, 2004), 194.

12. Lysander Spooner, *The Unconstitutionality of Slavery* (Boston: Bela Marsh, 1860), reprinted at Liberty Fund, https://oll.libertyfund.org/title/spooner-the-unconstitutionality-of-slavery-1860.

13. Frederick Douglass, "The Meaning

of July Fourth for the Negro," *Life and Writings Volume 2* (New York: International, 1950), 202.

14. Frederick Douglass, "Oath to Support the Constitution," *Life and Writings Volume 2* (New York: International, 1950), 118.

15. Michael Kent Curtis, *No State Shall Abridge: The Fourteenth Amendment and the Bill of Rights* (Durham: Duke University Press, 1986), 24.

16. *Nunn v. Georgia* 1 Ga. (1 Kel.) 243 (1846).

17. *Ibid.* "The right of the whole people, old and young, men, women and boys, and not militia only, to keep and bear arms of every description, and not such merely as are used by the militia, shall not be infringed, curtailed, or broken in upon, in the smallest degree; and all this for the important end to be attained: the rearing up and qualifying a well-regulated militia, so vitally necessary to the security of the free State."

18. *Congressional Globe*, 39th Congress, 1st Session, 176–77 (1866).

19. Stephen P. Halbrook, *Freedmen, the Fourteenth Amendment, and the Right to Bear Arms, 1866–1876* (Westport, CT: Praeger, 1998), 42.

20. *Ibid.*

21. Fourteenth Amendment, U.S. Constitution (1868).

22. Damon Root, *Overruled: The Long War for Control of the U.S. Supreme Court* (New York: Palgrave Macmillan, 2014), 28.

23. *Congressional Globe*, 39th Congress, 1st Session, 156–59, 1065. 1090 (1866).

24. Eric Foner, *The Second Founding: How the Civil War and Reconstruction Remade the Constitution* (New York: W.W. Norton, 2019), 75.

25. *Congressional Globe*, 39th Congress, 1st Session, 2765, 2961 (1866).

26. *Congressional Globe*, 39th Congress, 1st Session, 2549 (1866).

27. Stephen P. Halbrook, *Freedmen, the Fourteenth Amendment, and the Right to Bear Arms, 1866–1876* (Westport, CT: Praeger, 1998), 107.

28. Michael Kent Curtis, *No State Shall Abridge: The Fourteenth Amendment and the Bill of Rights* (Durham: Duke University Press, 1986), 91.

29. Eric Foner, *The Second Founding: How the Civil War and Reconstruction*

Remade the Constitution* (New York: W.W. Norton, 2019), 75.

30. Akhil Reed Amar, *America's Constitution: A Biography* (New York: Random House, 2005), 387.

31. *United States v. Hall* (1871), Et. Al., 3 Chi. Leg. News, 260; 13 Int. Rev. Rec. 181.

32. Randy Barnett, *Restoring the Lost Constitution: The Presumption of Liberty* (Princeton: Princeton University Press, 2004), 205.

33. *Slaughter-House Cases*, 83 U.S. (16 Wall.) 36 (1873).

34. Eric Foner, *The Second Founding: How the Civil War and Reconstruction Remade the Constitution* (New York: W.W. Norton, 2019), 133–134.

35. Michael Kent Curtis, *No State Shall Abridge: The Fourteenth Amendment and the Bill of Rights* (Durham: Duke University Press, 1986), 175.

36. Randy Barnett, *Restoring the Lost Constitution: The Presumption of Liberty* (Princeton: Princeton University Press, 2004), 323.

37. Eric Foner, *The Second Founding: How the Civil War and Reconstruction Remade the Constitution* (New York: W.W. Norton, 2019), 76.

38. *Ibid.*

Chapter Seven

1. Aurelius Augustine, *City of God*, reprinted in *The Works of Aurelius Augustine*, ed. Marcus Dodds, 2014, made available digitally through guntenburg.org, https://gutenberg.org/files/45304/45304-h/45304-h.htm. In the original Latin: "Lex iniusta non est lex." Martin Luther King, Jr., asserted this precept in his "Letter from Birmingham Jail" in 1963.

2. Thomas Aquinas, *Summa Theologica*, reprinted in *The Rights Retained by the People*, Volume 2 (Fairfax: George Mason University Press, 1993), 391.

3. *Ibid.*, 393.

4. Richard Tuck, *Natural Rights Theories: Their Origin and Development* (New York: Cambridge University Press, 1979),19.

5. Randy Barnett, *Restoring the Lost Constitution: The Presumption of Liberty* (Princeton: Princeton University Press, 2004), 50 (footnote).

6. Thaddeus Russell, *Unregistered Podcast*, Episode 43, with guest Dave Smith, February 6, 2018, https://www.youtube.com/watch?v=7t-LjjjYnCs.

7. Thomas Jefferson, "Letter to the Danbury Baptist Association (January 1, 1802)," reprinted in *Jefferson & Madison on Separation of Church and State: Writings on Religion and Secularism*, ed. Lenni Brenner (Fort Lee: Barricade Books, 2004), 163.

8. Thomas Jefferson, "A Bill for Establishing Religious Freedom, 18 June 1779," *Founders Online*, National Archives, https://founders.archives.gov/documents/Jefferson/01-02-02-0132-000--0082. Original source: *The Papers of Thomas Jefferson*, vol. 2, 1777–18 June 1779, ed. Julian P. Boyd (Princeton: Princeton University Press, 1950), 545–553.

9. Karl Marx, "The Jewish Question." First published February 1844 in Deutsch-Französische Jahrbücher. *Marxists.org*, https://www.marxists.org/archive/marx/works/download/pdf/On%20The%20Jewish%20Question.pdf, 13.

10. Jeremy Bentham, *Rights, Representation, and Reform: Nonsense upon Stilts and Other Writings on the French Revolution*, ed. P. Schofield, C. Pease-Watkin, and C. Blamires, *The Collected Works of Jeremy Bentham* (Oxford: Oxford University Press, 2002), 317–401.

11. *Ibid.*

12. Oliver Wendell Holmes, "Natural Law" (1918), *Collected Legal Papers*, 310. Reprinted in *Natural Law, Natural Rights, and the American Constitutional Tradition*, National Endowment for the Humanities, https://www.nlnrac.org/critics/oliver-wendell-holmes.

13. Bradley C.S. Watson, *Natural Law, Natural Rights, and the American Constitutional Tradition*, National Endowment for the Humanities, https://www.nlnrac.org/critics/oliver-wendell-holmes.

14. Oliver Wendell Holmes, "Natural Law," *Harvard Law Review* 32 (1918), 41.

15. Thomas Paine, "To Thomas Jefferson from Thomas Paine, spring 1788(?)," *Founders Online*, National Archives, https://founders.archives.gov/documents/Jefferson/01-13-02-0002. Original source: *The Papers of Thomas Jefferson*, vol. 13, March–7 October 1788, ed. Julian P. Boyd (Princeton: Princeton University Press, 1956), 4–8.

16. For a more in-depth exploration of the influence of social deference upon Colonial America, see Gordon S. Woods's *Radicalism of the American Revolution* (New York: A.A. Knopf, 1992).

17. Peter H. Wood, "Liberty is Sweet," *Beyond the American Revolution: Explorations in the History of American Radicalism* (DeKalb: Northern Illinois University Press, 1993), 187.

18. Gordon S. Wood, *Creation of the American Republic, 1776–1787* (Chapel Hill: University of North Carolina Press, 1969), 49.

19. J.G.A. Pocock, *The Machiavellian Moment: Florentine Political Thought and the Atlantic Republican Tradition* (Princeton: Princeton University Press, 1975), 54.

20. Leonardo Bruni, *De Studiis et Literis* (1405), reprinted in *Vittorino da Feltre and other humanist educators; essays and versions. An introduction to the history of classical education*, ed. William Harrison Woodward (Cambridge: Cambridge University Press, 1897), 128, https://archive.org/details/vittorinodafeltr00woodiala/page/128/mode/2up.

21. J.G.A. Pocock, *The Machiavellian Moment. Florentine Political Thought and the Atlantic Republican Tradition* (Princeton: Princeton University Press, 1975), 88.

22. Niccolò Machiavelli, *The Art of War* (1520), reprinted by Liberty Fund from *The Seven Books on the Art of War, by Niccolo Machiavelli, Citizen and Secretary of Florence*, trans. Henry Neville (1675), https://oll.libertyfund.org/titles/machiavelli-the-art-of-war-neville-trans.

23. Pocock, *The Machiavellian Moment*, 200.

24. *Ibid.*

25. *Ibid.*, 272.

26. Donato Giannotti, *Opere*, 3 vols., ed. G. Rosini (Pisa, 1819), 1, 51.

27. Pocock, *The Machiavellian Moment*, 288.

28. *Ibid.*, 291.

29. Gordon S. Wood, *Creation of the American Republic, 1776–1787* (Chapel Hill: University of North Carolina Press, 1969), 33.

30. Clinton Rossiter, *Seedtime of the Republic: The Origin of the American*

Tradition of Political Liberty (New York: Harcourt, Brace, 1953), 362.

31. Michael P. Zuckert, *The Natural Rights Republic: Studies in the Foundation of the American Political Tradition* (Notre Dame: University of Notre Dame Press, 1996), 206.

32. *Ibid.*, 207.

33. *Ibid.*

34. See Adam Smith, *The Wealth of Nations* (1776) and David Hume, *Treatise on Human Nature* (1739).

35. Jonathan Haidt, *The Righteous Mind: Why Good People are Divided by Politics and Religion* (New York: Vintage, 2012), 66.

36. Jonathan Haidt, *The Righteous Mind*, 1.

37. *Ibid.*

38. Charles de Secondat Montesquieu, *Considerations on the Causes of the Romans' Greatness and Decline* (1734), reprinted in *Montesquieu: Selected Political Writings*, edited and translated by Melvin Richter (Indianapolis: Hackett Publishing, 1990), 98.

39. Montesquieu, *The Spirit of the Laws* (1748), reprinted in *Montesquieu: Selected Political Writings*, 163.

40. *Ibid.*, 174.

41. Jack N. Rakove, *Original Meanings: Politics and Ideas in the Making of the Constitution* (New York: Vantage/Random House, 1996), 19.

42. It is surprising that *Discourses on Government* (1680), by Algernon Sidney, was not more influential upon the American founders. It argues similar natural rights claims as Locke ("That which is not just, is not Law; and that which is not Law, ought not to be obeyed") and was written, like Locke's *Two Treatises*, as a response to Robert Filmer's *Patriarcha*. Sidney was convicted of treason and executed on December 7, 1683. John Adams expressed his own surprise that Sidney had not loomed larger in American thought in a letter to Thomas Jefferson, dated September 18, 1823. "I have undertaken to read Algernon Sidney on Government ... as often as I have read it, and fumbled it over; it now excites fresh admiration, that this has excited so little interest in the literary world ... as for the proof it brings of the bitter sufferings of the advocates of Liberty from that time to this." Reprinted in *The Adams-Jefferson Letters: The Complete Correspondence Between Thomas Jefferson & Abigail & John Adams*, ed. Lester J. Sotiris

(Charlotte: University of North Carolina Press, 1959), 598. Years later, Adams's son, John Quincy, claimed Sidney (also Rousseau) was indeed an influence upon the American founding, stating that "Sidney and ... Locke, constitute the foundation of the North American Declaration of Independence, and together with the subsequent writings of Montesquieu and Rousseau, that of the Constitution of the Commonwealth of Massachusetts, and of the Constitution of the United States." John Quincy Adams, *The Social Compact* (Providence, RI: Knowles and Vose, 1842), 11–12, 29. It is possible John Quincy Adams in this context was speaking to Sidney's legacy rather than his direct influence. Rhode Island governor Stephen Hopkins was among the few in the colonies to quote Sidney, in his pamphlet "The Rights of the Colonies Examined" (1764).

43. John Locke, *Second Treatise on Civil Government* (1689), reprinted in *For the Record: A Documentary History of America, Volume 1*, eds. David E. Shi and Holly A. Mayer (New York: W.W. Norton, 2013), 87.

44. Locke, *Second Treatise on Civil Government*, 89.

45. James Otis, "The Rights of the British Colonies Asserted and Proved," reprinted in *The American Revolution: Writings from the Pamphlet Debate, 1764–1772*, ed. Gordon S. Wood (New York: Penguin Random House, 2015), 52.

46. *Ibid.*, 77.

47. Richard Bland, "An Inquiry into the Rights of the British Colonies," reprinted in *The American Revolution: Writings from the Pamphlet Debate, 1764–1772*, ed. Gordon S. Wood (New York: Penguin Random House, 2015), 313.

48. "Fryday May 10. 1776 ," *Founders Online*, National Archives, https://founders.archives.gov/documents/Adams/01-03-02-0016-0116. Original source: *The Adams Papers, Diary and Autobiography of John Adams*, vol. 3, Diary, 1782–1804; Autobiography, Part One to October 1776, ed. L.H. Butterfield (Cambridge: Harvard University Press, 1961), 382–384.

49. John Adams, *Thoughts on Government* (1776), *Adams Papers-Digital Edition*, reprinted from *Thoughts on Government*, Boston, 1776, itself reprinted from the Philadelphia edition of 1776, Massachusetts Historical Society, http://www.masshist.org/publications/adams-papers/index.php/view/PJA04dg2.

50. Writs of assistance were general warrants issued by courts and used by customhouse officers and British soldiers in the American colonies. The writs gave the police powers wide latitude due to their lack of including specific addresses to be searched or specific items to be seized. The writs were a major source of contention among resistors during the imperial crisis of the 1760s. James Otis became a vocal critic of the writs, calling them "the worst instrument of arbitrary power, the most destructive of English liberty and the fundamental principles of law" (Boston Superior Court, February 1761, Massachusetts Historical Society, *Adams Papers Digital Edition*, Legal Papers of John Adams, volume 2). Referring to Otis's legal challenge to the writs, eyewitness John Adams later stated, "Otis was a flame of fire!... American Independence was then and there born" (Massachusetts Records, "James Otis Arguing Against the Writs of Assistance in the Old Town House," https://malegislature.gov/VirtualTour/Artifact/79).

51. John Adams, *Thoughts on Government* (1776).

52. John Adams, "Fryday June 2. 1775," *Founders Online*, National Archives, https://founders.archives.gov/documents/Adams/01-03-02-0016-0045. Original source: *The Adams Papers, Diary and Autobiography of John Adams*, vol. 3, Diary, 1782–1804; Autobiography, Part One to October 1776, ed. L.H. Butterfield (Cambridge: Harvard University Press, 1961), 351–352.

53. "John Adams and the Massachusetts Constitution," Commonwealth of Massachusetts Official Website, https://www.mass.gov/guides/john-adams-the-massachusetts-constitution.

54. *Ibid.*

55. Gordon S. Wood, *Creation of the American Republic, 1776–1787* (Chapel Hill: University of North Carolina Press, 1969), 342.

56. Louis H. Pollak, ed., *The Constitution and the Supreme Court, A Documentary History: An Assessment, Through Documents and Commentary, of the Fundamental Powers of the Supreme Court*, Volume I (Cleveland: World, 1966), 20.

57. Thomas Tudor Tucker (Philodemus), *Conciliatory Hints, Attempting, by a Fair State of Matters, to Remove Party Prejudice* (1784), reprinted in *American Political Writing During the Founding Era, 1760–1805*, eds. Charles S. Hyneman and Donald S. Luts (Indianapolis: Liberty Fund, 1983), 627.

58. James Wilson, "On the Natural Right of Individuals (1791)," *Lectures on Law*, reprinted in *The Collected Works of James Wilson*, Volume II, eds. Kermit Hall and Mark David Hall (Indianapolis: Liberty Fund, 2007), 1057–1058.

Chapter Eight

1. Randy Barnett and Josh Blackman, *An Introduction to Constitutional Law: 100 Supreme Court Cases Everyone Should Know* (New York: Wolters Kluwer, 2020), 127.

2. *Whig history* subscribes to a belief of inevitable historical progress. It was influenced by Enlightenment thinkers and was a philosophy invested in the power of human reason to appropriate the empirical method for the science of making government. Its core liberalism has been tremendously influential in American intellectual history and politics, but the view of inevitable human progress and, for some, the possibility of human perfectibility, is troublesome and unrealistic for many modern historians. *Merriam-Webster* defines Whig history ("Whiggish") as "characterized by a view which holds that history follows a path of inevitable progression and improvement and which judges the past in light of the present." Whig history has thus been criticized by modern historians for its use of presentism: using the present to evaluate the past. https://www.merriam-webster.com/dictionary/Whiggish.

3. Ken I. Kersch, *Constructing Civil Liberties: Discontinuities in the Development of American Constitutional Law* (Cambridge: Cambridge University Press, 2004), 133.

4. *Buck* v. *Bell*, 274 U.S. 200 (1927).

5. *Korematsu* v. *United States*, 323 U.S. 214 (1944).

6. *Ibid.*

7. *Kelo* v. *City of New London*, 545 U.S. 469 (2005).

8. *Ibid.*

9. *Lochner* v. *New York*, 198 U.S. 45.

10. *Ibid.*

11. Randy Barnett, *Restoring the Lost Constitution: The Presumption of Liberty* (Princeton: Princeton University Press, 2004), 224.

12. *United States* v. *Carolene Products Company*, 304 U.S. 144 (1938), footnote four.

13. *Ibid.*

14. *Schenck* v. *United States*, 249 U.S. 47 (1919).

15. *Texas* v. *Johnson*, 491 U.S. 397 (1989).

16. Keith E. Whittington, *Political Foundations of Judicial Supremacy: The Presidency, the Supreme Court, and Constitutional Leadership in U.S. History* (Princeton: Princeton University Press, 2007), 140.

17. *Meyer* v. *Nebraska*, 262 U.S. 390 (1923).

18. Leo Pfeffer, *Church, State, and Freedom* (Boston: Beacon Press, 1953), 513.

19. *Pierce* v. *Society of Sisters*, 268 U.S. 510 (1925).

20. *Plessy* v. *Ferguson*, 163 U.S. 537 (1896).

21. *Brown* v. *Board of Education of Topeka*, 347 U.S. 483 (1954), oral arguments by Thurgood Marshall.

22. *Bolling* v. *Sharpe*, 347 U.S. 497 (1954).

23. Dwight D. Eisenhower, "Radio and Television Address to the American People on the Situation in Little Rock," *Debating the Civil Rights Movement, 1945–1968*, eds. Steven F. Lawson and Charles Payne (Lanham, MD: Rowman & Littlefield, 1998), 60.

24. *Ibid.*

25. *Cooper* v. *Aaron*, 358 U.S. 1 (1958).

26. *Ibid.*

27. *Ibid.*

28. Larry D. Kramer, *The People Themselves: Popular Constitutionalism and Judicial Review* (New York: Oxford University Press, 2004), 221.

29. *Ibid.*.

30. *Marbury* v. *Madison*, 5 U.S. (1 Cranch) 137 (1803).

31. Miscegenation laws prohibited the procreation of interracial children. Such laws included bans on marriage, dwelling in the same home, and other restrictions on behavior which may contribute to a mixing of the white and black races. *Merriam-Webster* defines miscegenation as "a mixture of the races; especially: marriage, cohabitation, or sexual intercourse between a white person and a member of another race." https://www.merriam-webster.com/dictionary/miscegenation.

32. *Loving* v. *Virginia*, 388 U.S. 1 (1967).

33. Erwin Chemerinsky, *The Case Against the Supreme Court* (New York: Penguin, 2014), 134–135.

34. *Ibid.*, 135.

35. *Ibid.*, 136.

36. *Ibid.*, 137.

37. Ninth Amendment, U.S. Constitution (1791).

38. *Griswold* v. *Connecticut* (1965), 381 U.S. 479, 486.

39. *Planned Parenthood* v. *Casey*, 505 U.S. 833 (1992).

40. Sotirios A. Barber, "The Ninth Amendment: Inkblot or Another Hard Nut to Crack?" 64 *Chicago-Kent Law Review* 67 (1988). Reprinted in *The Rights Retained by the People, Volume 2*, ed. Randy Barnett (Fairfax: George Mason University Press, 1993), 60–61.

41. *Lawrence* v. *Texas*, 539 U.S. 558 (2003).

42. Stephen Macedo, *The New Right v. The Constitution* (Washington, D.C.: Cato Institute, 1986), 27.

43. *District of Columbia* v. *Heller*, 554 U.S. 570 (2008).

44. Second Amendment, U.S. Constitution (1791).

45. *District of Columbia* v. *Heller*, 554 U.S. 570 (2008).

46. *McDonald* v. *Chicago*, 561 U.S. 742 (2010).

47. *Ibid.*

48. *Ibid.*

49. *McDonald* v. *Chicago*, 561 U.S. 742 (2010).

50. Keith Whittington, *Repugnant Laws: Judicial Review of Acts of Congress from the Founding to the Present* (Lawrence: University Press of Kansas, 2019), 274.

51. *Obergefell* v. *Hodges*, 576 U.S. 644 (2015).

52. *Ibid.*

53. *Ibid.*

54. *Ibid.*

55. *Citizens United* v. *Federal Election Commission*, 558 U.S. 310 (2010).

56. *Ibid.*

57. *Ibid.*

58. *Ibid.*

59. *Ibid.*

60. *Ibid.*

61. *Ibid.*

62. *Ibid.*

63. Keith Whittington, *Repugnant Laws: Judicial Review of Acts of Congress from the Founding to the Present* (Lawrence: University Press of Kansas, 2019), 282.

64. *Matal* v. *Tam*, 582 U.S. ___ (2017).

65. *Ibid.*

Bibliography

Primary Sources

Abrams v. United States. 250 U.S. 616 (1919).

Adams, Abigail. Letter to John Adams. 13 February 1797. Reprinted in Letter to Thomas Jefferson (with an addendum written by John Adams). 25 October 1804. Reprinted in *The Adams-Jefferson Letters: The Complete Correspondence Between Thomas Jefferson & Abigail & John Adams*. Edited by Lester J. Cappon. Charlotte: University of North Carolina Press, 1959.

_____. Letter to Thomas Jefferson. 1 July 1804. Reprinted in *The Adams-Jefferson Letters: The Complete Correspondence Between Thomas Jefferson & Abigail & John Adams*. Edited by Lester J. Cappon. Charlotte: University of North Carolina Press, 1959.

_____. Letter to Thomas Jefferson. 18 August 1804. Reprinted in *The Adams-Jefferson Letters: The Complete Correspondence Between Thomas Jefferson & Abigail & John Adams*. Edited by Lester J. Cappon. Charlotte: University of North Carolina Press, 1959.

_____. *My Dearest Friend: Letters of Abigail and John Adams*. Edited by Margaret A. Hogan and C. James Taylor. Cambridge: Harvard University Press, 2010.

Adams, John. "Fryday June 2. 1775." *Founders Online*. National Archives. https://founders.archives.gov/documents/Adams/01-03-02-0016-0045. Original source: *The Adams Papers, Diary and Autobiography of John Adams*, vol. 3, Diary, 1782–1804; Autobiography, Part One to October 1776. Edited by L.H. Butterfield. Cambridge: Harvard University Press, 1961, 351–352.

_____. "Fryday May 10. 1776." *Founders Online*. National Archives. https://founders.archives.gov/documents/Adams/01-03-02-0016-0116. Original source: *The Adams Papers, Diary and Autobiography of John Adams*, vol. 3, Diary, 1782–1804; Autobiography, Part One to October 1776. Edited by L.H. Butterfield. Cambridge: Harvard University Press, 1961, 382–384.

_____. Letter to Abigail Adams. 1 January 1797. Reprinted in *My Dearest Friend: Letters of Abigail and John Adams*. Edited by Margaret A. Hogan and C. James Taylor. Cambridge: Harvard University Press, 2010.

_____. Letter to Thomas Jefferson. 18 September 1823. Reprinted in *The Adams-Jefferson Letters: The Complete Correspondence Between Thomas Jefferson & Abigail & John Adams*. Edited by Lester J. Cappon. Charlotte: University of North Carolina Press, 1959.

_____. Letter to Thomas Jefferson. 6 December 1787. Reprinted in *The Debate on the Constitution: Federalist and Antifederalist Speeches, Articles, & Letters During the Struggle Over Ratification, September 1787 to August 1788*. Edited by Bernard Bailyn. New York: The Library of America, 1993.

_____. *Thoughts on Government*. 1776. *Adams Papers-Digital Edition*. Reprinted from *Thoughts on Government*, Boston, 1776, itself reprinted from the Philadelphia edition of 1776, Massachusetts Historical Society. http://www.masshist.org/publications/adams-papers/index.php/view/PJA04dg2.

Alien and Sedition Act. July 6, 1798. Fifth Congress. Enrolled Acts and Resolutions; General

Records of the United States Government; Record Group 11; *Our Documents.* National Archives. https://www.ourdocuments.gov/doc.php?flash=false&doc=16&page=transcript#.

Aquinas, Thomas. *Summa Theologica.* Reprinted in *The Rights Retained by the People,* Volume 2. Fairfax: George Mason University Press, 1993.

Augustine, St. Aurelius. *City of God.* Reprinted in *The Works of Aurelius Augustine.* Edited by Marcus Dodds. 2014. Made available digitally through guntenburg.org. https://gutenberg.org/files/45304/45304-h/45304-h.htm.

Barron v. *Baltimore.* 32 U.S. (7 Pet.) 243 (1833).

Bayard v. *Singleton.* 1 Martin (N. Car.) 42 (1787).

Bentham, Jeremy. *Rights, Representation, and Reform: Nonsense upon Stilts and Other Writings on the French Revolution.* In *The Collected Works of Jeremy Bentham.* Edited by P. Schofield, C. Pease-Watkin, and C. Blamires. Oxford: Oxford University Press, 2002, 317–401.

Berkshire Court of Common Pleas. *Manuscript Record Book 4A, 24.* Superior Court Clerk's Office, Pittsfield, Massachusetts. (Colonel John Ashley of Sheffield case, 1781/1782.)

Blackstone, William. *Commentaries on the Laws of England.* 1753. Notes selected from the editions of Archibold, Christian, Coleridge, Chitty, Stewart, Kerr, and others, Barron Field's Analysis, and Additional Notes, and a Life of the Author by George Sharswood. Philadelphia: J.B. Lippincott, 1893. Reproduced through Liberty Fund Online. https://files.libertyfund.org/files/2140/Blackstone_1387-01_EBk_v6.0.pdf.

Bland, Richard. "An Inquiry into the Rights of the British Colonies." Reprinted in *The American Revolution: Writings from the Pamphlet Debate, 1764–1772.* Edited by Gordon S. Wood. New York: Penguin Random House, 2015.

Bodin, Jean. *On Sovereignty.* Cambridge Texts in the History of Political Thought. Cambridge University Press, 1992.

Bolling v. *Sharpe.* 347 U.S. 497 (1954).

Bonham Case. Sir Edward Coke. 1610. Co. Rep. 113b. 118a, 77 Eng. Rep. 646, 652 (C.P. 1610).

Boston News-Letter. September 1, 1774. Reprinted in *Making the Revolution: 1763–1791.* Primary Source Collection. *America in Class.* National Humanities Center. http://americainclass.org/sources/makingrevolution/crisis/text7/coerciveactsresponse.pdf.

Brandenburg v. *Ohio.* 395 U.S. 444 (1969).

Brattle v. *Hinckley* (1786). https://constitutional.lawi.us/brattle-v-hinckley/.

Brom and Bett v. *Ashley* (1781). https://www.mass.gov/guides/massachusetts-constitution-and-the-abolition-of-slavery.

Brown v. *Board of Education of Topeka.* 347 U.S. 483 (1954).

Bruni, Leonardo. *De Studiis et Literis* (1405). Made available by Internet Archive and reprinted in *Vittorino da Feltre and other humanist educators; essays and versions. An introduction to the history of classical education.* Edited by William Harrison Woodward. Cambridge: Cambridge University Press, 1897. https://archive.org/details/vittorinodafeltr00woodiala/page/128/mode/2up.

Brutus. "Essay XII." 1788. *The Anti-Federalist Papers and the Constitutional Convention Debates.* Edited by Ralph Ketcham. New York: Signet Classics, 1986.

_____. "Essay XV." 1788. *The Anti-Federalist Papers and the Constitutional Convention Debates.* Edited by Ralph Ketcham. New York: Signet Classics, 1986.

Buck v. *Bell.* 274 U.S. 200 (1927).

Calder v. *Bull.* 3 U.S. 386 (1798).

"Centinel XVI." Centinel. 1788. Reprinted at *Teaching American History.* Documents Archive. https://teachingamericanhistory.org/library/document/centinel-xvi/.

Cherokee Nations v. *Georgia.* 30 U.S. (5 Pet.) 1 (1831).

Chisolm v. *Georgia.* 2 U.S. 419 (1793).

Citizens United v. *Federal Election Commission.* 558 U.S. 310 (2010).

Clay, Henry. "On the Boundaries of Texas." Senate debate. June 8, 1850. *The Speeches of Henry Clay, Volume 2.* Edited by Calvin Colton. New York: A.S. Barnes, 1857.

Congressional Globe. 35th Congress. 2nd Session (1859).

Congressional Globe. 38th Congress. 1st Session (1864).

Congressional Globe. 39th Congress. 1st Session (1866).

Cooper v. *Aaron.* 358 U.S. 1 (1958).

Corfield v. Coryell. 4 Wash. C.C. 371 (1823) 6 Fed. Case 546 (No. 3,230).

Coxe, Tenche. "An American Citizen (Parts I, II, and III)." September 26, 28, and 29, 1787. Reprinted in *The Debate on the Constitution: Federalist and Antifederalist Speeches, Articles, & Letters During the Struggle Over Ratification, September 1787 to August 1788.* Edited by Bernard Bailyn. New York: The Library of America, 1993.

Curtis, J. (Dissent). *Dred Scott v. Sanford.* 60 U.S. 393 (at 621), 1857.

Cushing, Justice William. Notes from the Quock Walker Case at the Supreme Judicial Court of Massachusetts. April 1783. *Massachusetts Historical Society.* MHS Collections Online. https://www.masshist.org/database/viewer.php?item_id=630&mode=transcript&img_step=13&br=1#page13.

Day v. Savadge. Hob. 84. K.B. 1614. Ruling by Sir Henry Hobart.

Debs v. United States. 249 U.S. 211 (1919).

Declaration of Independence (original draft). 1776. Thomas Jefferson. Reprinted in *For the Record: A Documentary History of America; Volume 1: From First Contact Through Reconstruction.* Edited by David E. Shi and Holly A. Mayer. New York: W.W. Norton, 1999.

Dickinson, John. "Letters from a Pennsylvania Farmer, No. VII." Reprinted in *The American Revolution: Writings from the Pamphlet Debate, 1764–1772.* Edited by Gordon S. Wood. New York: Penguin Random House, 2015.

_____. "Letters from a Pennsylvania Farmer, No. IX." Reprinted in *The American Revolution: Writings from the Pamphlet Debate, 1764–1772.* Edited by Gordon S. Wood. New York: Penguin Random House, 2015.

District of Columbia v. Heller. 554 U.S. 570 (2008).

Dr. Bonham's Case, 8 Co. Rep. 114. Court of Common Pleas. 1610. Ruling by Sir Edward Coke.

Douglass, Frederick. Frederick Douglass Biography. *Battlefields.* https://www.battlefields.org/learn/biographies/frederick-douglass.

_____. "The Meaning of July Fourth for the Negro." *Life and Writings Volume 2.* New York: International, 1970.

_____. "Oath to Support the Constitution." *Life and Writings Volume 2.* New York: International, 1970.

Drayton, William Henry. "A Letter from Freeman of South Carolina, To the Deputies of North America, Assembled in the High Court of Congress at Philadelphia." Reprinted in *The American Revolution: Writings from the Pamphlet Debate, 1773–1776.* Edited by Gordon S. Wood. New York: Penguin Random House, 2015.

Dred Scott v. Sandford. 60 U.S. (19 How.) 393 (1857).

Eisenhower, Dwight D. "Radio and Television Address to the American People on the Situation in Little Rock." Reprinted in *Debating the Civil Rights Movement, 1945–1968.* Edited by Steven F. Lawson and Charles Payne. Lanham, MD: Rowman & Littlefield, 1998.

Ellsworth, Oliver. Connecticut Ratification Convention. "Oliver Ellsworth Defends the Taxing Power and Comments on Dual Sovereignties and Judicial Review." 7 January 1788. Reprinted in *The Debate on the Constitution: Federalist and Antifederalist Speeches, Articles, & Letters During the Struggle Over Ratification, September 1787 to August 1788.* Edited by Bernard Bailyn. New York: The Library of America, 1993.

"Federalist No. 10." Publius (James Madison). 1788. The Federalist Papers. Edited by Clinton Rossiter). New York: Mentor/New American Library, 1961.

"Federalist No. 22." Publius (Alexander Hamilton). December 14, 1787. Reprinted in *Citizen Hamilton: The Wit and Wisdom of an American Founder.* Lanham, MD: Rowman & Littlefield, 2006.

"Federalist No. 34." Publius (Alexander Hamilton). 1788. *The Federalist Papers.* Edited by Clinton Rossiter. New York: Mentor/New American Library, 1961.

"Federalist No. 51." Publius (James Madison). 1788. *The Federalist Papers.* Edited by Clinton Rossiter. New York: Mentor/New American Library, 1961.

"Federalist No. 78." Publius (Alexander Hamilton). 1788. *The Federalist Papers.* Edited by Clinton Rossiter. New York: Mentor/New American Library, 1961.

First Convention Ever Called to Discuss the Civil and Political Rights of Women. Seneca Falls, New York, July 19, 20, 1848. Online Text. https://www.loc.gov/item/rbcmiller0011 07/.

Fitzhugh, George. *Cannibals All!, Or, Slaves without Masters.* 1856. Cambridge: Belknap Press of Harvard University Press, 1988. https://hdl-handle-net.proxy.lib.pdx.edu/2027/heb.04951. EPUB.

Germantown Petition Against Slavery. 1688. "A Minute Against Slavery, Addressed to Germantown Monthly Meeting, 1688." *Germantown Mennonite Historic Trust.* http://www.meetinghouse.info/uploads/1/9/4/1/19410913/a_minute_against_slavery.pdf.

Giannotti, Donato. *Opere.* 3 vols. Edited by G. Rosini. Pisa. 1819.

Gideon v. Wainwright. 372 U.S. 335 (1963).

Gitlow v. New York. 268 U.S. 652 (1925).

Griswold v. Connecticut (1965). 381 U.S. 479, 486. Justice Goldberg's Concurring Opinion.

Hamilton, Alexander. *Alexander Hamilton Papers:* Legal File, 1804; *Rutgers v. Waddington,* 1804, 1708. Manuscript/Mixed Material. https://www.loc.gov/item/mss246120632/.

_____. Letter to Oliver Wolcott, Junior. 29 June 1798. *Founders Online.* National Archives. Original source: *The Papers of Alexander Hamilton,* vol. 21, April 1797–July 1798. Edited by Harold C. Syrett. New York: Columbia University Press, 1974, 522–523. https://founders.archives.gov/documents/Hamilton/01-21-02-0296.

Hayburn's Case. 2 U.S. 409 (1792). Remarks by Associate Justice James Wilson.

Henry, Patrick. Virginia Ratification Convention. "Elaboration of His Main Objections." 12 June 1788. Reprinted in *The Debate on the Constitution: Federalist and Antifederalist Speeches, Articles, & Letters During the Struggle Over Ratification, September 1787 to August 1788.* Edited by Bernard Bailyn. New York: The Library of America, 1993.

Hoffy, Alfred M. Copied after Charles Bird King. *John Ross—A Cherokee Chief.* 1843. Hand-colored lithograph on paper. National Portrait Gallery, Smithsonian Institution. http://n2t.net/ark:/65665/sm458924554-53d8-4d7b-a2e2-1446f810ce01.

Holmes v. Walton (1780). "Holmes v. Walton: Case File Transcriptions and Other Materials." *New Jersey Digital Legal Library.* http://njlegallib.rutgers.edu/hw/.

Hylton v. United States. 3 U.S. 171 (1796).

Indian Removal Act of 1830. *A Century of Lawmaking for a New Nation: U.S. Congressional Documents and Debates, 1774–1875.* Library of Congress. http://memory.loc.gov/ammem/amlaw/lawhome.html.

Jackson, Andrew. "On Indian Removal." Message to Congress. December 6, 1830. *Records of the United States Senate, 1789–1990.* Record Group 46. National Archives. https://www.ourdocuments.gov/doc.php?flash=false&doc=25&page=transcript.

Jacobson v. Massachusetts. 197 U.S. 11 (1905).

Jefferson, Thomas. "A Bill for Establishing Religious Freedom, 18 June 1779." *Founders Online.* National Archives. https://founders.archives.gov/documents/Jefferson/01-02-02-0132-0004-0082. Original source: *The Papers of Thomas Jefferson,* vol. 2, 1777–18 June 1779. Edited by Julian P. Boyd. Princeton: Princeton University Press, 1950.

_____. Letter to Abigail Adams. 22 July 1804. Reprinted in *The Adams-Jefferson Letters: The Complete Correspondence Between Thomas Jefferson & Abigail & John Adams.* Edited by Lester J. Cappon. Charlotte: University of North Carolina Press, 1959.

_____. Letter to Abigail Adams. 11 September 1804. Reprinted in *The Adams-Jefferson Letters: The Complete Correspondence Between Thomas Jefferson & Abigail & John Adams.* Edited by Lester J. Cappon. Charlotte: University of North Carolina Press, 1959.

_____. Letter to Abigail Adams. 13 June 1804. Reprinted in *The Adams-Jefferson Letters: The Complete Correspondence Between Thomas Jefferson & Abigail & John Adams.* Edited by Lester J. Cappon. Charlotte: University of North Carolina Press, 1959.

_____. Letter to James Madison. 15 March 1789. *Founders Online.* National Archives. https://founders.archives.gov/documents/Jefferson/01-14-02-0410. Original source: *The Papers of Thomas Jefferson,* vol. 14, 8 October 1788–26 March 1789. Edited by Julian P. Boyd. Princeton: Princeton University Press, 1958,. 659–663.

_____. Letter to James Madison. 6 September 1789. *Founders Online.* National Archives. https://founders.archives.gov/documents/Madison/01-12-02-0248. Original source:

The Papers of James Madison, vol. 12, 2 March 1789–20 January 1790 and supplement 24 October 1775–24 January 1789. Ed. Charles F. Hobson and Robert A. Rutland. Charlottesville: University Press of Virginia, 1979, 382–388.

_____. Letter to John Breckinridge. 12 August 1803. *Founders Online.* National Archives. https://founders.archives.gov/documents/Jefferson/01-41-02-0139. Original source: *The Papers of Thomas Jefferson,* vol. 41, 11 July–15 November 1803. Edited by Barbara B. Oberg. Princeton: Princeton University Press, 2014,. 184–186.

_____. Letter to John Taylor. 26 November 1798. *Founders Online.* National Archives. Original source: *The Papers of Thomas Jefferson,* vol. 30, 1 January 1798–31 January 1799. Edited by Barbara B. Oberg. Princeton: Princeton University Press, 2003, 588–590. https://founders.archives.gov/documents/Jefferson/01-30-02-0398.

_____. Letter to the Danbury Baptist Association. 1 January 1802. Reprinted in *Jefferson & Madison on Separation of Church and State: Writings on Religion and Secularism.* Edited by Lenni Brenner. Fort Lee: Barricade Books, 2004.

_____. *Notes on the State of Virginia.* 1782. New York: Harper Torchbooks, 1964.

Jennison, Nathaniel. "Nathaniel Jennison to the House of Representatives." 18 June 1782. (11 Memorial of) H.R. doc. no. 956 (1782 session). Massachusetts Archives.

Joint Resolution of the Legislature of Wisconsin. March 19, 1859. Reprinted in *Nullification.* Edited by Thomas E. Woods. Washington, D.C.: Regnery, 2010.

Kelo v. City of New London. 545 U.S. 469 (2005).

Kentucky Resolution of 1798 (Thomas Jefferson). "Resolutions Adopted by the Kentucky General Assembly, In the House of Representatives, November 10th, 1798." *The Papers of Thomas Jefferson, Volume 30.* January 1, 1798 to January 31, 1799. Princeton University Press, 2003.

King, Martin Luther, Jr. "I Have a Dream." 1963. *Full Text March on Washington Speech.* NAACP. https://www.naacp.org/i-have-a-dream-speech-full-march-on-washington/.

_____. "Letter from Birmingham Jail." 1963. African Studies Center—University of Pennsylvania. https://www.africa.upenn.edu/Articles_Gen/Letter_Birmingham.html.

Korematsu v. United States. 323 U.S. 214 (1944).

Lawrence v. Texas. 539 U.S. 558 (2003).

Lincoln, Abraham. "A House Divided." Speech at Springfield, Illinois, June 16, 1858. *The Collected Works of Abraham Lincoln.* Edited by Roy P. Basler. New Brunswick: Rutgers University Press, 1953. 2:461 at 465.

Livingston, Edward. "Opposition to the Alien and Sedition Acts." Reprinted in *Logic of History. Five hundred political texts being concentrated extracts of Abolitionism; Also results of Slavery Agitation and Emancipation; Together with Sundry Chapters on Despotism, Usurpations and Frauds.* Published and edited by S.D. Carpenter, 1864.

Lochner v. New York. 198 U.S. 45 (1905).

Locke, John. *Second Treatise on Civil Government.* 1689. Reprinted in *For the Record: A Documentary History of America, Volume 1.* Edited by David E. Shi and Holly A. Mayer. New York: W.W. Norton, 2013.

Longacre, James Barton. Copied after Jean Pierre Henri Elouis. *James Wilson.* c. 1825. Sepia ink wash with watercolor on paper. National Portrait Gallery, Smithsonian Institution. http://n2t.net/ark:/65665/sm4a4a53ed3-ed0e-48f1-b350-c19823076b96.

Loving v. Virginia. 388 U.S. 1 (1967).

Machiavelli, Niccolò. *The Art of War* (1520). Made available by Liberty Fund from *The Seven Books on the Art of War, by Niccolo Machiavelli,* Citizen *and Secretary of Florence.* Translated by Henry Neville (1675). https://oll.libertyfund.org/titles/machiavelli-the-art-of-war-neville-trans.

Madison, James. Letter to George Washington. 30 September 1787. Reprinted in *The Debate on the Constitution: Federalist and Antifederalist Speeches, Articles, & Letters During the Struggle Over Ratification, September 1787 to August 1788.* Edited by Bernard Bailyn. New York: The Library of America, 1993.

_____. Letter to Thomas Jefferson. 24 October 1787. *Founders Online.* National Archives. Original source: *The Papers of James Madison,* vol. 10, 27 May 1787–3 March 1788. Edited by Robert A. Rutland, Charles F. Hobson, William M.E. Rachal, and Frederika J. Teute.

Chicago: University of Chicago Press, 1977, pp. 205–220.https://founders.archives.gov/documents/Madison/01-10-02-0151.

_____. *Notes of Debates in the Federal Convention of 1787 Reported by James Madison.* Athens: Ohio University Press, 1966.

_____. "Vices of the Political System of the United States." April 1787. *Founders Online.* National Archives. founders.archives.gov/documents/Madison/01-09-02-0187.

Marbury v. *Madison.* 5 U.S. (1 Cranch) 137 (1803). Ruling by Chief Justice John Marshall. *U.S. Reports.* Periodical. https://www.loc.gov/item/usrep005137/.

Martin, Luther. "Genuine Information" (1788). *The Complete Anti-Federalist.* 3 vols. Edited by Herbert J. Storing. Chicago: University Press of Chicago, 1981, 2.4.63– 71.

Matal v. *Tam.* 582 U.S. ___ (2017).

Maurin, Nickolas Eustache. Copied after Gilbert Stuart. *John Adams.* 1828. Lithograph on paper. National Portrait Gallery, Smithsonian Institution. http://n2t.net/ark:/65665/sm427f70617-410d-4b43-97a8-7d3b3e61b6b7.

McCulloch v. *Maryland.* March 6, 1819. "Minutes of the Supreme Court of the United States." Record Group 267. *National Archives.* https://www.ourdocuments.gov/doc.php?flash=false&doc=21&page=transcript.

McDonald v. *Chicago.* 561 U.S. 742 (2010).

Meyer v. *Nebraska.* 262 U.S. 390 (1923).

Montesquieu, Charles de Secondat. *Considerations on the Causes of the Romans' Greatness and Decline.* 1734. Reprinted in *Montesquieu: Selected Political Writings.* Edited and translated by Melvin Richter. Indianapolis: Hackett, 1990.

_____. *The Spirit of the Laws.* 1748. Reprinted in *Montesquieu: Selected Political Writings.* Edited and translated by Melvin Richter. Indianapolis: Hackett, 1990.

National Labor Relations Board v. *Jones & Laughlin Steel Corporation.* 301 U.S. 1 (1937).

New England Antislavery Society Constitution. 1832. Boston: Garrison and Knapp, 1832.

Newsam, Albert. Copied after Henry Inman. *John Marshall.* 1831. Lithograph on paper. National Portrait Gallery, Smithsonian Institution. http://n2t.net/ark:/65665/sm49bc7ac57-7fcc-4633-9fe3-06eeb8a895c2.

Nunn v. *Georgia.* 1 Ga. (1 Kel.) 243 (1846).

Obergefell v. *Hodges.* 576 U.S. 644 (2015).

O'Halloran, Thomas J. *Thurgood Marshall, attorney for the NAACP.* 1957. Photographic Portrait. Library of Congress. https://www.loc.gov/pictures/item/2003688132/.

Otis, James. "The Rights of the British Colonies Asserted and Proved." Reprinted in *The American Revolution: Writings from the Pamphlet Debate, 1764–1772.* Edited by Gordon S. Wood. New York: Penguin Random House, 2015.

Paine, Thomas. "To Thomas Jefferson from Thomas Paine, spring 1788(?)." *Founders Online.* National Archives. https://founders.archives.gov/documents/Jefferson/01-13-02-0002. Original source: *The Papers of Thomas Jefferson,* vol. 13, March–7 October 1788. Edited by Julian P. Boyd. Princeton: Princeton University Press, 1956, 4–8.

Pennsylvania House resolution refuting nullification. Reprinted in *American Sovereigns: The People and America's Constitutional Tradition before the Civil War.* Edited Christian G. Fritz. Oxford: Cambridge University Press, 2008. https://hdl-handle-net.proxy.lib.pdx.edu/2027/heb.07867. EPUB.

Pierce v. *Society of Sisters.* 268 U.S. 510 (1925).

Planned Parenthood v. *Casey.* 505 U.S. 833 (1992).

Plessy v. *Ferguson.* 163 U.S. 537 (1896).

Pollak, Louis H., ed. *The Constitution and the Supreme Court: A Documentary History, Volume I.* New York: Meridian Books, 1968.

_____, ed. *The Constitution and the Supreme Court: A Documentary History, Volume II.* New York: Meridian Books, 1968.

Ramos v. *Louisiana.* 590 US ___ (2020).

Redick, David. Letter to William Irvine. 24 September 1787. Reprinted in *The Debate on the Constitution: Federalist and Antifederalist Speeches, Articles, & Letters During the Struggle Over Ratification, September 1787 to August 1788.* Edited by Bernard Bailyn. New York: The Library of America, 1993.

Report of 1800. 7 January 1800. *Founders Online*. National Archives. Original source: *The Papers of James Madison*, vol. 17, 31 March 1797–3 March 1801 and supplement 22 January 1778–9 August 1795. Edited by David B. Mattern, J.C.A. Stagg, Jeanne K. Cross, and Susan Holbrook Perdue. Charlottesville: University Press of Virginia, 1991, 303–351. https://founders.archives.gov/documents/Madison/01-17-02-0202.

"Resolutions Adopted by the Kentucky General Assembly, In the House of Representatives, November 10th, 1798." *The Papers of Thomas Jefferson*, Volume 30: 1 January 1798 to 31 January 1799. Princeton: Princeton University Press, 2003, 550–56.

Roman Catholic Diocese of Brooklyn, New York v. Andrew Cuomo, Governor of New York. 592 U.S. ____ (2020).

Rousseau, Jean-Jacques. *The Social Contract and The First and Second Discourses*. Edited by Susan Dunn. New Haven: Yale University Press, 2002.

Russell, Thaddeus. *Unregistered Podcast*. Audio/Video. Episode 43. With guest Dave Smith. February 6, 2018. https://www.youtube.com/watch?v=7t-LjjjYnCs.

Rutgers v. *Waddington* (1784).

Saint-Mémin, Charles Balthazar Julien Févret de. *Thomas Jefferson*. 1804. Engraving on paper. National Portrait Gallery, Smithsonian Institution. http://n2t.net/ark:/65665/sm415d87bf7-blec-442c-aa39-532cff1ee849.

Schenck v. *United States*. 249 U.S. 47 (1919).

Schultze, Louis. Copied after a photograph by John H. Fitzgibbon. *Dred Scott*. C. 1890s. Oil on canvas. Missouri Historical Society. https://mohistory.org/collections/item/1897-009-0001.

Sedgwick, Susan Anne Livingston Ridley. *Elizabeth Freeman*. 1811. Oil pastel on ivory. Massachusetts Historical Society. https://en.wikipedia.org/wiki/Elizabeth_Freeman#/media/File:Mumbett70.jpg.

Sidney, Algernon. *Discourses on Government*. 1698. Reprinted through Liberty Fund Online. https://oll.libertyfund.org/titles/sidney-discourses-concerning-government.

Slaughter-House Cases. 83 U.S. (16 Wall.) 36 (1873).

Smith, Melancton. *The Anti-Federalist Writings of the Melancton Smith Circle*. Edited by Michael Zuckert and Derek Webb. Indianapolis: Liberty Fund, 2009.

South Bay United Pentecostal Church v. Gavin Newsom, Governor of California. 590 U.S. (2020).

Spooner, Lysander. *The Unconstitutionality of Slavery* (Boston: Bela Marsh, 1860), reprinted at Liberty Fund. https://oll.libertyfund.org/title/spooner-the-unconstitutionality-of-slavery-1860.

State v. *Harden*. 29 S.C.L. (2 Speers) 151n, 155n (1832).

Story, Joseph. *Commentaries on the Constitution of the United States: with a Preliminary Review of the Constitutional History of the Colonies and States Before the Adoption of the Constitution*. Boston: Little, Brown, 1873 (first printing 1833).

Stromberg v. *California*. 283 U.S. 359 (1931).

Texas v. *Johnson*. 491 U.S. 397 (1989).

Trevett v. *Weeden* (1786). Rhode Island Supreme Court.

Tucker, Thomas Tudor (Philodemus). *Conciliatory Hints, Attempting, by a Fair State of Matters, to Remove Party Prejudice*. 1784. *Reprinted in American Political Writing During the Founding Era, 1760–1805*. Edited by Charles S. Hyneman and Donald S. Lutz. Indianapolis: Liberty Fund, 1983.

Unidentified Artist. *Dr. Elizabeth M. Baer*. C. 1916. Photographic illustration on newsprint. Philadelphia: The WWI Years. http://philadelphiawwiyears.com/philadelphia-history-the-world-war-i-years-april-19-1916/.

_____. *Frederick Douglass*. 1856. Quarter-plate ambrotype. National Portrait Gallery, Smithsonian Institution. http://n2t.net/ark:/65665/sm4edbc86d9-ca8e-4512-b840-0fe22f2d299b.

_____. *James Madison*. C. 1801–1810. Stipple engraving on paper. National Portrait Gallery, Smithsonian Institution. http://n2t.net/ark:/65665/sm451832610-bb74-4021-84df-5d0f626e1384.

United States v. *Carolene Products Company*. 304 U.S. 144 (1938).

United States v. *Darby Lumber Co.* 312 U.S. 100 (1941).

United States v. *Hall* (1871). Et. Al. 3 Chi. Leg. News, 260; 13 Int. Rev. Rec. 181.

Vannerson, Julian. *John A. Bingham, Representative from Ohio, Thirty-fifth Congress.* 1859. Photograph on salted paper. Library of Congress. https://www.loc.gov/pictures/item/2010649352/.

Vattel, Emer de. *The Law of Nations, Or, Principles of the Law of Nature, Applied to the Conduct and Affairs of Nations and Sovereigns, with Three Early Essays on the Origin and Nature of Natural Law and on Luxury.* Republication of the 1797 translation of Vattel's work, along with new English translations of three early essays. Edited and introduced by Béla Kapossy and Richard Whatmore. Indianapolis: Liberty Fund, 2008.

Virginia Declaration of Rights. June 12, 1776. George Mason. National Archives. *Founding Documents.* https://www.archives.gov/founding-docs/virginia-declaration-of-rights.

Virginia Resolution of 1798 (James Madison). "Virginia Resolutions, 21 December 1798." *Founders Online.* National Archives. https://founders.archives.gov/documents/Madison/01-17-02-0128. Original source: *The Papers of James Madison, vol. 17,*.31 March 1797–3 March 1801 and supplement 22 January 1778–9 August 1795. Edited by David B. Mattern, J.C.A. Stagg, Jeanne K. Cross, and Susan Holbrook Perdue. Charlottesville: University Press of Virginia, 1991.

West Coast Hotel Co. v. *Parrish.* 300 U.S. 379 (1937).

Williamson v. *Lee Optical Co.* 348 U.S. 483 (1955).

Wilson, James. "On the Natural Right of Individuals (1791)." *Lectures on Law.* Reprinted in *The Collected Works of James Wilson.* Volume II. Edited by Kermit Hall and Mark David Hall. Indianapolis: Liberty Fund, 2007.

_____. Pennsylvania Ratification Convention. "Response to [William] Findley." 1 December 1787. Reprinted in *The Debate on the Constitution: Federalist and Antifederalist Speeches, Articles, & Letters During the Struggle Over Ratification, September 1787 to August 1788.* Edited by Bernard Bailyn. New York: The Library of America, 1993.

_____. Remarks at the Pennsylvania Ratification Convention. December 3, 1787. Reprinted in *Collected Works of James Wilson Volume 1.* Edited by Kermit L. Hall and Mark David Hall. Indianapolis: Liberty Fund, 2007.

Wisconsin Joint Resolution. March 19, 1859. *General Laws Passed by the Legislature of Wisconsin.* Wisconsin State Legislature official website. https://docs.legis.wisconsin.gov/1859/related/joint_resolutions/4.pdf.

Worcester v. *Georgia.* 31 U.S. (6 Pet.) 515 (1832).

Secondary Sources

Ackerman, Bruce. *The Failure of the Founding Fathers: Jefferson, Marshall, and the Rise of Presidential Democracy.* Cambridge: Belknap Press of Harvard University Press, 2007.

"Africans at the End of Slavery in Massachusetts." *Massachusetts Historical Society.* https://www.masshist.org/endofslavery/index.php?id=54.

Amar, Akhil Reed. *America's Constitution: A Biography.* New York: Random House, 2005.

Bailyn, Bernard. *The Ideological Origins of the American Revolution.* Cambridge: Belknap Press of Harvard University Press, 1967.

Baker, Keith Michael. *Inventing the French Revolution: Essays on French Political Culture in the Eighteenth Century.* New York: Cambridge University Press, 1990.

Barber, Sotirios A. "The Ninth Amendment: Inkblot or Another Hard Nut to Crack?" 64 *Chicago-Kent Law Review* 67 (1988). Reprinted in *The Rights Retained by the People, Volume 2.* Edited by Randy Barnett. Fairfax: George Mason University Press, 1993.

Barnett, Randy. "The Ninth Amendment and Constitutional Legitimacy." 64 *Chicago-Kent Law Review* 67 (1988). Reprinted in *The Rights Retained by the People, Volume 2.* Fairfax: George Mason University Press, 1993.

_____. *Our Republican Constitution: Securing the Liberty and Sovereignty of We The People.* New York: Broadside Books/HarperCollins, 2016.

_____. *Restoring the Lost Constitution: The Presumption of Liberty.* Princeton: Princeton University Press, 2004.

Barnett, Randy, and Josh Blackman. *An Introduction to Constitutional Law: 100 Supreme Court Cases Everyone Should Know.* New York: Wolters Kluwer, 2020.

Bartlett, Irving H. *The American Mind in the Mid-Nineteenth Century.* Northbrook: AHM Publishing, 1967.

Beard, Charles A. "The Supreme Court—Usurper or Grantee?" *Political Science Quarterly* 27, no. 1 (March 1912), 1–35. https://www.jstor.org/stable/2141105.

Beeman, Richard. *Plain, Honest Men: The Making of the American Constitution.* New York: Random House, 2009.

Bernstein, R.B. *Thomas Jefferson.* New York: Oxford University Press, 2003.

Bickel, Alexander M. *The Least Dangerous Branch.* New Haven: Yale University Press, 1986.

Bilder, Mary Sarah. "Idea or Practice: A Brief Historiography of Judicial Review." *Journal of Policy History* 20, no. 1, 6–25. Cambridge: Cambridge University Press, 2008.

Black, Jason Edward. *American Indians and the Rhetoric of Removal and Allotment.* Jackson: University Press of Mississippi, 2015.

Bodin, Jean. *On Sovereignty (Four Chapters from the Six Books of the Commonwealth).* Edited by Julian H. Franklin. New York: Cambridge University Press, 1992.

Boudin, Louis B. "Government by Judiciary." *Political Science Quarterly* XXVI, June 1, 1911, Internet Archive (238–270). https://archive.org/details/jstor-2141031/page/n15/mode/2up.

Brown, Robert E. "Charles Beard and the Constitution: A Critical Analysis of 'An Economic Interpretation of the Constitution.'" *Harvard Law Review* LXX (June 1957). Reprinted in *Men of Little Faith: Selected Writings of Cecelia Kenyon.* Boston: University of Massachusetts Press, 2002.

Burgess-Jackson, Keith. *Natural Law: Objections and Replies.* January 30, 2016. University of Texas Arlington. Philosophy of Law. https://www.uta.edu/philosophy/faculty/burgess-jackson/Natural%20Law%20(Objections%20and%20Replies).pdf.

Cappon, Lester J., ed. *The Adams-Jefferson Letters: The Complete Correspondence Between Thomas Jefferson & Abigail & John Adams.* Charlotte: University of North Carolina Press, 1959.

Chemerinsky, Erwin. *The Case Against the Supreme Court.* New York: Penguin, 2014.

Chernow, Ron. *Alexander Hamilton.* New York: Penguin, 2004.

_____. *Washington: A Life.* New York: Penguin, 2010.

"Circuit Riding." *Federal Judicial Center.* Definition entry. U.S. Supreme Court Education Center. USCourts.gov. https://www.fjc.gov/history/timeline/circuit-riding.

Clinton, Robert Lowery. "Game Theory, Legal History, and the Origins of Judicial Review: A Revisionist Analysis of *Marbury* v. *Madison*." *American Journal of Political Science* 38 no. 2 (May 1994), 285–302. https://www.jstor.org/stable/2111405.

Countryman, Edward. "To Secure the Blessings of Liberty." *Beyond the American Revolution: Explorations in the History of American Radicalism.* DeKalb: Northern Illinois University Press, 1993.

Curtis, Michael Kent. *No State Shall Abridge: The Fourteenth Amendment and the Bill of Rights.* Durham: Duke University Press, 1986.

Cushing, John D. "The Cushing Court and the Abolition of Slavery in Massachusetts: More Notes on the 'Quock Walker Case.'" *The American Journal of Legal History* 5, no. 2, 1961.

Davidson, Cathy N. "The Novel as Subversive Activity." *Beyond the American Revolution: Explorations in the History of American Radicalism.* DeKalb: Northern Illinois University Press, 1993.

Duke, George. "The Weak Natural Law Thesis and the Common Good." *Law and Philosophy* 35 (2016): 485–509.

Dyer, Justin Buckley. *Natural Law and the Antislavery Constitutional Tradition.* New York: Cambridge University Press, 2012.

Epstein, Richard A. *The Classical Liberal Constitution: The Uncertain Quest for Limited Government.* Cambridge: Harvard University Press, 2014.

Ferling, John. *Adams vs. Jefferson: The Tumultuous Election of 1800.* New York: Oxford University Press, 2004.

Finkelman, Paul. "James Buchanan, Dred Scott, and the Whisper of Conspiracy." *James Buchanan and the Coming of the Civil War.* Edited by John W. Quist and Michael J. Birkner. Gainesville: University Press of Florida, 2013. Accessed November 13, 2020. ProQuest Ebook Central.

_____. *Slavery & the Law,* ed. Lanham, MD: Rowman & Littlefield, 1998.

Finkelman, Paul, and Tim Garrison. "U.S. Indian Policy: Congress and the Executive, 1803–1848." *Encyclopedia of United States Indian Policy and Law.* Washington, D.C.: CQ Press, 2009.

Foner, Eric. *The Second Founding: How the Civil War and Reconstruction Remade the Constitution.* New York: W.W. Norton, 2019.

Garrison, Tim Alan. *Legal Ideology of Removal: The Southern Judiciary and the Sovereignty of Native American Nations.* Athens: University of Georgia Press, 2002.

Germantown Mennonite Historic Trust. http://www.meetinghouse.info/1688-petition-against-slavery.html.

Gienapp, Jonathan. "How to Maintain a Constitution: The Virginia and Kentucky Resolutions and James Madison's Struggle with the Problem of Constitutional Maintenance." *Nullification and Secession in Modern Constitutional Thought.* Edited by Sanford Levinson. Lawrence: University Press of Kansas, 2016.

Ginzberg, Lori D. *Women in Antebellem Reform.* Wheeling: Harlan Davidson, 2000.

Gordon-Reed, Annette and Peter Onuf. *"Most Blessed of the Patriarchs": Thomas Jefferson and the Empire of the Imagination.* New York: W.W. Norton, 2016.

Graber, Mark A. *Dred Scott and the Problem of Constitutional Evil.* Cambridge: Cambridge University Press, 2006.

Greeley, Horace. *The American conflict : a history of the great rebellion in the United States of America, 1860-'64 : it's causes, incidents, and results, intended to exhibit especially its moral and political phases, with the drift and progress of American opinion respecting human slavery, from 1776 to the close of the War for the Union.* Hartford: O.D. Case & Co.; Chicago: Geo. & C.W. Sherwood, 1865.

Grey, Thomas C. "The Uses of an Unwritten Constitution." 64 *Chicago-Kent Law Review* 67 (1988). Reprinted in *The Rights Retained by the People, Volume 2.* Edited by Randy Barnett. Fairfax: George Mason University Press, 1993.

Haidt, Jonathan. *The Righteous Mind: Why Good People are Divided by Politics and Religion.* New York: Vintage, 2012.

Halbrook, Stephen P. *Freedmen, the Fourteenth Amendment, and the Right to Bear Arms, 1866–1876.* Westport, CT: Praeger, 1998.

Hall, Kermit L., and Mark David Hall, eds. *The Collected Works of James Wilson, Volume 1.* Indianapolis: Liberty Fund, 2007.

Helmholzl. R.H. "Bonham's Case, Judicial Review, and the Law of Nature." *Journal of Legal Analysis* 1, no. 1 (Winter 2009), 325–346.

Hoffer, Peter Charles. *Rutgers v. Waddington: Alexander Hamilton, the End of the War for Independence, and the Origins of Judicial Review.* Lawrence: University Press of Kansas, 2016.

Hogan, Margaret A., and C. James Taylor, eds. *My Dearest Friend: Letters of Abigail and John Adams.* Cambridge: Harvard University Press, 2010.

Holmes, Oliver Wendell. "Natural Law." *Harvard Law Review* 32, no. 1 (1918): 40–44. Accessed April 13, 2021. doi:10.2307/1327676.

_____. *Natural Rights, and the American Constitutional Tradition.* Collected Legal Papers. National Endowment for the Humanities. https://www.nlnrac.org/critics/oliver-wendell-holmes.

Holton, Woody. *Abigail Adams: A Life.* New York: Free Press, 2009.

Hyneman, Charles S. *The Supreme Court On Trial: How the American Justice System Sacrifices Innocent Defendants.* New York: Atherton Press, 1963.

Isenberg, Nancy. *Fallen Founder: The Life of Aaron Burr.* London: Penguin, 2007.

"John Adams and the Massachusetts Constitution." Commonwealth of Massachusetts Official Website. https://www.mass.gov/guides/john-adams-the-massachusetts-constitution.

Johnson, Joel. "'Brutus' and 'Cato' Unmasked: General John Williams's Role in the New York Ratification Debate." *Proceedings of the Antiquarian Society.* October 2008. https://www.americanantiquarian.org/proceedings/45147499.pdf.

Kennedy, Roger G. *Mr. Jefferson's Lost Cause: Land, Farmers, Slavery, and the Louisiana Purchase.* New York: Oxford University Press, 2003.

Kenyon, Cecelia M. "Men of Little Faith: The Anti-Federalists on the Nature of Representative Government." *William and Mary Quarterly* 12, no. 1 (Jan. 1955): 3–43. http://www.jstor.org/stable/1923094.

Kersch, Ken I. *Constructing Civil Liberties: Discontinuities in the Development of American Constitutional Law.* Cambridge: Cambridge University Press, 2004.

Kornblith, Gary J., and John M. Murrin. "The Making and Unmaking of an American Ruling Class." *Beyond the American Revolution: Explorations in the History of American Radicalism.* DeKalb: Northern Illinois University Press, 1993.

Kramer, Larry D. *The People Themselves: Popular Constitutionalism and Judicial Review.* New York: Oxford University Press, 2004.

Lazarus, Edward. "Why the Tenth Amendment 'Nullification' Arguments Against the Stimulus Bill Are Sheer Folly—and Why It's Disturbing that So Many Years After the Civil War, They Are Still Being Raised." March 12, 2009. *FindLaw.* https://supreme.findlaw.com/legal-commentary/why-the-tenth-amendment-nullification-arguments-against-the-stimulus-bill-are-sheer-folly-and-why-its-disturbing-that-so-many-years-after-the-civil-war-they-are-still-being-raised.html.

Levinson, Sanford, ed. *Nullification and Secession in Modern Constitutional Thought.* Lawrence: University Press of Kansas, 2016.

Long Road to Justice: The African American Experience in the Massachusetts Courts. http://www.longroadtojustice.org/topics/slavery/quock-walker.php.

Macedo, Stephen. *The New Right v. The Constitution.* Washington, D.C.: Cato Institute, 1986.

Magliocca, Gerard N. *American Founding Son: John Bingham and the Invention of the Fourteenth Amendment.* New York: New York University Press, 2013.

Maier, Pauline. *American Scripture: Making the Declaration of Independence.* New York: Alfred A. Knopf, 1997.

_____. *Ratification: The People Debate the Constitution, 1787–1788.* New York: Simon & Schuster, 2010.

Martin, Asa Earl. *History of the United States: Volume I.* Boston: Ginn and Company, 1928.

Massey, Calvin R. "Federalism and Fundamental Rights: The Ninth Amendment." *Hastings Law Journal* 38, no. 305. Reprinted in *The Rights Retained by the People, Volume 1.* Edited by Randy Barnett. Fairfax: George Mason University Press, 1989.

McConnel, Michael W. "A Moral Realist Defense of Constitutional Democracy." 64 *Chicago-Kent Law Review* 67 (1988). Reprinted in *The Rights Retained by the People, Volume 2.* Edited by Randy Barnett. Fairfax: George Mason University Press, 1993.

McDonald, Forrest. *Novus Ordo Seclorum: The Intellectual Origins of the Constitution.* Lawrence: University Press of Kansas, 1985.

Meigs, William M. *The Relation of the Judiciary to the Constitution.* New York: Neale, 1919.

Moore, George H. *Notes on the History of Slavery in Massachusetts.* New York: D. Appleton & Co., 1866.

Nelson, William E. *Marbury v. Madison: The Origin and Legacy of Judicial Review.* Lawrence: University Press of Kansas, 2018.

O'Brien, William. "Did the Jennison Case Outlaw Slavery in Massachusetts?" *The William and Mary Quarterly* 17, no. 2 (Apr., 1960), 219–241.

O'Connor, Sharon Hamby, and Mary Sarah Bilder. "Appeals to the Privy Council Before American Independence: An Annotated Digital Catalogue." *Law Library Journal* 104, no. 1, 2012.

Orren, Karen, and Christopher Walker. "Cold Case File: Indictable Acts and Officer Accountability in *Marbury* v. *Madison*." *The American Political Science Review* 107, no. 2 (May 2013), 241–258.

Orth, John V. "Did Sir Edward Coke Mean What He Said?" *Constitutional Commentary.*

Spring 1999, 33. Gale Academic OneFile (accessed August 5, 2020). https://link-gale-com.proxy.lib.pdx.edu/apps/doc/A56885629/AONE?u=s1185784&sid=AONE&xid=21de5030.

Ostler, Jefferey. *Surviving Genocide: Native Nations and the United States from the American Revolution to Bleeding Kansas*. New Haven: Yale University Press, 2019.

Pennock, J. Roland, and John W. Chapman, eds. "Constitutionalism in Revolutionary America." *Nomos XX: Constitutionalism*. New York: New York University Press, 1979. Reprinted in *Men of Little Faith: Selected Writings of Cecelia Kenyon*. Boston: University of Massachusetts Press, 2002.

Pfeffer, Leo. *Church, State, and Freedom*. Boston: Beacon Press, 1953.

Pocock, J.G.A. *The Ancient Constitution and the Feudal Law: A Study of English Historical Thought in the Seventeenth Century; A Reissue with a Retrospect*. New York: Cambridge University Press, 1987.

Pollak, Louis H. *The Constitution and the Supreme Court: A Documentary History*, Volumes I and II. New York: World, 1966.

_____. *The Machiavellian Moment. Florentine Political Thought and the Atlantic Republican Tradition*. Princeton: Princeton University Press, 1975.

Powe, Lucas A., Jr. *America's Lone Star Constitution: How Supreme Court Cases from Texas Shape the Nation*. Oakland: University of California Press, 2018.

Ragsdale, Bruce. "Judicial Independence and the Federal Courts." *Federal Judicial History Office*. Federal Judicial Center, 2006.

Rakove, Jack N. *Original Meanings: Politics and Ideas in the Making of the Constitution*. New York: Vantage/Random House, 1996.

Rapaczynski, Andrzej. "The Ninth Amendment and the Unwritten Constitution: The Problems of Constitutional Interpretation." 64 *Chicago-Kent Law Review* 67 (1988). Reprinted in *The Rights Retained by the People, Volume 2*. Edited by Randy Barnett. Fairfax: George Mason University Press, 1993.

Root, Damon. *A Glorious Liberty: Frederick Douglass and the Fight for an Antislavery Constitution*. Lincoln: Potomac Books/University of Nebraska Press, 2020.

_____. *Overruled: The Long War for Control of the U.S. Supreme Court*. New York: Palgrave Macmillan, 2014.

Rorabaugh, W.J. "I Thought I Should Liberate Myself from the Thraldom of Others." *Beyond the American Revolution: Explorations in the History of American Radicalism*. DeKalb: Northern Illinois University Press, 1993.

Ross, William G. *A Muted Fury: Populists, Progressives, and Labor Unions Confront the Courts, 1890–1937*. Princeton: Princeton University Press, 2014.

Rossiter, Clinton. *1787: The Grand Convention; The Year That Made A Nation*. New York: Macmillan, 1966.

_____. *Seedtime of the Republic: The Origin of the American Tradition of Political Liberty*. New York: Harcourt, Brace.

Russell, Thaddeus. *Unregistered Podcast*. Episode 43, with guest Dave Smith. February 6, 2018. https://www.youtube.com/watch?v=7t-LjjjYnCs.

Schultz, David, and John R. Vile. *The Encyclopedia of Civil Liberties in America*. New York: Taylor & Francis Group, 2005. ProQuest Ebook Central. http://ebookcentral.proquest.com/lib/psu/detail.action?docID=2011180.

Sherry, Suzanna. "The Ninth Amendment: Righting an Unwritten Constitution." 64 *Chicago-Kent Law Review* 67 (1988). Reprinted in *The Rights Retained by the People, Volume 2*. Edited by Randy Barnett. Fairfax: George Mason University Press, 1993.

Smith, James Morton, "Alexander Hamilton, the Alien Law, and Seditious Libels." *The Review of Politics* 16, no. 3 (July 1954), 305–333. Cambridge University Press for the University of Notre Dame on behalf of *Review of Politics*. http://www.jstor.com/stable/1405146.

Smith, Tara. *Judicial Review in an Objective Legal System*. New York: Cambridge University Press, 2015.

Stites, Francis N. *John Marshall: Defender of the Constitution*. Boston: Little, Brown, 1981.

Storing, Herbert J. *What the Anti-Federalists Were For: The Political Thought of the Opponents of the Constitution*. Chicago: University of Chicago Press, 1981.

Strauss, David A. *The Living Constitution.* New York: Oxford University Press, 2010.

Taylor, Alan. *American Revolutions: A Continental History, 1750–1804.* New York: W.W. Norton, 2016.

_____. *Colonial America: A Very Short Introduction.* New York: Oxford University Press, 2013.

Thayer, James Bradley. "The Origin and Scope of the American Doctrine of Constitutional Law." *Harvard Law Review* VII, no. 3. October 25, 1893 (129–156). Doi: 10.2307/1322284.

"Timeline of Events Relating to the End of Slavery." *The Case for Ending Slavery. Massachusetts Historical Society.* 2020. https://www.masshist.org/teaching-history/loc-slavery/essay.php?entry_id=504.

Tocqueville, Alexis de. *The Ancien Régime and the French Revolution.* Edited by Jon Elster and Arthur Goldhammer. Cambridge: Cambridge University Press, 2011.

Treanor, William Michael. "Judicial Review Before Marbury." *Stanford Law Review* 58, no. 455 (2005), 455–462.

Tuck, Richard. *Natural Rights Theories: Their Origin and Development.* New York: Cambridge University Press, 1979.

Tushnet, Mark. *Taking the Constitution Away from the Courts.* Princeton: Princeton University Press, 1999.

Van Kley, Dale K. *The Damiens Affair and the Unraveling of the Ancien Regine, 1750–1770.* Princeton: Princeton University Press, 1984.

Waldren, Jeremy. "The Core of the Case Against Judicial Review." *The Yale Law Journal* 115 no. 6 (April 2006), 1346–1406. https://www.jstor.org/stable/20455656.

Watson, Bradley C.S. *Natural Law, Natural Rights, and the American Constitutional Tradition.* National Endowment for the Humanities. https://www.nlnrac.org/critics/oliver-wendell-holmes.

West, Thomas G. (Ed.) *Discourses on Government* (Editor's Introduction). 1698. Reprinted through Liberty Fund Online. https://oll.libertyfund.org/titles/sidney-discourses-concerning-government.

Whittington, Keith E. *Political Foundations of Judicial Supremacy: The Presidency, the Supreme Court, and Constitutional Leadership in U.S. History.* Princeton: Princeton University Press, 2007.

_____. *Repugnant Laws: Judicial Review of Acts of Congress from the Founding to the Present.* Lawrence: University Press of Kansas, 2019.

Wolfe, Christopher. *Natural Law Liberalism.* New York: Cambridge University Press, 2006.

Wood, Gordon S. *Creation of the American Republic, 1776–1787.* Chapel Hill: University of North Carolina Press, 1969.

_____. *Empire of Liberty: A History of the Early Republic, 1789–1815.* New York: Oxford University Press, 2009.

_____. *Radicalism of the American Revolution.* New York: A.A. Knopf, 1992.

_____. *Revolutionary Characters: What Made the Founders Different.* New York: Penguin Publishing, 2006.

_____. "The Trials and Tribulations of Thomas Jefferson." *Jeffersonian Legacies.* Edited by Peter Onuf. Charlottesville: University Press of Virginia, 1993.

Wood, Peter H. "Liberty is Sweet." *Beyond the American Revolution : Explorations in the History of American Radicalism.* DeKalb: Northern Illinois University Press, 1993.

Woods, Thomas E. *Nullification.* Washington, D.C.: Regnery, 2010.

Young, Alfred F. "Afterword." *Beyond the American Revolution : Explorations in the History of American Radicalism.* DeKalb: Northern Illinois University Press, 1993.

Zilversmit, Arthur. "Quok Walker, Mumbet, and the Abolition of Slavery in Massachusetts." *The William and Mary Quarterly* 25, no. 4 (1968): 614–24. doi:10.2307/1916801.

Zuckert, Michael P. *The Natural Rights Republic: Studies in the Foundation of the American Political Tradition.* Notre Dame: University of Notre Dame, 1996.

Index